BOOKS BY MALCOLM FORBES

Women Who Made a Difference
What Happened to Their Kids?
More Than I Dreamed: A Lifetime of Collecting
They Went That-a-way . . .
Around the World on Hot Air and Two Wheels
The Further Sayings of Chairman Malcolm
The Sayings of Chairman Malcolm
Fact and Comment
The Forbes Scrapbook of Thoughts on the Business of Life

MALCOLM FORBES

with JEFF BLOCH

WOMEN WHO MADE A DIFFERENCE

SIMON AND SCHUSTER
NEW YORK • LONDON • TORONTO
SYDNEY • TOKYO • SINGAPORE

SIMON AND SCHUSTER
Simon & Schuster Building
Rockefeller Center
1230 Avenue of the Americas
New York, New York 10020

Designed by Edith Fowler
Manufactured in the United States of America

10 9 8 7 6 5 4 3 2 1

Library of Congress Cataloging in Publication Data

Forbes, Malcolm S.
Women who made a difference/Malcolm Forbes: with Jeff Bloch.
p. cm.
1. Women—Biography—Dictionaries.
I. Bloch, Jeff. II. Title.
CT3202.F67 1990
920.72—dc20
[B] 90-43970
CIP

ISBN 0-671-69552-5

CONTENTS

L

M

N

O

P

R

S

FOREWORD

Besides his motorcycles, his balloons and his business, our father loved history. He loved the surprise of it—uncovering facts and anecdotes that have slipped through the cracks of the history books. As he wrote in the introduction of *They Went That-a-Way*, "When some well-known name comes up in conversation, how many times have we said, 'Whatever became of him/her?' " And usually, answering that question yielded fascinating results.

Pop was working on *Women Who Made a Difference* when he died in February. Like *They Went That-a-Way* and *What Happened to Their Kids?* this book asks, "Whatever became of . . . ?" But in this case, the fame of most of these women—if they ever actually achieved any degree of fame—faded long before their accomplishments did. And yet many of the marks they made still affect us all.

Most of us have never heard of Katharine McCormick, but without her financial backing, the birth control pill—and the sexual revolution it caused—might not have come along until years later. More than a century earlier, it took a genteel British woman, Lady Mary Wortley Montagu, to awaken the

British medical establishment to the benefits of smallpox inoculation.

Historians have written, of course, of many "women behind the men." But the women working alongside men, or in the forefront, were often overlooked. When it came time to dole out the credit, they went unnoticed because the men—including later historians—weren't in the habit of recognizing the accomplishments of the other half of the population. You have to read quite a lot about Eli Whitney to learn that he probably couldn't have invented the cotton gin without Catherine Greene. And most biographies of John Jacob Astor don't say much about the crucial role that his wife, Sarah, played in building his fur empire.

Pop was certainly a big believer in doing what "turned him on," in living the best life he could. Many of the women in this book were driven by the same spirit, and thus they became the first female doctors, the first women to pursue a particular business, or the first women to speak up for their rights.

Our father loved showing visitors to his office a favorite present from his granddaughter, an ashtray with the inscription "The best man for the job is often a woman!" He also took great pleasure in working on this project, and we hope you enjoy the results.

MOIRA FORBES MUMMA

MALCOLM S. FORBES, JR.

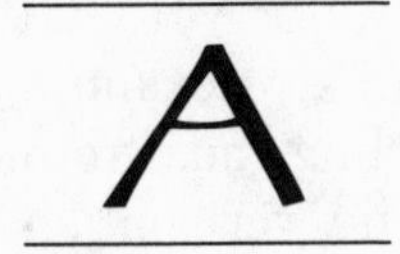

QUEEN ALEXANDRA

THE MARATHON IS LONGER
BECAUSE OF THIS BRITISH QUEEN

Anyone who has ever run a marathon knows that near the end, every step is more agonizing than all the ones that fell before it. Runners may take some comfort in reminding themselves that they are retracing the legendary distance of an ancient Greek messenger who in 490 B.C. ran from the battlefield at Marathon to Athens to proclaim the Greek victory. But in fact, modern marathoners run farther than did Pheidippides. And they do so at the whim of an English queen.

Actually, some historians today question whether anyone really ran from Marathon to Athens. But the legend was popular enough that organizers of the first modern Olympics in Athens in 1896 established the course—a distance of twenty-four miles—as the final race of the games. For the next twenty-five years, the distance of the marathon varied depending on the city in which it was held, though it remained around twenty-five miles.

In London in 1908, the marathon was supposed to be run from downtown Windsor to the White City Stadium, a distance of nearly twenty-six miles. Queen Alexandra, however, had another idea. The wife of the affable but ineffectual King Edward VII and daughter of Denmark's King Christian IX, Alexandra planned to watch the end of the grueling race from her royal box in the stadium. But she very much wanted her children and grandchildren to be able to view the start of the marathon. So the starting line was extended to the lawn of Windsor Castle, where Alexandra's brood could watch from the windows.

That made the distance of the London marathon 26 miles plus 385 yards. It might seem like a minor addition, but it wasn't to Dorando Pietri, the twenty-three-year-old Italian confectioner who led for most of the race. As he entered White City Stadium, less than 100 yards from the finish, Pietri collapsed. As the crowd roared and Queen Alexandra thumped her umbrella in the excitement, Pietri struggled to his feet, stumbled a few yards, and then fell again. American John Hayes had almost caught up with him before Pietri's fellow Italian athletes hoisted their exhausted compatriot and dragged him across the finish line.

It was the most dramatic marathon race so far. And even though Pietri was disqualified because he didn't run the final few yards alone, Queen Alexandra awarded him a golden cup anyway because of his thrilling effort. Of course, had Queen Alexandra allowed her family to leave the castle to watch the start of the race, Pietri would not have been faced with the extra distance that caused him to collapse.

The distance of the marathon continued to vary until 1921, when the International Amateur Athletic Federation chose the distance of the London Olympic marathon—26 miles, 385 yards—as the standard course. So the next time you run or watch the final, punishing moments of a marathon, think not of the heroic Greek runner. Think of that capricious queen —though she most certainly was not thinking of you.

VIRGINIA APGAR

DEVISED VITAL MEDICAL TESTS FOR NEWBORNS

"Every baby born in a modern hospital anywhere in the world is looked at first through the eyes of Virginia Apgar," a doctor once said, and he was not exaggerating. Because every one of those babies, before he or she is wrapped in a blanket and handed back to its mother, is given an "Apgar score" sixty seconds after birth. The quick evaluation of the baby's heart rate, breathing, muscle tone, reflexes, and skin color provides doctors with the first evidence of whether the newborn needs special help to stay alive.

It makes perfect sense, and yet it did not become a systematic part of delivery room procedure until Dr. Apgar developed her scoring system in 1952. Apgar came up with the test as a sidelight to her primary work. Originally one of the few female medical students at Columbia University in the early 1930s, Apgar was studying to be a surgeon, but switched to anesthesiology when a doctor convinced her that female surgeons couldn't make a living. Even "women won't go to a woman surgeon," Apgar said. "Only the Lord can answer that one."

Apgar became director of the anesthesiology department at Columbia-Presbyterian Medical Center in New York and was the school's first female professor. It was by working as the anesthesiologist during thousands of deliveries that Apgar realized doctors and nurses gave more immediate attention to the mother than to her newborn baby. "I kept wondering who was really responsible for the newborn," she said. "Birth is the most hazardous time of life."

In Apgar's test, the doctor or nurse evaluates each of the five vital signs with a score of zero to two. A total score of eight to ten usually means the baby is doing well, while lower scores alert doctors that the baby might need special attention. In medical schools, Apgar's name has become the acronym for teaching her test: Appearance (skin color), Pulse, Grimace (reflexes), Activity (muscle tone), and Respiration.

Apgar made no money on her test, which was in fact a fairly minor facet of her exemplary career. A doctor who once carried a child up nine flights of stairs because he was afraid of elevators, Apgar in 1959 became director of birth defects research for the March of Dimes. She traveled a hundred thousand miles a year, lecturing mothers on the dangers of drugs and urging them to seek early prenatal care. She sometimes carried a tiny preserved fetus in her purse to show parents. She taught students about the anatomy of the spinal cord by letting them feel her own bony spine.

Apgar, who said she never married because "I haven't found a man who can cook," lived in an apartment in Tenafly, New Jersey, where she cared for her mother in the same building. In her fifties she took up flying and also had a hobby of building musical string instruments, which she played in the Teaneck, New

Jersey, Symphony. She died of cirrhosis of the liver in 1974 at the age of sixty-five. She had delivered some twenty thousand babies during her career, but countless thousands more owe her their lives.

ASPASIA

WIFE OF PERICLES AND
INSPIRATION FOR PLATO AND SOCRATES

From the Golden Age of Athens, we remember the men—Socrates and Plato for their philosophy, Euripides for his plays, Thucydides for his histories, and Pericles for his leadership and oratory. Women don't make the list because they weren't allowed to. With barely more privileges than slaves, wives were kept secluded. They did not go out with their husbands to the theater or to parties, and even at home they couldn't share the same dinner table. Greek wives were supposed to take care of the household.

And yet, despite the restrictions, there is one woman whom Socrates and Plato credit as one of their teachers. Pericles, whose speeches were said to carry thunder and lightning, may well have been speaking her words. Her name was Aspasia, and of her President John Adams wrote, "I wish some of our great men had such wives."

Aspasia was one of a special group of Greek women who had vastly more privileges and influence than their married sisters. They were called "hetaerae," a class of unmarried female companions often described as courtesans but who were in fact much more. Because men's wives were so restricted, the hetaerae accompanied men to lectures, studied with them, debated with them.

Historians don't know when Aspasia was born or died, but she is believed to have arrived in Athens in about 450 B.C. from the eastern Greek city of Miletus. Legend has it that she was a great beauty, but the only surviving descriptions of her appearance say that she had a "small, high-arched foot," "a silvery voice," and golden hair. As a foreigner, Aspasia was not permitted to marry, so she opened a school of philosophy and rhetoric. Her home became the most popular salon in the city, attended by great artists, scholars, and politicians. Plato said that Aspasia taught him the theory of love; Socrates said he learned from her the art of eloquence.

Of all the great men who gathered at her home, the greatest was the most smitten of all. Pericles, the city's chief magistrate who ruled Athens for much of its Golden Age, fell so in love with Aspasia that he divorced his wife and moved in with her. Historians still debate how much her inspiration and counsel influenced the rule of Pericles, but it is more certain that she wrote some of his speeches including his most famous, the funeral oration he delivered for soldiers slain in the Peloponnesian War.

But although Aspasia undoubtedly enhanced Pericles' rule, the citizens of Athens were less impressed. It was one thing for the city's men to enjoy the companionship of the hetaerae, but Pericles broke the rules when he left his wife for Aspasia. He began staying home so often that people complained he had become aloof.

Still, Pericles was too powerful to criticize directly,

so Athenians attacked Aspasia instead. She was made the butt of many theatrical satires and lewd poems. More seriously, she was accused of seducing Pericles into waging war on behalf of her hometown. Finally, she was put on trial for blaspheming the gods.

Pericles gave such an impassioned defense at her trial that he wept, and his tears moved the judges to drop the charges against Aspasia. But the affair severely damaged the reputation of the great leader. He died a few years later, a broken man. As a consolation, Athenian rulers allowed him to leave his estate to his son by Aspasia, even though the boy was illegitimate.

The fate of Aspasia is lost to history, but her place is not. She was, said one twentieth-century historian, "one of the first women to be forced to run through the whole gamut of scorn, satire, and abuse because of her independence, her self-reliance, and her freedom from ordinary prejudice."

SARAH TODD ASTOR

JOHN JACOB'S WIFE KNEW MORE ABOUT FUR THAN HE DID

John Jacob Astor, whose fur and real estate fortune was worth $20 million at a time when Cornelius Vanderbilt only had a million and a half, was not known for his charity. Legendary for squeezing rent out of his impoverished immigrant tenants, this was also the man whom John James Audubon had to visit six times to collect the one thousand dollars Astor owed him for his "Birds of America" series. "Money is very scarce," Astor told him.

So presumably when Astor spent money on something, he thought it was worth it. Consider, then, historian John Scoville's account of Astor's wife, Sarah. "When they became very affluent," he wrote, "she used to make him pay her $500 an hour for using her judgment and knowledge of furs to promote his commercial plans. He paid her whatever she asked." Maybe Astor didn't drive a hard bargain with his wife, but considering what Sarah had done for him, he got off cheap.

The son of a German butcher, Astor was twenty-two in 1784 when he got off the boat in Baltimore with twenty-five dollars in his pocket. He declined to join his brother's butcher shop in New York and instead went to work for a baker there, but only until he could get into the fur business, which some passengers on the ship had told him was very lucrative. Astor was selling cakes on the street when he met Sarah Todd, who was cleaning the doorstep of her widowed mother's boardinghouse. He took a job with a furrier, then married Sarah in 1785.

Years later, when one of Astor's grandchildren asked him why he married Sarah, he replied, "Because she was so pretty." But she gave him much more. It was his wife's three-hundred-dollar dowry that financed Astor's first business, which began in two ground-floor rooms of his mother-in-law's boardinghouse. Actually, Sarah herself opened the store in the front room—selling musical instruments made by Astor's brother in London—while Astor trudged through the woods of upstate New York and Canada buying furs from Indians and trappers.

Astor would sell many of the furs in the Albany

markets, but he sent the best ones back to Sarah, who had to beat the smelly pelts, clean them, and try to convince the music customers to buy them. She continued to manage the successful store, which expanded and moved several times, until Astor sold it in 1802. By that time, Sarah had given birth to eight children, five of whom lived to adulthood.

Though it is Astor who is remembered as America's most successful furrier, even he admitted that his wife was a better judge of fur. Long after his business had made him a very wealthy man, Astor still had his wife examine each shipment. That's when she began billing him for her work, and he paid promptly. It was said she spent her earnings on charity.

Besides her money and her sweat, Sarah also gave her husband vital social connections. She insisted he go to church each Sunday so he would "know the right people." She regularly took him to a fashionable boardinghouse, where Astor met Aaron Burr and other up-and-coming young men. Sarah also was distantly related to one of New York's wealthiest families, the Brevoorts, and Astor used that connection on several occasions when he needed money for his business deals. When Astor wanted to get into the profitable China trade, two of Sarah's nephews, both sea captains who had sailed the route, helped him get started.

Some enthusiastic historians say it was Sarah's idea for her husband to start trading in the Orient. Some even give her credit for Astor's move into Manhattan real estate, which created the vast bulk of his fortune. But give Astor—who died in 1848, fourteen years after his wife—his due. He wasn't a puppet; he just didn't pull all the strings.

B

DELIA BACON

CLAIMED WILLIAM SHAKESPEARE WAS A FRAUD

Peruse modern writings on the works of William Shakespeare, and likely as not, you'll run across the argument that the Bard was a fraud, that he didn't pen his plays. Most writers give short shrift to the idea, yet the fact that they feel the need to deal with it at all is primarily the result of Delia Bacon's efforts. A few before her had questioned Shakespeare's authorship, but Bacon, with her notion that the plays actually were written by the more worldly Sir Francis Bacon (no relation), catalyzed the attack. "Will you tell me what one mortal thing [Shakespeare] did do?" wrote Bacon. "Do such things as these [experiences], that the plays are full of, begin in the fingers' end? Can you find them in an ink-horn? Can you sharpen them out of a goose-quill? Has your Shakespeare wit and invention enough for that?"

What is ironic is that while Bacon's theory has flourished, the mental torment that drove her to call Shakespeare "Will the Jester" is far less well known.

Bacon was born in 1811 to a Congregationalist minister who failed in his attempt to create a Puritan farming community in Ohio. After he died, she was raised by another family in Hartford, Connecticut, who gave her a much better education than most women received at the time. One of her classmates was Harriet Beecher Stowe, and Bacon exhibited her own talent when one of her short stories beat out the then-unknown Edgar Allan Poe in a contest. In the 1830s, Bacon began lecturing on history and culture, and her well-spoken, thoughtful discourses drew large crowds in Hartford and New Haven, and later even in Boston and New York.

And so she might have continued, had she not met Alexander MacWhorter, a theology student at Yale. Though she was thirty-five and he only twenty-three, MacWhorter courted Bacon passionately, to the point that her family felt the need to announce their engagement to protect her reputation. But after MacWhorter still wouldn't propose, Bacon's brother levied charges of misconduct against him with the New Haven ministerial association. A bitter, messy investigation ended with his acquittal—by a vote of twelve to eleven—and Bacon was left crushed. "The purposes that had become a part of my being are broken off," wrote Bacon after she withdrew from lecturing. "God does not need my labor, he appoints me to suffer."

Bacon sought refuge in reading, and the more she read about Shakespeare, the more she came to believe that he couldn't have written his plays. The works reflected someone who was very familiar with ancient history, as well as law and medicine and even court manners through the ages. And yet there was no record that Shakespeare ever was in a position to receive such an education. She concluded that Shakespeare was nothing more than an actor, and that the plays must have been written by the most learned men of the day—mostly Sir Francis Bacon, but also Sir Walter Raleigh, Edmund Spenser, and other "high-born wits and poets." Their motive, she alleged, was to spread the radical concept of democracy, which she said was the hidden theme of many of the plays.

Bacon began lecturing on the subject, and was so obsessed that one hostess felt she had to "put her copy of Shakespeare's works out of sight." Bacon called Shakespeare "the great myth of the modern age," an idea that "has become too gross to be endured any further."

Amazingly, Bacon found support from Ralph Waldo Emerson. "I am deeply gratified to observe the power of statement and the adequateness to the problem which this sketch of your argument evinces," Emerson wrote her. The famous author helped Bacon find wealthy donors to finance a trip to England for research. Once she got there, Emerson's recommendation also got her in to see the famous historian Thomas Carlyle. Bacon said that after she told him her theory, Carlyle "began to shriek. You could have heard him a mile." But he did recommend some papers she could review to help build her case.

But Bacon never looked at the papers. In fact, she did no research at all except read and re-read the plays, ferreting out hidden meanings and the signs of various authors. In her obsession, she became a recluse, living in unheated rooms and eating little food. For three years she moved between London, Stratford-upon-Avon, and St. Albans, where Sir Francis had lived. Once, she became convinced that there were papers hidden in Shakespeare's tomb that would prove her case. She even got the vicar's permission to remove the flagstone and look inside, but instead she just sat at the tomb for several nights, staring at the stones.

"The reason I shrink from seeing anyone now," Bacon wrote, "is that I used to be somebody, and whenever I meet a stranger I am troubled with a dim reminiscence of the fact, whereas now I am nothing but this work, and don't wish to be."

Ultimately, she wrote an article that Emerson helped her get published in *Putnam's Monthly* in the United States. It was supposed to be a five-part series, but the magazine canceled the contract after the first part. Emerson wrote to her, "I am sure you cannot be aware how voluminously you have cuffed and pounded the poor pretender, and then again, and still again, and no end."

And yet Bacon found another convert, none other than Nathaniel Hawthorne, who at the time was an American diplomat in Liverpool and the brother-in-law of one of her friends. On his recommendation, *The Philosophy of the Plays of Shakespeare Unfolded* was published in 1857. At seven hundred pages, Bacon's book was endlessly repetitive and disorganized. Hawthorne, who had had his wife read it for him, called it a "ponderous octavo volume." Critics were no more charitable.

But by then, for Bacon it barely mattered. Exhausted by her book and her obsession, Bacon lost her mind. Her nephew escorted her back to the United States, where she was put in an asylum. She died in 1859 at the age of forty-eight.

But her accusation has lived on. Mark Twain said he had read Bacon's book while he was an apprentice pilot on the Mississippi, and he believed it. And the last century has produced a whole series of literary efforts that attempt either to bolster her theory about Sir Francis Bacon, or proffer additional substitute authors. But Bacon was the first Baconian. Says the *Dictionary of American Biography*, "To its author remains the credit, or discredit, of having first inaugurated the most absurd, and, in other hands, the most popular of literary heresies."

DR. JAMES BARRY

A TOP BRITISH ARMY MEDICAL OFFICER
WHO TURNED OUT TO BE A WOMAN

When Dr. James Barry, Inspector General of the British Army Medical Department, died in 1865, officials were prepared to pay proper respect to a high-ranking officer who had given forty-six years of distinguished service for the good of the Crown. They were not prepared, however, when the Irish charwoman who laid out the body exclaimed, "The devil, a general. It's a woman. And a woman that has had a child!"

How could anyone fool everyone for nearly half a century? In fact, more than a few people suspected that Dr. Barry was not what he seemed. But in nineteenth-century England, when doctors often conducted physical examinations from the decent side of a nightgown, Barry escaped inquiries because what she did was literally unspeakable.

There is no record of Barry's true identity, her birthdate, or her family. It has been speculated that she was the daughter of a Scottish earl or an exiled Venezuelan general, or even that she was a bastard child of British royalty. Most likely, some historians say, she was the daughter of the sister of artist James Barry and was born about 1795. Whoever she was, in 1810 she was enrolled as a male medical student at Edinburgh University. Barely a teenager, Barry was probably aided in her disguise by her youth.

Barry entered the army as a hospital assistant at a time when a physical exam was not required. In 1815 she was sent to Cape Town in South Africa, where she became physician to the governor of the colony. She was, by all accounts, an excellent doctor, and was so successful with the governor and his family that her care was sought by most leading members of the colony. One lady wrote that Dr. Barry was "a perfect dancer who won his way into many a heart with impeccable bedroom manners. In fact he was a flirt."

But Barry clearly made a strange picture. One British lord who spent time in Cape Town wrote—after Barry's death—that Barry was "the most skillful of physicians and the most wayward of men; in appearance a beardless lad, with an unmistakably Scotch type of countenance, reddish hair, and high cheek bones. There was a certain effeminacy in his manner which he was always striving to overcome. His style of conversation was greatly superior to that one usually heard at a mess-table in those days."

Barry was said to have quite a hot temper. Once she challenged another officer to a duel, though both parties missed their shots. She frequently fought with military bureaucrats who opposed her reforms, which included efforts to provide better sanitation in the colony and improve the treatment of slaves. She once stood trial for disobeying her superiors, and apparently the only reason she kept her job as long as she did was because the governor liked her so well.

Eventually, Barry had offended so many in Cape Town that in 1828 she was sent to the British outpost of Mauritius, an island in the Indian Ocean. She spent nearly the next thirty years as a surgeon throughout the British Empire, including stints in Corfu, Malta, and Jamaica. If Barry did indeed give birth to a child—of which there is no record—it would have to have occurred during one of her long trips between these assignments.

Wherever she went, Barry had a reputation as something of an eccentric. She traveled with a black male servant (who after she died said he had no idea of anything amiss) and a series of small poodles, all of whom were named Psyche. When she was forced to share quarters with another male officer, she always insisted he leave the cabin while she dressed. One officer wrote, "The impression and general belief was that he was a hermaphrodite and as such escaped much comment or observation in places where everyone was used to him."

In 1857 Barry was sent to Canada as Inspector General, the top medical officer in the colony. After forty years in the tropics, however, the aging doctor became ill in the cold climate. She retired in 1859 and returned to London. She died in the summer of 1865 during a diarrhea epidemic. An army doctor, who brusquely had certified the death as that of a seventy-year-old man before the charwoman saw the body, said defensively that it was only his job to identify the body, not examine it. Later, a doctor and a nurse who had treated Barry for yellow fever in 1845 admitted they had seen that she was a woman, but had promised to keep her secret.

The army, at a time when women in England were not even allowed to attend medical school, was loath to issue an official report on its forty-six-year female veteran. Her tombstone said, ambiguously, "Dr. James Barry—Inspector General of Army Hospitals." Dr. G. W. Campbell, who had treated Barry in Canada and later became dean of the McGill Medical School, told his students, "If I had not stood in awe of Inspector General Barry's rank and medical attainments, I would have examined him—that is, her—far more thoroughly. Because I did not and because his—confound it, her—bedroom was always in almost total darkness when I paid my calls, this, ah, crucial point escaped me."

SYLVIA BEACH

SHE PUBLISHED JOYCE'S *ULYSSES*

When James Joyce's *Ulysses* was published in 1922, it became an almost instant classic. But that the sprawling, complex novel actually made it into print was almost as momentous. One woman in England and two women in the United States had been banned from publishing Joyce's book because it was considered obscene. Its appearance, finally, in a small bookstore in Paris "has been regarded by authoritative critics as one of the greatest literary events of this century," said *The New York Times*.

And the credit belongs to Sylvia Beach. The daughter of President Wilson's Presbyterian minister, Beach in 1919 opened the first American bookstore in Paris, called Shakespeare & Co. She quickly became the den mother of the city's thriving clique of expatriate writers, including F. Scott Fitzgerald, Ezra Pound, Sherwood Anderson, and Gertrude Stein. Beach's bookshop—in the days before paperbacks when most customers rented books—was their post office, bank, and literary salon, a place where writers, editors, publishers, and critics all mingled under Beach's enthusiastic nurturing. Wrote Ernest Hemingway in *A Moveable Feast*, "No one that I ever knew was nicer to me."

Beach adored them all, but she reserved her greatest admiration for Joyce. They had met in 1920 at a dinner party, where Beach saw Joyce slumped in a corner. "Is this the great James Joyce?" she said. "James Joyce," he replied, and then, she recalled, "he put his limp, boneless hand in my tough little paw—if you can call that a handshake." The next day, Joyce stopped by Shakespeare & Co., on the rue de l'Odéon, and soon he began visiting daily. Throughout their long friendship, Joyce addressed her as "Miss Beach," though everyone else called her Sylvia. For her part, Beach called him "Mr. Joyce," but "Melancholy Jesus" behind his back.

Their relationship (not romantic) was cemented by the news that *Ulysses* had been banned from publication in England and the United States. Joyce, who had worked on *Ulysses* since 1914, told Beach, "My book will never come out now." Beach spent the next eleven months helping Joyce edit his disjointed manuscript, a task that was hindered by his worsening glaucoma. Joyce continued revising and expanding *Ulysses* even as the text was in its final stages at the printer, ultimately writing an additional one-third of the novel on the page proofs. Beach proofread the massive work and meanwhile sold subscriptions to pay for the first edition of one thousand copies. To avoid the obscenity troubles, she found a printer in Dijon who didn't understand English.

The book sold well from the start, especially among American tourists. To get it through customs, Beach sold many copies with false covers entitled *Shakespeare's Works Complete in One Volume* or *Merry Tales for Little Folks.* Hemingway helped her arrange for copies to be smuggled from Canada to the United States.

Besides assisting with Joyce's writing, Beach began handling Joyce's personal life as well. She read him his mail, accompanied him to the doctor, took dictation of his letters, found him money when he and his wife were broke, and carried out a daily "grocer's list" of errands that Joyce set out for her. Beach said simply, "I worshiped James Joyce."

Beach published eleven editions of *Ulysses,* though she never had a contract with Joyce. That took its toll in 1933 when the U.S. Supreme Court ruled that the book was not obscene. Joyce sold the book to a U.S. publisher with no provision that Beach also get a share of the royalties. Beach was quoted as saying, "I understood from the first that, working with or for James Joyce, the pleasure was mine—an infinite pleasure; the profits were for him." But in private she was deeply hurt and it was a grave blow to their friendship.

Joyce did indeed get rich. Beach, meanwhile, nearly went broke. As her writer friends left Paris in the 1930s, Beach's bookshop suffered. In 1936, the year she was awarded the French Legion of Honor, some of her friends, including Hemingway and T. S. Eliot, held benefit readings to keep Shakespeare & Co. from failing. In 1941 a German officer threatened to confiscate all her books after Beach refused to sell him her personal copy of Joyce's *Finnegans Wake.* In two hours, Beach and some friends removed all the books, photographs, and memorabilia from the shop and stored it in Beach's apartment upstairs. She never reopened her bookshop.

Beach was imprisoned for seven months during World War II. After the war she made a career giving speeches and interviews on literary life in Paris during the 1920s. In June 1962 Beach helped dedicate a center for Joyce studies (Joyce had died in 1941). On October 6 she was found dead in her apartment above her former bookshop. Officials said she had died of a heart attack a day or two before. She was seventy-five.

AMELIA BLOOMER

NAMESAKE OF THAT CRAZY UNDERGARMENT

What the bra-burners were to the 1960s, Amelia Bloomer was a century before. Other women's rights leaders like Susan B. Anthony and Elizabeth Cady Stanton were more central to the cause, but it was Bloomer who so catalyzed the movement with a pair of Turkish-style pants that they became her namesake. At a time when women wore dresses that dragged the ground and so many undergarments that the total weight of the costume often reached fifteen pounds, "bloomers" focused the debate for women's rights on the fundamental issue: just who would wear the pants in the family?

The irony is that Amelia Bloomer wasn't exactly on the front lines of feminism, and in fact, she didn't even invent the seemingly shocking costume that came to bear her name. On the other hand, when, as a school teacher, Amelia Jenks married Dexter Bloomer, a lawyer in Seneca Falls, New York, in 1840, she did insist on deleting the word "obey" from their vows. Her husband later bought the Seneca Falls newspaper, and Bloomer began writing articles. It was that experience more than any feminist fervor that caused her to be given the task of starting a women's newspaper after the historic Women's Rights Convention in Seneca Falls in 1848.

Bloomer began publishing the *Lily* on January 1, 1849. The first women's journal actually produced by a woman, the *Lily* initially found only a few hundred subscribers. Then one day in 1851 Bloomer was visited by her neighbor, Elizabeth Cady Stanton, and Stanton's cousin, Elizabeth Miller. It was Miller who, after being uncomfortable in her heavy dresses while traveling Europe, had designed a lighter outfit consisting of a shorter skirt (four inches below the knees) that revealed a pair of pantalets that reached her ankles. Stanton, too, had become delighted with the comfort and flexibility of the outfit, and both women were so dressed when they visited Bloomer.

Bloomer then had an outfit made for herself and wrote about it in the *Lily*. "Fit yourselves for a higher sphere," she wrote, "and cease groveling in the dirt. Let there be no stain of earth upon your soul or apparel." Almost overnight, hundreds of women sent letters asking for dress patterns. Newspapers around the country picked up on the story, mockingly referring to the fad as "Bloomerism," and later coining the phrase "bloomers."

The media had their fun—London musicales

spoofed the new dress and somebody wrote "The Bloomer Waltz." But the feminists turned it to their advantage. Bloomer began appearing at women's rights lectures, and she later wrote, "If the dress drew the crowds that came to hear me, it was well. They heard the message I brought them. Until the papers had ceased writing squibs at my expense, I wore no other costume." By 1853 the *Lily* had more than six thousand subscribers, and Bloomer began publishing the monthly newspaper twice a month.

And yet for all the splash they made, bloomers soon faded from fashion almost as quickly as they had appeared. Bloomer and other women's movement leaders eventually decided the costume was detracting from other issues. Bloomer and her husband, joining the drive to settle the West, moved to Council Bluffs, Iowa, in 1855. She sold the *Lily* and it folded the following year. Bloomer continued to write occasional articles and make speeches; in 1856 she failed to convince the Nebraska territorial legislature to give women the vote.

Bloomer died of a heart attack at the age of seventy-six in 1894, about the time her "bloomers" came back in vogue for a while. Of course, what has happened to fashion since then probably would make even Mrs. B blanch.

NELLIE BLY

THE ORIGINAL MUCKRAKER

Before the muckrakers, there was Nellie Bly. At a time when newspapers generally were ignoring the burgeoning urban slums and sweatshops, she got herself hired in a factory and wrote about the abuses firsthand. She had herself committed to New York's horrible insane asylum on Blackwell's Island, and got arrested so she could report on a women's prison. Her exposés forced public officials to enact major reforms. But after she had embarked on her most famous assignment—a race to beat the pace of Jules Verne's *Around the World in Eighty Days*—Verne, greeting her in France, took one look at the dainty, five-foot-five young woman and said, "Why, she is a mere baby."

Actually, Nellie Bly was her pen name, taken from a Stephen Foster song. The real woman, Elizabeth Cochrane, was born at the end of the Civil War in a mining town near Pittsburgh that was named for her father. The sixth of ten children, Cochrane and her family were forced to move into the city after her father died and his estate was depleted. As she neared the end of her teens, Cochrane had two choices. She could either get married or she could become a domestic worker in a wealthy home.

The *Pittsburgh Dispatch* said as much in an editorial in 1885 entitled "What Girls Are Good For," which opposed women's suffrage and the idea that women might have careers. With only one year of formal education, Cochrane wrote such an angry yet articulate reply that the *Dispatch*'s editor placed an advertisement to find out who had sent the anonymous letter. Cochrane showed up and soon she became the only woman in the newsroom.

Refusing to write a society column, Cochrane wrote about Pittsburgh's slums, its dangerous factories, and one of its most taboo subjects, divorce. In 1886, the *Dispatch* agreed to send her to Mexico after she promised to take along her mother as a chaperone. Her stories about Mexico's desperately poor and corrupt rich got her expelled from the country.

Cochrane then set her sights on Joseph Pulitzer's *World*, the most popular paper in New York and the nation. She caught Pulitzer's attention with her idea of getting committed to Blackwell's Island, which she prepared for by practicing emotional breakdowns in front of the mirror in her hotel room. Cochrane checked into a women's hotel and began babbling in Spanish and bursting into tears for no apparent reason. After she was committed, other newspapers began reporting the tale of this strange, probably Cuban, woman who kept asking for a gun.

The *World* remained silent until it rescued Cochrane a week later. Calling the asylum a "human rat trap," Cochrane wrote, "Take a perfectly sane and healthy woman. Shut her up, make her sit from 6 A.M. to 8 P.M. on straight benches; do not allow her to talk or move during these hours; let her know nothing of the world or its treatment; and see how long it will take to make her insane." The city quickly allocated $3 million to clean up Blackwell's Island.

Ironically, after bringing so much attention to the worst problems, Cochrane is best remembered for a publicity stunt. On November 14, 1889, she sailed from Jersey City for England wearing a two-piece dress, a plaid coat, a cap and gloves, and carrying one small bag. At a time when women didn't travel alone,

Cochrane's immodest goal was to circle the globe and return to Jersey City from the west in less time than it took Verne's fictional Phileas Fogg in his 1873 novel. "A Veritable Feminine Phileas Fogg!" the *World* blared, and newspapers across the country joined the breathless coverage of Cochrane's journey.

It was as if astronauts today were to make a three-month trip to Mars, only Cochrane traveled by steamer, train, rickshaw, and sampan. She wrote about places and experiences that most Americans knew nothing about. She visited a Hindu temple, saw a Chinese funeral, and rode a burro in the Suez. Back home, there were songs written about her, toys named for her, clothes and games patterned after her. When her ship arrived in San Francisco on January 21, she was greeted by a huge crowd, and people stood to meet her train at every stop across the country. She reached Jersey City on January 25, seventy-two days, six hours, and eleven minutes from the time she left. "Father Time Outdone!" blazoned the *World*.

Nellie Bly would never be as famous again. After an exhausting, year-long speaking tour, Cochrane returned to her writing. In April 1895, she was returning from the Midwest, where she had been covering a two-year drought, when she met a New York businessman on her train. She married Robert Seaman—he was seventy-two, she not quite thirty—a few days later. In reporting her departure from the newspaper, the *World* said, "Miss Bly will become the mistress of a metropolitan residence, a magnificent country seat, a whole stableful of horses, and nearly everything the good fairy of the story books always pictures."

They lived quietly in New York until Seaman died in 1910. Cochrane then took over her husband's Ironclad Manufacturing Company and quickly ran it into the ground. Determined to make it her own, she had expanded rapidly, and then discovered that some of her employees were stealing from her. They accused her of fraud, and the ensuing legal battle left her nearly bankrupt. Perhaps to flee her creditors, Cochrane traveled to Austria-Hungary early in World War I and transferred her remaining properties into Austrian holding companies. When the United States entered the war, she lost everything.

In 1919, one of her old colleagues gave her a job at the *New York Evening Journal*. But by then, the muckrakers of the early 1900s had institutionalized investigative reporting, and Cochrane's stories didn't make nearly the splash they used to. With few friends and no family, Cochrane died of pneumonia in 1922 at the age of fifty-six. In the *World*, where she had practically owned the front page during the height of her career, her obituary garnered only a half-column on an inside page.

BOUDICCA

THE EARLY BRITISH QUEEN WHO TURNED BACK THE ROMAN EMPIRE

In 43 A.D., the boundaries of the Roman Empire were expanded when its powerful troops invaded Britain and conquered its primitive tribes. Less than twenty years later, the Empire was almost swept off the island by an angry woman.

Boudicca (or Boadicea) was queen of the Iceni, a

Celtic tribe that ruled what is now the county of Norfolk, north of London. Her husband, King Prasutagus, had made a deal with the invading Romans: he would give them half his lands when he died if they let him keep his throne until then. But instead, when Prasutagus died in the year 59, the Roman overlords seized all of the king's lands, flogged Boudicca, and raped her two daughters.

Already outraged by high Roman taxes and other abuses, the native tribesmen heeded Boudicca's call for revenge. She amassed a force estimated at over one hundred thousand people, though that included a large share of women and children. Still, it was more than enough, since the Roman governor, Suetonius, was off fighting the Druids in Wales.

Standing before her legions, Boudicca did indeed cut the figure of a military leader. Wrote a Roman historian, "She was huge of frame, terrifying of aspect, and with a harsh voice. A great mass of bright red hair fell to her knees. She wore a great twisted golden torc [necklace], and a tunic of many colors, over which was a thick mantle, fastened by a brooch. Now she grasped a spear, to strike fear into all who watched her." And what she told them would have pleased General Patton: "Let us show them that they are hares and foxes trying to rule over dogs and wolves."

First Boudicca marched on what is now the city of Colchester but was then a colony of twenty thousand Roman settlers. Boudicca and her angry Britons killed them all and burned the town to the ground. They did the same to the twenty thousand inhabitants of London, where even today excavation reveals a black layer of ashes from her onslaught. Next she wiped out thirty thousand Romans at St. Albans. Wrote another

Roman historian, "The Britons were not interested in taking prisoners or selling them as slaves, nor in any of the usual commerce of war, but only in killing by the sword, the gibbet (hanging), by fire, and the cross."

Boudicca was able to forge her wrath with ease because she was unopposed. But finally Suetonius gathered some ten thousand Roman soldiers north of London, where he drew Boudicca and her mob in pursuit. It was here where Boudicca's anger was no match for the Roman Empire. Suetonius set the battle on a hill bordered by trees. Clogged by their carts of women and children, the attacking Britons had nowhere to turn in retreat.

The battle ranks as the biggest slaughter ever on the island of Britain. The Romans estimated that some eighty thousand Britons were killed—probably more than one-tenth of all Celts in Britain—while only about four hundred Roman soldiers died. Boudicca, whose name was derived from a word meaning "victorious," escaped back to her home country, where she killed herself with poison.

Although she lost, Boudicca came closer than anyone to pushing the Romans out of Britain, and she remains a folk heroine there. The battle did cause Rome to reconsider its treatment of the colony. Suetonius was replaced by a more conciliatory governor who tried to Romanize the Britons instead of merely rule over them. Ironically, then, Boudicca's righteous anger probably hastened the westernization of the British Isles.

LOUISE BOYD

SOCIALITE TURNED ARCTIC EXPLORER

Louise Boyd, a San Francisco debutante, was perfectly willing to wear breeches and boots as she trekked through the ice and slush of the barren Arctic, but she had her limits. "At sea, I don't bother with my hands, except to keep them from being frozen," she said. "But I powder my nose before going on deck, no matter how rough the sea is. There is no reason why a woman can't rough it and still remain feminine."

However incongruous a picture it may have presented, the woman who always wore a corsage ("Even in Greenland, I'd find something and wear it with a safety pin") and traveled with her maid also contributed more fundamental information on the conditions and cartography of the Arctic than did many of the male explorers who reached the territory ahead of her.

Boyd was born thousands of miles and worlds away from the Arctic lands she would explore. The daughter of a wealthy mining operator in idyllic Marin County, California, she was educated in private girls' schools, made her debut at the age of twenty in 1907, and was presented at court in England. Throughout her Arctic career, and long afterward, she remained a central figure in San Francisco's society scene, noted by *The New York Times* in 1963 as one of its grande dames.

For a woman who would lead such a rugged life in the North, Boyd came from an unhealthy family. Both her brothers died in their teens of rheumatic fever, and both her parents were dead by the time she was thirty-two. It was after that when Boyd began traveling, first along the usual grand tour of Europe and then, on a whim in 1924, to Spitsbergen, an island between Norway and Greenland. When she was later asked why she kept on returning to the frigid region, Boyd barely seemed to understand the question. The Arctic, she said, presents "a picture of such majesty and on so vast a scale that no explanation need be given by any explorer for wishing to revisit such a scene."

Boyd's second Arctic trip was in 1928, when she took some friends to hunt polar bears. The newspapers, covering the voyage on the society page, reported that Boyd shot twenty-nine of the animals, though she later denied it. "That's a crazy story," she said. "I think it was only five or six, and that was for food."

It was Boyd's third Arctic expedition that moved the newspaper stories about her from the society columns to the front page. She was sailing in the region when it was reported that the explorer Roald Amundsen, famous for discovering the South Pole, was missing in the Arctic. Boyd and her crew joined the rescue effort, searching for three months and ten thousand miles before the early winter forced officials to give up. For her work, Boyd was awarded the French Legion of Honor and Norway's Order of St. Olaf, becoming the first foreign woman to receive that honor.

After that, Boyd got serious. She bought the SS *Veslekari*, a 125-foot wooden seal ship built in 1918, and equipped it with the best scientific instruments and experts that her family fortune could buy. During the 1930s Boyd organized four scientific expeditions to the Arctic. Each trip uncovered vast new information about the region. Boyd returned with samples of its microscopic plants and animal life. Her crew measured the depths of Greenland's eastern fjords, and they corrected substantial map errors of the earlier explorers. In 1938 she sailed farther north on Greenland's eastern shore than anyone ever had.

Boyd herself handled all the photography on her voyages, collecting thousands of images that remain a valuable record of the Arctic. That skill proved to be particularly important during World War II, when the U.S. War Department, worried that Germany might invade the region, hired Boyd as a technical expert and declared her materials confidential.

Boyd made one last trip to the Arctic in 1955, when she chartered an airplane and at the age of sixty-seven became the first woman to fly over and around the North Pole. She remained active both in San Francisco society and in the geography profession until her last years, which she spent convalescing with intestinal cancer. By then, mostly because of her Arctic expeditions, Boyd's fortune was depleted. When she died in 1972, two days before her eighty-fifth birthday, she was staying in a nursing home, paid for by her friends.

LAURA BRIDGMAN

THE FIRST DEAF-MUTE TAUGHT TO COMMUNICATE

The story of Helen Keller is a remarkable one, to say the least. Completely deaf and blind, she not only learned to communicate, but also went on to graduate from Radcliffe and became an international symbol of human achievement. Her life, however, may not have been so heroic had it not been for Laura Bridgman. Fifty years before Helen Keller discovered the meaning of "water," Laura Bridgman was the first deaf-mute ever to be brought out of her dark, silent shell.

Laura was the third of eight children of a successful New Hampshire farmer who later became a state legislator. Born healthy in 1829, at the age of two she suffered scarlet fever in an epidemic that killed her two older sisters. Laura survived, but she completely lost her sight and hearing, and as often happens, her senses of smell and taste also were severely damaged. As five younger siblings arrived over the next few years, Laura's mother had too little time to give her silent daughter much attention. Laura simply followed her mother around all day, clinging to an old boot that was her favorite toy.

When Laura was seven, a newspaper story about her life caught the attention of Dr. Samuel Gridley Howe, director of the Perkins Institute, a Boston school for the blind. At the time, the experts firmly believed that those who were both deaf and blind could not be taught to communicate, and there were a few failed cases that supported that belief. Laura, too, was drifting away from contact. Her family was at a loss to control her, and by the time Howe took Laura to his school, she responded only when her father stamped his foot hard on the floor. "She seemed quite bewildered at first," Howe wrote of Laura's first days at Perkins, "but soon grew contented, and began to explore her new dwelling. Her little hands were continually stretched out, and her tiny fingers were in constant motion, like the feelers of an insect."

Howe (later married to suffragette Julia Ward Howe) and his assistants began by placing raised letters on everyday objects such as dishes and silverware.

Soon, Laura was able to match the labels to the objects, even if she didn't understand what she was doing. But then one day, after only several weeks, she made the connection. Wrote Howe, "She perceived that here was a way by which she could make herself up a sign of anything that was in her own mind, and show it to another mind; and at once her countenance lighted up with a human expression. It was no longer a dog or parrot—it was an immortal spirit, eagerly seizing upon a new link of union with other spirits!"

Though Laura caught on quickly, her instruction was painstaking. This was before Braille or sign language, so she had to slowly run her fingers over the letters of the alphabet to form new words. It took an hour to teach her left from right, and several hours for her teacher to explain the difference between "in" and "on." When Laura was correct, her teacher patted her on the head; a tap on the elbow meant she had made a mistake. She learned to write on grooved paper and within a few months Laura was able to write to her mother. It took her four years to learn the rudiments of grammar but eventually she wrote poetry and an autobiography.

Early on, Howe published articles about Laura's achievements, and soon her progress was followed throughout the United States and Europe. Exhibition days at the school drew crowds of people who stood behind barriers and watched Laura—wearing a plain dress and a green ribbon wrapped around her eyes—as she sewed or wrote letters. Charles Dickens added to her fame by including her in his *American Notes* in 1843. "Self-elected saints with gloomy brows, this sightless, earless, voiceless child may teach you lessons you will do well to follow," Dickens wrote. "Let that poor hand of hers lie gently on your hearts."

Except for visits to her family, Laura lived at Perkins

for the rest of her life. She knitted, cleaned, and taught sewing, strictly requiring her blind students to pull out incorrect stitches and start again.

It was said that Laura was one of the most widely studied individuals in the nineteenth century. Howe once even tried using electric charges to re-start her senses. After Laura died of pneumonia at the age of sixty, a doctor performed an anatomical study of her brain that was cited in neurology books for decades. Also among those who learned from her case was Anne Sullivan, a teacher who trained at Perkins before she went to work with her most famous student —Helen Keller.

MARGARET BROWN

OTHERWISE KNOWN AS THE "UNSINKABLE" MOLLY BROWN

Perhaps there were two Molly Browns. One, the well-known subject of a popular movie musical starring Debbie Reynolds, was a high-spirited if rough-edged country girl who survived the *Titanic* and won the hearts of high society. The other, which better reflects Molly's reputation while she was alive, was an ill-mannered eccentric whose pathetic attempts to enter the upper class left her the laughingstock of Denver and many wealthy ports of call. The real Molly Brown, born Margaret, did much to fuel both legends. "Sure I'm eccentric," she said. "But I have a heart as big as a ham!"

There are so many different versions of the life of Molly Brown—most launched by her—that the only certain fact is that she was a hell of a storyteller. Born in 1867 in Hannibal, Missouri (she would claim an unlikely acquaintance with the town's most famous native, Mark Twain), the daughter of a ditchdigger, Molly followed her brother to Leadville, Colorado, when she was seventeen. While she was waiting tables, her bright red hair caught the eye of James Brown, the manager of a local mine. Molly hesitated to marry him because he wasn't rich, but he soon obliged her. The legend is that Brown, after selling his share of one mine, brought home three hundred thousand dollars, which he later accidentally incinerated after Molly hid the money in the stove. In truth, the amount was seventy-five dollars in gold coins which were merely blackened in the flames. Molly was happy to see the legend flourish. "Oh, hell," she said. "What difference does it make? It's a damn good story!"

Brown eventually did strike the mother lode, earning an estimated $2.5 million for his one-eighth share of the Little Jonny Mine. At Molly's insistence, they moved to Denver and built a garish mansion, called "The Lion House" for all the stone beasts that surrounded it. Molly had arrived but she was not welcomed by Denver's elite, dubbed the "Sacred Thirty-Six." She was not invited to their parties, they were always not at home when she called, and they did not even respond to invitations to her lavish feasts. Once she called in neighborhood children to eat her sumptuous, neglected buffet.

Indeed, the harder she tried, the more humiliating her failure became. Her gaudy dresses were described as Christmas trees. She wore so many bulky fur capes that she was called "a unique fur-bearing animal." She sent letters and poems to the Denver newspapers, which they printed intact with all her spelling errors and uneducated grammar.

Molly fought back by hiring tutors who taught her proper English, French, and etiquette. When that wasn't enough—and after her husband got tired of her social climbing and left her—Molly moved to Paris. On her frequent return visits, Molly would claim friendships with artists, writers, and royalty, including Sarah Bernhardt and the Vanderbilts. In truth, her popularity was less secure. In Paris she staged a play, *L'Aiglon*, that the critics savaged. And though she claimed she delighted passengers on her transatlantic cruises with her newly acquired operatic, yodeling, and poetic talents, she was pointedly dissuaded from performing on her most famous voyage—aboard the *Titanic*.

Probably more than anyone else, Molly Brown thanked her lucky stars to be on the ill-fated luxury liner, which sank with 1,513 of its 2,224 passengers. Even her worst Denver enemies had to admit she behaved heroically, though her heroism grew more colorful every time she recounted it. When the luxury steamer rammed an iceberg on the evening of April 15, 1912, Molly was exercising in her black velvet suit. Aware of the danger, she returned to her cabin, and, according to most versions, clad herself in woolen underwear, a pair of heavy bloomers, two wool petticoats, a four-thousand-dollar sable muff and a sixty thousand dollar chinchilla cape.

After marshaling dozens of shivering women and children into the few lifeboats, Molly boarded the last one. Said one passenger, "She delivered orders like a deckhand." She threatened to throw the listless seaman overboard unless he started rowing, then she picked up an oar herself. "I'll row," she said. "I haven't for years—but I learned when I was a child on the banks of the Mississippi. I bet I still can." When the twenty-three other women preferred to cry rather than row, Molly barked, "Row, you sons of bitches. Row or I'll let daylight into you!" It was said that after she gave most of her clothing to chilled passengers, they were faced with a view of Molly clad in her underwear and waving her Colt automatic pistol.

Molly's lifeboat was rescued after seven hours in the twenty-eight-degree North Atlantic, and Molly stepped onto the New York pier a national hero. "I had typical Brown luck," she told reporters. "I'm unsinkable."

And yet in Denver, she remained little more than tolerated. Admitted to one society matron's home, she wanted to know how much everything cost and then whistled when she heard the prices. Molly took her show on the road, traveling to exotic spots all over the world, always carrying her too-tall walking cane draped with flowers. "I'm getting to be more of a lady every day," she reported. "In Honolulu I learned to play the ukelele. In Siam I mastered the native dances. In Switzerland I learned how to yodel. Want to hear me?"

She donated to many charities: a children's library, a hospital wing, families of striking Colorado miners. After she was rejected by the Army Nursing Corps during World War I, she went over to Europe at her own expense to sing for the soldiers. But all of that ended after her estranged husband died in 1922. Her son and daughter fought to claim the estate that Molly was blithely giving away. They won, and Molly was left with a trust that provided her one hundred thousand dollars a year.

In somewhat diminished style, Molly continued her

regular resort tours until she died suddenly of a stroke at the Barbizon Hotel in New York on the day after Christmas in 1932. She was sixty-five. The sweetened version of Molly Brown survives in the Broadway musical, first staged in 1960, and the 1964 movie. Also, when *Gemini 3*, the first two-man spacecraft, was launched in 1965, it bore the name *Molly Brown*.

C

ANNA CARROLL

SHE CLAIMED HER MILITARY STRATEGY
WON THE CIVIL WAR

Any history book about the Civil War will recount the military achievements of the great generals like Grant and Lee. But only a few mention Anna Carroll, a woman whom some have called President Lincoln's "secret weapon," and whom some even credit with devising the critical military course that helped the Union win the war. Her tombstone in Cambridge, Maryland, calls her "A great humanitarian and a close friend of Abraham Lincoln." But when Carroll told the president she wanted to be paid fifty thousand dollars for her services, Lincoln abruptly told her that her demand was "the most outrageous one ever made to any government on earth."

Carroll, whose ancestors include a signer of the Declaration of Independence and the first American Catholic bishop, was born in 1815 and grew up amidst the law volumes and political discussions in her father's study on the Eastern Shore of Maryland. She was Thomas Carroll's favorite daughter, and during his brief term as governor in 1830, the vivacious redhead became his secretary, calling herself "Princess Anne" at social functions. As her family's political and financial fortunes diminished, Anna Carroll receded from view until the 1850s, when she emerged as a leading spokesman for the anti-Catholic, anti-foreign Know-Nothing Party.

Carroll gained national attention when the Civil War broke out in 1861. She wrote a pamphlet called "The War Powers of the Government," which articulately set forth the president's legal justification for sending the military against the Confederacy, a matter that was much disputed at the time. Lincoln was so impressed that he had Carroll's pamphlet distributed to all members of Congress. Assistant Secretary of War Thomas Scott went beyond that. He paid Carroll $1,250 out of his own pocket and printed ten thousand copies.

And that is where the truth and legend of Anna Carroll began to muddy. Scott took it upon himself to arrange with Carroll to write more Unionist literature, and they agreed to work out the finances later. Carroll's second pamphlet, "The Relations of the National Government to the Revolted Citizens," along with her first piece is credited by historians as making a significant contribution to constitutional thought.

But because of her alliance with Scott, Carroll decided to do more for the Union side. Accompanied by Lemuel Jones, a government agent whose relationship with her is not clear, Carroll traveled to St. Louis in the fall of 1861. At the time, Union military leaders believed that the key to defeating the Confederacy was to gain control of the Mississippi River, which would cut off shipments from the west. Carroll met a river captain, Charles Scott, who told her it was the Tennessee River, which flowed through the middle of the South, that was far more vital to a Union victory.

Carroll submitted a report on the Tennessee River plan in November to her friend Thomas Scott at the War Department. In February, General Grant began marching down the Tennessee River valley, an effort that ultimately paved the way for Sherman's march to the sea. Based on the timeliness of Carroll's report, a few historians—especially feminist writers in the late 1800s—claimed that she had devised the most important military strategy of the war. But in fact, others at the same time were discussing the Tennessee River plan and the specific course of action was proposed by Grant himself.

Still, Carroll went to Lincoln in 1862 to seek her $50,000, which is when he called her "outrageous." She was paid $750. In 1865 Carroll said in a magazine interview, "I deem it a pleasant duty to make known to the American people how much they are indebted to Captain Charles M. Scott for the crowning victory which now thrills with joy every patriot." But in 1870 she was calling it the "Carroll Plan" and when she asked Congress for compensation, she upped her fee to $250,000.

Carroll pressed her claim for fourteen years to no avail. In 1893 she died at the age of seventy-seven in her spinster sister's home in Washington, D.C. But her cause did not die with her. Suffragists took up her claim, and a few novels have enhanced her role, portraying her as an unofficial member of Lincoln's Cabinet whom the president himself had sent to St. Louis to evaluate the Union's war strategy.

Though it wouldn't satisfy her, Carroll's place in the history books belongs in the footnotes.

MARY CHESNUT

AUTHOR OF A FAMOUS CONFEDERATE
CIVIL WAR DIARY

If you wish to find out about the Confederacy, there is an ample supply of dates and documents that will tell you everything about the military and governmental maneuvers. But to find out what was really happening—what Southerners were doing while the battles were going on—historians turn to the writings of Mary Chesnut. Though she was nearly forgotten when she died, Chesnut left behind a four-hundred-thousand-word journal that Edmund Wilson called "an extraordinary document—in its informal department, a masterpiece." Historian Lyman Butterfield said it was "the best written by a woman in the whole range of our history . . . in the same top bracket with that of Sewall, Byrd, Cotton Mather, and John and John Quincy Adams."

Mary Chesnut was perfectly positioned to record the rise and fall of the South. The oldest daughter of South Carolina Governor and U.S. Senator Stephen Decatur Miller, Mary received an excellent education in a Charleston boarding school. In 1840, when she was seventeen, she married James Chesnut, heir to one of the wealthiest plantations in the state. Her husband, too, went to Washington as a senator, but they left in 1860 when their state became the first to secede from the Union.

It was then that Mary began keeping a diary, noting conversations, thoughts, and developments of the coming war. She wasn't sure exactly how, but she thought that her journal might "at some future day afford facts about these times and prove useful to more important people."

Many, of course, kept similar journals, but none had the privileged view of Mary Chesnut. It was her husband who delivered the demand to surrender Fort Sumter. He served in the Confederate congress and was the liaison between the rebel government and South Carolina. He also was an aide to President Jefferson Davis which, along with Mary's close friendship with Davis's wife, Varina, gave Mary such a unique perspective that, said one historian, "her account must always be a prime source of understanding the man and his administration."

Mary accompanied her husband throughout the war and often was in the right place to hear revealing conversations: Confederate Vice President Alexander Stephens talking about the dangers of secession, General Winfield Scott complaining about the lack of Southern discipline. But unlike the military journals, her tone was far from reverent. "Old Pick was there with a better wig," she wrote of one general. In the early days of the Confederacy, she wrote, "Jeff Davis ill and shut up, and none but *noodles* have the world in charge."

The Chesnuts lived in Richmond when the city became the Confederate capital, and Mary made their home the center of its social life. Almost nightly, she hosted evenings of charades, dances, or amateur theatricals that were attended by all the top Confederate officials. Her husband scolded her for throwing so many parties, but she argued that in the face of so many slain soldiers it was either "distraction or death." Her stories about the parties tell much about the frantic, desperate pace of the Southern capital as the war wore on. The diary, begun with descriptions of jubilant Southerners, ends with a recounting of Varina Davis and her four young children seeking refuge in Mary's home to hide from the Yankees.

After the war, Mary and her husband returned to Camden, South Carolina. While he rebuilt their plantations and was involved in reorganizing the state's government, Mary slowly worked on the scattered pages of her diary. It was not until 1884 that she finished revising her journal, which she recopied into fifty notebooks, totaling four hundred thousand words. There it remained when she died of a heart attack two years later, following her husband's death in 1885. As she left no children, her death brought little notice.

And for twenty years, neither did her diary. Mary left the manuscript to a younger friend, a schoolteacher named Isabella Martin, who kept the notebooks in a box under her bed. Martin found little interest in publishing the weighty journal until she condensed it drastically with the help of a New York writer. In 1905 *A Diary from Dixie* was published following five excerpts in the *Saturday Evening Post*. It was only 150,000 words in length and it had been watered down. Where Mary had described someone as "ugly as sin," the first edition said "she was not pretty."

A revised edition, twice as long, was published in 1949, and an even more complete edition came out in 1981. Her diary is now considered, among historians at least, the most famous journal of the Confederacy. Mary had thought her diary might be found useful "at some future day." It took a century, but she was right.

D

ELSIE DE WOLFE

TREND-SETTING INTERIOR DECORATOR

Of the wealthy, sometimes tasteless clients whose homes she decorated, the zestful Elsie de Wolfe once said, "There is often a lot of pig's ear left in those silk purses." She was no less direct in her decorating. In the early 1900s, when homes were laden with dark-walled Victorian chambers cluttered with velvet curtains and potted palms, de Wolfe swept it all away and ushered in cream-colored walls, mirrors, and most of all, light chintz fabric. Looking back, that may seem like a minor accomplishment. But at a time when interior decorating was strictly a man's job, de Wolfe not only came to dominate the profession but she also spread her innovations well beyond the mansion set. "Elsie de Wolfe," said *House & Garden*, "is a woman who has imposed her taste on one generation and lived to see it taken for granted by another."

With her motto "Never Complain, Never Explain" embroidered on a silk pillow, de Wolfe had a knack for being at the center of things that was not limited to her decorating career. Born in 1865, the daughter of a Canadian doctor, she managed to be presented at the court of Queen Victoria when she was seventeen because her mother's cousin was the queen's chaplain. From there she was introduced to London's social set, and they became her devoted fans when she took to the stage in London and later in New York. Noted, in fact, less for her talent than for the glittering audiences she drew, even de Wolfe admitted, "It was clear I was not Sarah Bernhardt." Still, before she retired in 1905, she did play opposite John Drew and was understudied by his niece, Ethel Barrymore.

Her decorating career began in her own home, a New York townhouse on Irving Place that she shared with her longtime companion, Elisabeth Marbury, the biggest theatrical agent at the turn of the century. De Wolfe's refreshingly simple designs drew instant attention from the Sunday salon she and Marbury hosted there and at their second home in Versailles, with guests including Bernhardt, Oscar Wilde, architect Stanford White, and Anne Morgan, J. P.'s sister. Her friends helped her win the important commission to decorate the new Colony Club, New York's first women's club, though White, who had designed the building, had to allay the doubts of those concerned that de Wolfe had no actual training as an interior decorator. "Let the girl alone," he said. "She knows more than any of us."

De Wolfe went on to decorate the mansions of several industrialists. She arranged for coal magnate Henry Clay Frick to furnish his Fifth Avenue mansion with the coveted $3 million Wallace collection of French antiques ("My ten percent commission made me a rich woman," she said). But her biggest coup was the Park Avenue penthouse of Condé Nast, publisher of *Vogue, Vanity Fair,* and *House & Garden.* Nast's magazines proceeded to feature her work, and de Wolfe's taste was imitated across the country. Her use of delicate eighteenth-century furniture made antiquing popular as never before. Her most copied innovation—a light, inexpensive, glazed cotton fabric called chintz—was used on so many walls, furniture, and curtains that de Wolfe became known as "the Chintz Lady."

"A woman's environment will speak for her life, whether she likes it or not," de Wolfe wrote in her 1913 best-seller, *The House in Good Taste*. "A house is a dead giveaway." Her rules were simple: comfort and suitability. "I believe in plenty of optimism and white paint," she said. Also, "don't make each room a different color in a small apartment or you'll make yourself nervous," she said. And "don't choose colors for rooms according to fashion. You can't get rid of curtains at the end of the year."

De Wolfe became such a trendsetter that even her silliest innovations found their following. She started the fashion of wearing little white gloves, and in 1924 she was the first woman to tint her gray hair blue. In all things, her desire was to find something new and pursue it with vigor. She went up in Wilbur Wright's flimsy airplane in 1908. A strict vegetarian who practiced yoga, she stood on her head every morning into her seventies. And when she was seventy, Paris dressmakers voted her the best-dressed woman in the world.

In 1926, to the surprise of many, de Wolfe married a British diplomat, Sir Charles Mendl. It was a marriage of convenience that allowed her to become an international hostess, throwing lavish parties at their homes in Beverly Hills, New York, and Versailles. De Wolfe continued to host parties into her eighties, though her painful arthritis and a heart attack left her confined to a wheelchair. Her last party came three weeks before she died in 1950 at the age of eighty-four. On her deathbed, the woman with undying vitality came out of a coma long enough to say, "They can't do this to me. I don't want to go."

ABIGAIL DUNIWAY

SHE HELPED BRING WOMEN THE VOTE, LONG BEFORE THE NINETEENTH AMENDMENT

By the time the Nineteenth Amendment was ratified in 1920, giving women the right to vote, women had already been casting ballots for years in several states. As early as 1869, Wyoming and Utah had granted women's suffrage, and the issue was hotly contested in several other western states as well. Stoking many of those battles was a witty, self-educated farmer's wife who had arrived on the Oregon Trail. Abigail Scott Duniway never gained the national reputation of eastern feminists like Susan B. Anthony, but, said one historian, "her feminist victories generally preceded those won elsewhere. They were a spearhead glinting across the Rockies and influencing the entire nation."

Duniway's fight for women's rights was born out of her own experiences. She saw her mother, who hadn't wanted to make the arduous journey, die on the Oregon Trail. After she got married in 1853 when she was eighteen, Duniway not only had six children over the next fifteen years, but she also ended up cooking meals for the many bachelor farmers "who found comfort in mobilizing at mealtimes at the homes of the few married men in the township." Her husband lost their farm near Salem when a friend defaulted on bank notes that he had endorsed, and Duniway was appalled that she could do nothing about it. "I was my husband's silent partner—a legal nonentity," she said, "with no voice or power for self-protection under the sun."

After her husband was disabled by a runaway wagon, Duniway opened a millinery shop to support the family. The store became a gathering place for women—whom the law treated as property of their husbands—to trade their tribulations. One woman's husband abandoned her and their children and then sold their home out from under them. "Those farm women worked as hard as their husbands, yet were treated like children," said Duniway.

It was Duniway's husband who convinced her that things would never change until women could vote. So in 1871, Duniway moved her family to Portland and started a weekly newspaper, *New Northwest*. The lively journal, typeset by two of her sons, was a quick success and lasted sixteen years, largely because of Duniway's practical approach to the issues. She advised one woman, who signed her letter "Nervous Sufferer," "You need rest. Get your decaying teeth extracted. Let Molly's face go dirty and John's knee peep out. These things will surely happen when you are dead and gone."

For twenty-five years Duniway lectured throughout the Northwest. Ironically, she found it easier to win over male audiences than female. She was once challenged by a man who said, "I have often known a hen to try to crow, but I've never known one to succeed at it yet." Duniway replied, "I once saw a rooster try to set, and he made a failure, too."

In 1872 Duniway spoke before a joint session of the

Oregon legislature and convinced the men to pass laws which allowed married women to go into business by themselves and protected their property if their husbands left. She later won Oregon women the right to sue and the power to control their own earnings.

In 1883 she even convinced the legislature to approve a state constitutional amendment granting women's suffrage, but the measure failed at the polls. She fought for a similar amendment across the border in Washington, but the territory's Supreme Court rejected it. Her speeches were instrumental in gaining the women's vote in Idaho in 1896 and Washington voters eventually went along in 1910.

But Oregon posed Duniway's most difficult battle. After male voters again rejected her campaign in 1900, national suffrage leaders moved in to mount another drive. Duniway split bitterly from the national suffragettes, who linked their campaign with prohibition, pledging that women would vote to outlaw liquor. But the national leaders fared no better than Duniway, and Oregon men defeated the suffrage amendment for a third time in 1906. Duniway herself tried again in 1908 and 1910; the final loss was by a lopsided 58,000 to 37,000.

When the measure appeared again on the ballot two years later, Duniway, seventy-eight and confined to a wheelchair by rheumatism, did not lead the drive. But when it was approved—by a slim margin of 61,000 to 57,000—it was Duniway who was asked to write the official proclamation and sign it with the governor.

Duniway died in 1915, five years before the nation followed her lead and gave all women the right to vote. "Excited?" Duniway had responded to reporters when she became Oregon's first registered female voter. "No, I am not excited. I *knew* it would come."

E

MARGARET EATON

AT THE CENTER OF A SCANDAL THAT ALMOST DESTROYED ANDREW JACKSON'S PRESIDENCY

"I have heard that a drowning man will sometimes see, at a glance, his whole past life, and, at these words of my wife, it seemed to me the future was shown me in as sudden and as vivid a manner," wrote John Calhoun, vice president under Andrew Jackson. "The rupture with General Jackson; the Administration changing from a Free Trade policy to that of Protection; the failure to adjust the Tariff difficulties; Executive patronage brought to bear upon the States' Rights leaders; personal popularity influencing the masses; certain nullification by South Carolina, and almost certain attempt at coercion by the Federal Government—this was the panorama which passed like a flash before my eyes."

What could Mrs. Calhoun have said to prompt her husband's frightening visions? She had told him that Mrs. Margaret Eaton, wife of the Secretary of War, had paid her a call, and Mrs. Calhoun had decided not to return the visit. It hardly sounds dire, but in its day it was a grave snub. And while it didn't cause all of Calhoun's nightmares, what became known as the "Eaton Affair" shaped the first term of the Jackson presidency more than any other matter.

"While I was still in pantalets and rolling hoops with other girls, I had the attentions of men, young and old, enough to turn a girl's head," Peggy Eaton wrote in her memoirs. And it got her in trouble throughout her life. The daughter of William O'Neale, proprietor of the fashionable Franklin boardinghouse in Washington, D.C., Peggy enjoyed a childhood surrounded by the powerful, doting congressmen who stayed there when the legislature was in session. A beautiful girl, Peggy caused her first small scandal simply by the fact that her father allowed her to work in the tavern, an all-male preserve.

Peggy got married in 1816 when she was sixteen, which was not so unusual except that by then she had already rejected one suitor, who killed himself, and she had tried to elope with an Army major. Her husband, whom she married after a two-week courtship, was a naval purser named John Timberlake. He proved to be unreliable, and after he failed at several business ventures, he began to drink heavily. They had three children.

Meanwhile, in 1818, Senator John Eaton of Tennessee took a room at Franklin House. A wealthy twenty-eight-year-old widower, Eaton helped Timberlake get commissions to resume his naval career. That left Peggy, while her husband was sailing abroad for years at a time, free to escort Eaton to Washington parties. The rumors of their romance began as early as 1821 and were widespread enough that President Monroe's wife snubbed Peggy at a White House gathering. But after Jackson, then a senator, joined Eaton at Franklin House in 1823, he wrote to his wife,

Rachel, that he found Peggy "much maligned, amiable, free of the vices of which she is accused."

After Jackson was elected president in 1828, Eaton, one of his strongest supporters, was an obvious Cabinet choice. But the gossip about Peggy had gotten so bad that after her husband died earlier that year in the Mediterranean, it was rumored that he had committed suicide over her affair with Eaton. Yet when Eaton told Jackson he was worried how Jackson's enemies might take advantage of the matter, the president-elect told him, "If you love Margaret Timberlake, go and marry her at once and shut their mouths."

Eaton and Peggy were married by the Senate chaplain on January 1, 1829, but that did not silence their critics. When it became clear that Jackson would name Eaton Secretary of War, the entire Tennessee delegation hurried to the White House to protest. But Jackson, whose own late wife had suffered the Washington gossips because of her previous divorce, was not about to back down. "This makes me well," he said. "I was born for a storm and a calm does not suit me."

It was then that Mrs. Calhoun made her husband's life pass before his eyes. She refused to socialize with Mrs. Eaton, and most Washington hostesses—including the wives of three of Jackson's six Cabinet members—followed suit. They didn't invite her to their parties and declined to attend ones where she would be. Jackson countered by placing Peggy at his right—the seat of honor—at a White House dinner.

Peggy, for her part, was as stubborn as Jackson. She declined to defuse the matter by traveling abroad, and when Eaton suggested he take an ambassadorship to get out of Washington, she forbade it. In an interview late in her life, Peggy said, "I was fond of society, gay as a lark, full of fun and nonsense—sometimes, maybe, a little original and lawless in my remarks, but, sir, before heaven and my God, as innocent of actual wrong to anyone as an unborn babe."

"The Ladies War," as the *Times* of London called it, ruined the Washington social season, but worse, it cast a heavy pall over Jackson's administration. Jackson spent much of his first year sending staff members to investigate the allegations against Peggy Eaton. Finally, in September 1829, Jackson called a Cabinet meeting solely for the purpose of discussing Mrs. Eaton, "to obtain justice for her, for myself and for our country," the president said. Jackson presented affidavits from dozens of witnesses supporting Mrs. Eaton's character, and he personally questioned and discredited those who had spoken against her. "She is chaste as a virgin!" Jackson exclaimed, and he told his Cabinet members to either behave or resign.

When the situation did not improve, Eaton submitted his resignation in April 1831. Secretary of State Martin Van Buren, a widower who had been gracious to Mrs. Eaton all along, also resigned. Jackson then demanded the resignations of the three Cabinet members whose wives had snubbed Mrs. Eaton, leaving all but one of his Cabinet posts vacant.

Calhoun kept his job, but only temporarily. When Jackson sought a second term in 1832, the vice-presidential slot went to Van Buren. Calhoun never regained his momentum toward the White House, and Van Buren was elected president in 1836. There were, to be sure, many political issues that caused Jackson and the two men to shift their alliances, but the Eaton affair was not a small one among them. Some believed Calhoun to be the last hope for conciliation with the

South, and there is even a book called *Peggy O'Neale, or the Doom of the Republic*.

Eaton lost his Senate bid in 1833, but was governor of Florida from 1834 to 1836 and ambassador to Spain from 1836 to 1840. Eaton and his wife were with Jackson at the Hermitage when he died in 1845. After Eaton died in 1856, Peggy was left to raise the four children of one of their daughters who had died. In 1859 she shocked Washington all over again when she married the children's nineteen-year-old Italian dancing instructor. They moved to New York in 1865 and a year later, her young husband stole her fortune and married her youngest granddaughter.

Mrs. Eaton spent her last years in Washington, where her earlier scandals had grown dim enough that she was invited to parties again. She died of dropsy in 1879, just before she turned eighty. Shortly before she died, Peggy Eaton had asked that her tombstone read, "She was never dull." Her family did not comply.

SARAH EMMA EDMONDS

"THE BEARDLESS BOY"

In the diary that he kept during the Civil War, Union soldier Jerome Robbins wrote of a fellow recruit named Frank Thompson. They had trained together, camped together, and marched side by side into battle, and Robbins wrote, "Though never frankly asserted by her, it will be understood that my friend

Frank is a female, which accounts for the singularity of the use of pronouns."

Frank, it was later discovered, was really Sarah Emma Edmonds, a Canadian-born woman who served with the Union army for two years in the Potomac region. While it was not unheard of for women to pose as soldiers during the Civil War—it was estimated some four hundred tried it—Emma Edmonds succeeded well beyond the others.

Her ruse began before the war when, in 1859 at the age of seventeen, she ran away from home in New Brunswick to escape her hard-driving father, a farmer. She dressed as a man, since that was less conspicuous, and got a job selling Bibles door-to-door. By 1861 Edmonds—that is, Frank Thompson—was selling books in Flint, Michigan. Her guise was so convincing that she escorted young women out riding in her horse and carriage. When President Lincoln issued his first call for volunteer troops, Edmonds enlisted along with the rest of her male friends. At first, the army—which didn't require a physical—rejected the five-foot six-inch "beardless boy" (as one officer called Thompson) for being too small. But soon Thompson was allowed to join and was sent with the Michigan regiment to the Potomac.

Edmonds later wrote, "I went to war with no other ambition than to nurse the sick and care for the wounded." She never fully explained why she posed as a man to accomplish that, but some historians guess that she simply had come to enjoy the freedom that her disguise gave her. Edmonds apparently spent most of her military career behind the front lines. One soldier wrote, "He seemed happiest when caring for the sick, and after the first fights at Blackburn's Ford and Bull Run [in Virginia], spent much of his time in the various hospitals."

But she had her harrowing moments. Twice Edmonds was sent to spy behind Confederate lines. Once she posed as a black boy, the second time she was "disguised" as a peddler woman. During one mission, Edmonds said, she shot a rebel farm wife through her hand after the woman had shot at her first. "I told her that if she uttered another word or scream she was a dead woman," Edmonds said. Her spying provided Union officers with information about Confederate troop movements and, more importantly, identified several spies in the Union camps.

Edmonds clearly was well thought of by her commanders. She was appointed an aide to Colonel Orlando Poe, who later testified "that her sex was not suspected by me or anyone else in the regiment." She also was the brigade's mail-carrier, and she said she "was more than once obliged to swim my horse across the swift-running streams in going back and forth with the mail."

Edmonds once was thrown from her horse, seriously injuring her ribs, but she didn't seek medical treatment because that would have ended her ruse. She later said it was that same fear that caused her to desert the army in the spring of 1863 when she developed a severe fever. However, her friend, Jerome Robbins, said in his diary that Edmonds deserted because of a failed romance with a Union officer.

Whatever caused her to give up her soldier career, Edmonds also gave up her male guise. As a woman, she went back to the battlefront as a nurse. She wrote a fictionalized account of her life called *Nurse and Spy in the Union Army* that was widely popular, selling some 175,000 copies when it was published in 1865.

In 1867 Edmonds went back to New Brunswick and married a carpenter, Linus Seelye. Their three children all died young and they adopted two boys. In

1882, after she and Seelye had moved several times and never successfully settled anywhere, Edmonds finally went public with her soldier's story to qualify for a veteran's pension. Her captain wrote on her behalf, "She followed that regiment through hard-fought battles, never flinched from duty, and was never suspected of being else than what she seemed. The beardless boy was a universal favorite."

Her army buddies invited her to their reunion in 1884, and that same year Congress granted her a pension of twelve dollars a month. After she died of malaria in 1898 at the age of fifty-six, Edmonds was buried with full military honors in the Grand Army of the Republic Cemetery in Houston—the only woman there. Her tombstone read, "Emma E. Seelye—Army Nurse."

MARY MOODY EMERSON

RALPH WALDO'S AUNT AND INSPIRATION

Ralph Waldo Emerson dealt the church a blow from which it has never recovered. With his philosophy of Transcendentalism, the great essayist and poet convinced many to move beyond organized religion in their search for God. With Henry David Thoreau and Walt Whitman, Emerson spawned a liberal revolt against strict church doctrine and hierarchy in favor of individualism and equality.

How ironic, then, that the father of such radical ideas would say that the person who influenced him the most was his Aunt Mary, a painfully orthodox spinster who refused to speak to him after he broke with the church. "She was as great an influence in my life as Greece or Rome," Emerson said of Mary Moody Emerson. "I who cling always to her writings, forget everything else very fast. Her genius was the purest." Added one historian, "Without her, he might have become simply another estimable Reverend Mr. Emerson, in the pattern of so many Waldos, Bulkelys, Emersons and Moodys."

Mary Emerson's entire life was shaped by her severe childhood. Born in 1774, she was the descendant of six generations of New England preachers, the period's most esteemed profession. But after her father died, she was raised by an ill-tempered aunt and her shiftless husband on an impoverished farm with no other children. "Rose before light every morn," Mary wrote in her journal. "Commented on scriptures, touched Shakespeare, washed, carded, cleaned house, baked." Mostly self-educated, Mary pursued for herself the Bible, *Paradise Lost*, and the works of Plato and Byron.

After her brother died in 1811, Mary moved to Boston to help his widow raise their six children. All the children under ten years old, the middle of three sons was Ralph Waldo, an intelligent if not overly ambitious boy. Mary changed that. Only four feet three inches tall because of her malnourished childhood, Emerson's aunt was nevertheless an imposing teacher. "Scorn trifles," she would tell them over and over. "Lift your arms. Do what you are afraid to do."

Emerson remembered that his aunt talked with him constantly, kept journals that he read and reread, and always pushed him harder than did his schoolteachers. "Aunt Mary wrote the prayers which first my brother William and then I read aloud morning and evening," Emerson wrote. "And they still sound in my ear with their prophetic and apocalyptic ejaculations."

Emerson was admitted to Harvard in 1817, which made everyone proud but Aunt Mary. "Would to God thou wouldst not to Cambridge," she wrote him. "True, they use the name Christo, but it is but a garnished sepulchre where may be found some relics of the body of Jesus—some grosser parts which he took not at his ascent!"

As he matured, Mary's pupil moved farther and farther away from her. Emerson was ordained a minister in 1829, but he left the church three years later after his wife died. Wrote Mary, "It is far sadder than the translation of a soul by death of the body to lose Waldo as I have lost him." After Emerson gave his heretical Harvard Divinity School address in 1838, Mary refused to enter his home for years.

Despite their religious differences, there is much of Aunt Mary's staunch independence in Emerson's doctrine of self-reliance, though as she grew older, Mary pushed the concept to the limit. Wearing short-cropped yellow hair, a funeral shroud, and the result of an extensive search for a pointedly odd bonnet, Mary spent years wandering among cheap New England boardinghouses. One Concord, Massachusetts, resident wrote of her, "A person at war with society as to all its decorums, she eats and drinks what others do not, and when they do not; dresses in a white robe these October days, enters into conversation with everybody, and talks on every subject."

One newspaper said after she died, "She was thought to have the power of saying more disagreeable things in a half hour than any person living." Mary would have agreed. "To live to give pain rather than pleasure (the latter so delicious) seems the spider-like necessity of my being on earth," she wrote. Still, Thoreau said of her, "She is singular among women, at least, in being really and perseveringly interested to know what thinkers think."

Mary eventually lived with a niece in Brooklyn, where she died in 1863 at the age of eighty-eight. Emerson, who lived another nineteen years, never forgot his aunt. "Though I have learned to discriminate and drop her huge alloy of theology and metaphysics," he wrote, "her letters and journals charm me still as thirty years ago, and honor the American air."

DOROTHY EUSTIS

SHE INTRODUCED THE SEEING EYE DOG TO AMERICA

Morris Frank, the first blind person to be guided by a Seeing Eye dog, explained the difference the German shepherd made in his life. "Back in Nashville, getting a haircut was a major event. Some days Father would drop me at the barbershop on his way to work and leave me there all morning until he could pick me up on his way home to lunch. Today, Buddy took me to get my haircut. For the first time in four years, I'm free."

Dorothy Eustis was responsible for thousands of stories like that. She was a Philadelphia Main Line girl, the daughter of the head of a sugar refining company, who put her fortune to work. After marrying in

1906 when she was twenty, she and her first husband, an upstate New York businessman, created an experimental dairy farm to demonstrate that selective breeding could develop cows that would produce more milk. They were so successful that their cattle tripled in value.

It was while she was working on the farm that Dorothy became impressed with the intelligence of her pet German shepherd, Hans. After her husband died, she moved to Switzerland in 1921 and began breeding shepherds to try to enhance the breed's qualities. The results were good, and Dorothy, along with her second husband, George Eustis, and a horse breeder named Jack Humphrey, began training the dogs for the Swiss police and army.

In 1927, her husband was in Germany to study dog-training techniques when he visited a school at Potsdam where dogs were taught to guide blind war veterans. Dorothy wrote an article about the program for the *Saturday Evening Post:* "I shall never forget the change that came over one man as he turned away from that gate [where he harnessed his dog]. One moment it was an uncertain, shuffling blind man, tapping with a cane, the next it was an assured person, with his dog firmly in hand and his head up, who walked toward us quickly and firmly, giving his orders in a low, confident voice . . . Gentlemen, again without reservation, I give you the shepherd dog!"

Looking back, it seems like the most natural, obvious idea. But American experts on the blind didn't agree. The head of the prestigious Perkins School for the Blind in Boston said guide dogs were preposterous, "a dirty little cur dragging a blind man along at the end of a string, the very index of incompetence and beggary."

But Morris Frank, a blind insurance salesman who had heard about Eustis's article, entitled "The Seeing Eye," wrote her to ask how he could get such a dog. Eustis and her husband and Humphrey began training German shepherds as Seeing Eye dogs, and then she brought Frank to Switzerland to teach him how to use the dog to guide him. When she sent him back to the United States, reporters were waiting at the pier in New York City. They were won over after Frank and his dog walked off the ship and, without assistance, crossed West Street, a murderous stretch of heavy traffic.

But American blind organizations still weren't convinced, so Eustis, by then divorced, raised the money to establish The Seeing Eye School. After a brief effort failed in Nashville in 1930, she moved to Morristown, New Jersey, where the school still trains dogs today. By the time Eustis died of cancer in 1946 at the age of sixty, some 1,300 dogs—mostly German shepherds, but also Labradors and boxers—had been trained. Since then, thousands more blind people—and those who benefit from their mobility—are the richer for her.

MINNA AND AIDA EVERLEIGH

PROPRIETORS OF THE WORLD'S MOST LAVISH WHOREHOUSE

When Prince Henry of Prussia arrived in New York in 1902, reporters asked him what he most wanted to see in America. "I would like to visit the Everleigh Club in Chicago," he replied. It is not ordinary for a prince to announce that he wants to go to a whorehouse, but then the Everleigh Club was no ordinary brothel. "No house of courtesans in the world was so richly furnished, so well advertised, and so continuously patronized by men of wealth and slight morals," said the *Chicago Tribune*, which was well-situated to report such facts. A reporter at the newspaper later wrote that when he was working the night desk, his editor told him that if any major news broke after 1 A.M., he could round up reporters and editors by calling Calumet 412—the phone number of the Everleigh Club.

In a later time, Minna and Aida Everleigh, the club's proprietresses, might have become the star executives of a Forbes 500 company. But there were few such opportunities at the turn of the century. In fact, although prostitution is hardly more acceptable now than it was then, some historians now say that in an era when women were barred from most businesses, the Everleigh sisters were simply an example of women who found their niche and succeeded at it.

Minna and Aida were raised to be Southern belles. The daughters of a successful lawyer in a small Virginia town, they attended finishing school and then promptly married a pair of brothers whose last name was Lester. But the marriages lasted less than a year, and in 1898, when Minna was twenty and Aida was twenty-three, they joined a traveling theater troupe.

Their acting careers ended later that year after they inherited a small fortune—$35,000—and found themselves in Omaha, Nebraska—the site of the Trans-Mississippi Exposition. Minna and Aida opened a brothel and doubled their money in two years. No longer Minna and Aida Lester, they chose the name Everleigh from their grandmother, who signed her many letters to them, "Everly yours."

When business died down after the fair closed, the Everleigh sisters moved on to Chicago. In 1900, prostitution and other vices were centered in a section of the city's South Side called the Levee. In an area with an estimated five hundred brothels, Minna and Aida leased one of the largest mansions, at 2131 S. Dearborn Street, from a madam who was retiring. They agreed to pay $500 a month plus $55,000 for the furnishings, which they promptly discarded.

After extensive renovations, the fifty-room Everleigh Club opened in February 1900. If you didn't go upstairs, you might have thought you were in the slightly garish home of some new-monied coal baron. There was a music room with a gold-leaf piano where chamber groups performed, a library stuffed with classics, and an art gallery. There were also twelve soundproof parlors, among them the Blue Room, which featured college pennants and pictures of Gibson Girls. Each had a $650 gold spittoon, and perfume wafted through all the rooms. Upstairs were forty to fifty finely crafted brass beds.

While the blond-haired Aida ran the business side, red-headed Minna, wearing a silk gown, a large diamond necklace, bracelets, and rings, and a ruby and emerald stomacher, greeted their guests. Writer Edgar Lee Masters recalled, "She was remarkably thin. Her hair was dark and frizzled, her face thin and refined. 'How is my boy?' was her cordial salutation." But beyond her graciousness, Minna never lost sight of the business. She told her staff, "There shall be no cry, 'In the parlor, girls,' when visitors arrive. And remember that the Everleigh Club has no time for the rough element, the clerk on a holiday or a man without a checkbook."

At a time when most prostitutes charged a dollar for their services, it cost ten dollars just to walk into the Everleigh Club. Customers were expected to spend a minimum of one hundred dollars during the evening, which wasn't difficult, since dinner—pheasant, capon, or broiled squab for an early supper, or fried oysters, lobster, and caviar at midnight—cost fifty dollars a plate and wine was twelve dollars a bottle. The price for going upstairs started at twenty-five dollars.

On an average night, the sisters raked in over $2,500. It came from bankers, politicians, business tycoons like John "Bet-a-Million" Gates, and famous men such as actor John Barrymore. But the Everleigh Club also profited from many a corporate expense account, and was particularly busy during Chicago's annual auto show.

For a long time, the Everleigh Club seemed immune to the periodic reform movements that pledged to clean up the Levee. Probably that was because the Everleigh sisters paid twenty thousand dollars a year to the district's aldermen. They also provided the girls for the annual masked ball of the First Ward Democratic Club and, just to be fair, took out a half-page ad in the Cook County Republican Marching Club's annual reception booklet.

Even by 1911, when the club's fame had made it the focus of reform-minded politicians and nearly every preacher in the city, the sisters blithely sent out an advertising brochure that called the Everleigh Club one of the "two outstanding points of interest in Chicago," the other being the stockyards. But it was that pamphlet, combined with the mysterious death of a young heir shortly after he had left the club, which finally led city officials to shut down the Everleigh Club in October 1911. It was the first blow to the Levee and led to the district's decline.

Minna and Aida, still in their mid-thirties, retired from their business, taking with them some one million dollars in cash and two hundred thousand dollars in jewels. After another Chicago neighborhood refused to let them settle down, the sisters moved to New York, where they lived in a fashionable brownstone near Central Park for more than thirty years. Using their former married name, Lester, and saying nothing about their past, they joined several women's clubs, organized a poetry reading group, and often went to the theater.

Minna died in 1948 at the age of seventy, and Aida then moved back to Virginia. She remained there until she died in 1960 at the age of eighty-four.

F

FANNIE FARMER

COOKING BY THE BOOK

If you tried to cook something by adding a "handful" of this, a "heaping spoonful" of that, and a lump of butter "the size of an egg," the odds of producing a tasty dish would definitely be against you. Especially if you were using somebody else's recipe, the meal could flop simply because your spoons and eggs didn't match theirs. Yet for countless generations, that's how people cooked. It wasn't until less than a century ago that Fannie Farmer brought precision into the kitchen.

"The Mother of Level Measurements" was herself said to be a pretty poor cook in her youth. The daughter of a Boston printer, Farmer ended her schooling in high school when she suffered a stroke that disabled her for several years and left her with a limp for the rest of her life. When she recovered in her late twenties, Farmer went to work as a "mother's helper" to help support her father's failing business.

It was while she was cooking one day that the family's daughter asked her whether it wouldn't be more consistent to use two level spoonfuls instead of one heaping spoonful. In 1887, at the age of thirty, Farmer enrolled in the Boston Cooking School. After two years of training, she became assistant principal, and in 1894 she was put in charge of the school.

Two years later she published *The Boston Cooking-School Cook Book.* Unlike any other previous cookbook, Farmer's was precise. Every recipe—which she had tested in the school's kitchen time and again to make sure each dish turned out the same every time—contained specific measurements down to one-eighth of a teaspoon. Further, the seven-hundred-page cookbook assumed its readers knew nothing. "To bake is to cook in an oven," it explained, and offered eight ways to generate heat, including using wood, kerosene, and coal.

Farmer emphasized the nutritional value of foods, saying in her introduction, "It is my wish that it may not only be looked upon as a compilation of tried and tested recipes, but that it may awaken an interest through its condensed scientific knowledge which will lead to deeper thought and broader study of what to eat."

Her publisher, Little, Brown & Co., thought Farmer's cookbook was so unlikely that it required Farmer to pay for the first printing of three thousand copies. It did not feature the most haute-cuisine recipes. The dishes were well-known, traditional fare, but Farmer's early editions were criticized as too provincial, concentrating on New England at the expense of other regions' specialties. Even in 1930, H. L. Mencken called the latest edition "too feminine and a shade too Yankee." But it has consistently found its audience. Now in its twelfth edition—revised to take into account kitchen devices that she never dreamed of—Fannie Farmer's cookbook has sold millions.

As far as Farmer was concerned, her cookbook was a sidelight. In 1902 she opened her own cooking school, and while she trained her share of professional cooks, she mostly sought to teach housewives. The red-haired, bright-blue–eyed woman performed weekly cooking demonstrations that were reported in newspapers nationwide. Farmer also developed diets for the sick and invalid, and she lectured at Harvard Medical School to present her findings.

Farmer suffered a second stroke in 1908, but she continued to lecture and perform cooking demonstrations from a wheelchair. Her last lecture came ten days before she died in 1915 of kidney disease and hardening of the arteries. She was fifty-seven.

Farmer had written in her cookbook, "The time is not far distant when a knowledge of the principles of diet will be an essential part of one's education. Then mankind will eat to live, will be able to do better mental and physical work, and disease will be less frequent." Though many of her original recipes might be out of date, that statement—for many—has yet to come true.

JANE, LADY FRANKLIN

HER SEARCH FOR HER MISSING HUSBAND PROVED THAT HE HAD FOUND THE NORTHWEST PASSAGE

What Columbus's discovery of America meant five hundred years ago, what the *Apollo* astronauts' landing on the moon meant to us, the search for the Northwest Passage was to the nineteenth century. At a time when the only way to cross between the Atlantic and Pacific oceans was to sail thousands of miles southward around Cape Horn, seamen—especially the British—were obsessed with finding a northern route through the Arctic islands of Canada.

Ultimately, it was Sir John Franklin who discovered the much-sought passage. Though the effort killed him, his name has survived on a bay, a strait, a lake, and a mountain range. And for that it is his wife who deserves the credit. In fact, without Jane, Lady Franklin, the history books probably would record that someone else found the passage. One Arctic historian even goes so far as to say that this driven woman, not her husband, "might be said to have discovered the Northwest Passage. More than any naval explorer it was she who was responsible for combing the Arctic solitudes until the last trace of her missing husband was found."

Actually, Lady Franklin, not Sir John, was the more adventurous of the two. Born in 1792, she grew up traveling widely with her father, a wealthy silk weaver. After she married Franklin—a naval commander already knighted for his Arctic explorations—in 1828, she frequently accompanied him on his Mediterranean voyages. In 1837, when her husband was lieutenant governor of Van Damien's Land, now Tasmania, Lady Franklin set out on her own and became the first woman to scale the four-thousand-foot Mount Wellington in New Zealand. "You have completely eclipsed me, and almost every other traveler—females certainly," her husband wrote to her.

Sir John proved to be a less able colonial administrator than ship officer, and he was soon recalled from Tasmania. By then in his late fifties, he could well have retired after a distinguished career, which in the 1820s had included several Arctic missions to chart the Canadian coast. But his wife would not have it. "The character and position you possess in society, and the interest—I may say celebrity—attached to your name, belong to the expeditions," she wrote him. "Nor indeed can I properly enjoy your society if you are living in inactivity when you might be in active employ."

So at fifty-nine, Sir John Franklin claimed command of a highly prestigious expedition to find the Northwest Passage. Previous explorations had come close to unlocking the icy course, so the HMS *Erebus* and the HMS *Terror* were launched with great anticipation. Sir John and his crew of 128 sailed in July 1845, their ships stocked with provisions to last three years.

There was some concern when no word of the expedition came in 1846 or 1847, but it wasn't until 1848 when rescue efforts were mounted. Even then, it was largely due to the prodding of Lady Franklin. She marshaled the press, wrote letters to world leaders, and practically laid siege on the British Admiralty. Further, she offered a reward of two thousand pounds for information about her husband's fate and even tried to go on search missions herself. When she was denied, she wooed sea captains to search for her husband. "I will be for you a son," replied a French naval lieutenant, who would later drown in the Arctic searching for her husband.

The search for Franklin and his crew soon became the largest and most widely followed of the era. Five expeditions were launched in 1848, three in 1849, and ten in 1850. By 1857, a total of thirty-eight ships had combed the Arctic islands of Canada, including some sponsored jointly for the first time by England and the United States. Five of the ships were financed by Lady Franklin herself, whom the press called the "English Penelope," after the faithful wife of Odysseus of Greek mythology. Ironically, though none of the rescue ships found Franklin, their voyages added great depth to the scarce knowledge of the geography of the Arctic.

In 1850, one rescue ship returned with evidence of Franklin's voyage from an Arctic island. The searchers found large stacks of food supplies which Franklin's crew apparently had dumped after they had been found spoiled, indicating the expedition would have run out of supplies in a much shorter time than three years. In 1854, another search team heard Eskimos tell of a group of white men they had seen a few years earlier traveling over the ice on King William Island. The Eskimos said they had later seen the white men's dead bodies, and the natives were carrying many small silver pieces—including a plate with Franklin's name engraved on it.

After that, the British Admiralty declared Franklin's mission lost and the official search was ended. But Lady Franklin was not ready to give up. In 1857 she put up seven thousand pounds to launch the HMS *Fox*. The ship endured two long winters in the Arctic with no success, but finally in 1859 the crew found what everyone had been looking for. They discovered a small boat from Franklin's expedition containing skeletons, instruments from the original ships, and most importantly, a written paper. The document recorded that Franklin's mission, after proceeding on course, had been stranded by ice during the winter of 1846–47. There was no thaw in the summer of 1847, and Franklin himself had died that June. The surviving crew had finally abandoned their ice-locked ships in 1848 and attempted to trudge southward across King William Island. All perished.

The evidence showed that although Franklin and his crew had died, it was not before he had discovered the crucial strait between King William Island and Victoria Island that led to the western side of the Northwest Passage. It would be fifty years before Roald Amundsen would sail the complete passage, but Franklin was recognized as its discoverer.

Lady Franklin spent part of her seventies traveling around the world, including a trip to Alaska at the age of seventy-eight after hearing reports of survivors from her husband's expedition. The Royal Geographical Society awarded her its Founder's Medal for finding the truth about Franklin's fate. Said one newspaper, "What the nation would not do, a woman did."

ROSALIND FRANKLIN

THOUGH SLIGHTED BY HER FELLOW SCIENTISTS, SHE CO-DISCOVERED DNA

In 1953 a group of British scientists announced that they had discovered the structure of DNA. Literally the stuff of life, deoxyribonucleic acid holds the key to our genetic code, and its discovery has led scientists to pinpoint the cause of all sorts of inherited traits, especially diseases. The British finding of the double-helix structure of DNA was one of the most important advances of the twentieth century, and in 1962, three of the scientists were awarded the Nobel Prize for Medicine and Physiology.

In fact there was a fourth scientist integrally involved in the discovery of DNA. Had Rosalind Franklin lived that long, the Nobel committee—whose prize cannot be awarded posthumously, or to more than three people—would have had a much more difficult time deciding whom to honor.

Franklin, from a family of Jewish socialists, had proven her keen scientific merit at an early age. After being admitted to Cambridge to study chemistry at eighteen, she later won a fellowship in Paris, where she learned a complicated new technique, called x-ray crystallography, that was used to study molecular structures. Using that technique, Franklin made ground-breaking discoveries in the field of industrial carbons.

In 1951, at the age of thirty-one, Franklin was invited to apply her x-ray procedure to a DNA research project at King's College in London. Though her research was separate, it was assumed that Franklin would collaborate with another prominent scientist in the field at King's College, Maurice Wilkins. The trouble was, the two of them didn't get along. As Franklin's friend and biographer later wrote, "the history of molecular biology might be rather different from what it is today if Rosalind and Maurice Wilkins had not hated one another at sight."

Who can say who was at fault? Franklin, an intense, fiercely single-minded scientist, certainly was not one to smooth things over. Said Aaron Klug, who collaborated with her some years later, "I can't say she was like a man, not like that at all, but one didn't think of her being particularly like a woman. She wasn't shy or self-effacing—but she wasn't blustering either. She spoke her opinions firmly. I think people were unaccustomed to dealing with that in a woman. I think they expected women to behave rather differently, quieter. She expected reason to dominate."

Franklin proceeded to produce a series of unique x-rays of DNA material. There was much debate at the time over what exactly DNA looked like, but Franklin refused to guess. She continued her painstaking research, unaware that she already had created the information that would yield the discovery. A doctoral student who worked with her recalled, "I felt repeatedly that Maurice [Wilkins] was trying various ways to stimulate Rosalind into saying something about the structure, but she, for her part, would say, 'We are going to wait, we are going to let the spots on this photograph tell us what the structure is.' And so, since there was nobody here Maurice could talk to who was willing to speculate about the structure, he talked to Crick and Watson about it."

Francis Crick and James Watson were conducting DNA research at Cambridge. Franklin got along with them no better than she did with Wilkins, and the feeling was mutual. Watson, in his 1968 book, *The Double Helix*, which portrays Franklin as little more than an over-zealous lab assistant, wrote, "The real problem was Rosy [a derogatory nickname they called her behind her back]. The thought could not be avoided that the best home for a feminist is in another person's lab."

Wilkins, without asking Franklin, showed her x-rays to Watson. "Perhaps I should have asked Rosalind's permission and I didn't," said Wilkins, who in one letter called her "our dark lady." "Things were very difficult . . . I had this photograph, and there was a helix right on the picture, you couldn't miss it. I showed it to Jim [Watson], and I said 'Look, there's the helix, and that damned woman just won't see it.' He picked it up, of course."

Indeed, Watson had written earlier, "We are certainly a long way from proving its correctness [the double helix structure]. To do this we must obtain collaboration from the group at King's College, London, who possess very excellent photographs." After Wilkins showed him Franklin's x-rays, Watson wrote, "The instant I saw the picture my mouth fell open and my pulse began to race. The pattern was unbelievably simpler than those obtained previously."

Based on their own extensive research—and also on Franklin's—Watson and Crick wrote a scientific paper stating their conclusion that the structure of DNA was a double helix—two interlocking spirals—which has proven to be the foundation of all genetic research. Franklin, who had seen their visual model, wrote her own paper based on her research, as did Wilkins. All three reports were published in the scientific journal, *Nature*, on April 25, 1953.

Watson and Crick's breakthrough, however, was only the initial step in unlocking the genetic code. Franklin and others produced additional evidence afterward that confirmed their finding. But largely because of her animosity with Wilkins, Franklin left King's College and embarked on a new research project on the structure of viruses. She continued her research until she died of cancer in 1958 at the age of thirty-seven.

Watson, Crick, and Wilkins were awarded the Nobel Prize in 1962. The debate over Franklin's role in their research erupted after Watson published his one-sided account in 1968. Crick, for his part, was angered by Watson's book. He and Franklin became friends after 1953, and Franklin stayed with Crick and his wife for a time during her final illness.

The point is not that Franklin deserves all the credit for discovering the structure of DNA, just a good share of it. Her later colleague, Klug, said, "She needed a collaborator, and she didn't have one. Somebody to break the pattern of her thinking, to show her what was right in front of her, to push her up and over. You know, in a way, Watson was her collaborator."

JESSIE BENTON FRÉMONT

HER WRITINGS ENCOURAGED THOUSANDS OF PIONEERS TO TRAVEL WEST

Until the 1840s, just about the only Americans who had ventured to the Far West were fur trappers and a few explorers. The surge of pioneers who followed hitched up their wagon trains for several reasons, but one important factor was a series of expeditions led by Lieutenant John Charles Frémont. Returning with more than the usual mundane record of his missions, Frémont presented the government with vivid, vigorously written accounts of his journeys to Wyoming, the Columbia River valley, and California.

His reports—which were distributed widely and reprinted in many newspapers—fueled the frontier spirit, and many settlers recalled that reading them had prompted their trek. Said one historian of the Columbia River report, "More than any other work of its time, it dramatized the West and made it both alluring and accessible to a generation of restless Americans."

But although Frémont did see and do everything contained in his reports, it was his wife who wrote them. Having traveled no farther west than St. Louis, Jessie Benton Frémont wrote of the "savage sublimity" of the Rockies. Without pictures, she painted the West in all its awesome beauty and fertility. She blended the drama of her husband's near starvation in the Sierras with practical information about the best westward routes and the most desirable lands. Of California, the explorer's wife reported, "It is true. This valley is a paradise."

In a way that characterized Jessie's life with her husband, the reports made Frémont famous (and made his guide, Kit Carson, a legend), though they were submitted in Jessie's handwriting. In a later era, Jessie probably would have made a name for herself. The oldest daughter of the powerful, five-term Missouri Senator Thomas Hart Benton, she grew up amidst a lively blend of Washington politics and Missouri pioneers. Well-schooled by her father, she translated confidential Spanish documents for the State Department while her husband was traveling.

Ironically, the senator had tried to prevent Jessie from marrying Frémont, a mid-level government officer, by arranging for him to be sent on his first western expedition. But Jessie waited, Frémont's trip was a success, and the two were secretly married in 1841 when she was seventeen and he was twenty-eight.

Benton then turned around and used his influence to put his son-in-law at the helm of the explorations that would make him famous. But upon his return from Wyoming in 1842, Frémont found that he couldn't get started writing his report. So Jessie, eighteen at the time, sat with him every day for four hours beginning at 9 A.M. He would tell her about his experiences, and she would craft them into an adventure. "Without her sharp eye for a good story," said her biographer, Pamela Kerr, "the report, if completed at all, would have been another dry treatise." Jessie was twenty-one when she wrote her husband's second report, the one most credited for sending immigrants westward.

Frémont's career as an explorer ended abruptly in 1847 when he was court-martialed for helping to lead a revolt against Mexican rule in California. Jessie pleaded her husband's case directly to President Polk, but to no avail. She also stood closely by his side when he became the Republican party's first presidential nominee in 1856. It was the first time in the nation's history that a candidate's wife campaigned with him, and Jessie proved to be so popular that one campaign song was about "Frémont and our Jessie" instead of the vice-presidential candidate.

Frémont, of course, lost that election. And after he failed to quell Civil War disturbances in Missouri in 1861, he was fired as head of the Department of the West, though again Jessie had taken her plea directly to President Lincoln. Frémont proceeded to lose his entire fortune, made in the California mines, by speculating in railroad stocks.

Jessie was left to support the family, including two children, by her writing. "I am like a deeply built ship," she said. "I drive best under a strong wind." In the 1870s and 1880s she wrote many articles, mainly reminiscences, for magazines such as *The Atlantic Monthly* and *Harper's* and she also compiled four memoirs. She also wrote most of Frémont's memoir in 1887. Never again wealthy, Jessie and her husband moved among furnished rooms in New York before they settled in Los Angeles. After Frémont died in 1890, Jessie and her daughter moved into a modest home built for them by a committee of ladies in southern California.

Jessie, who died in 1902 at the age of seventy-eight, often quoted Alfred, Lord Tennyson. " 'For man is man and master of his fate,' " she recited, then added, "That is poetry. When one is not a man but a woman, you follow in the wake of both man and fate, and the prose of life proves one does not so easily be 'master' of fate."

G

MYRA CLARK GAINES

THE MOST LITIGIOUS AMERICAN IN THE NINETEENTH CENTURY

Daniel Clark, the man without whom Thomas Jefferson said the Louisiana Purchase might not have been completed, died in 1813. Seventy-eight years later, the U.S. Supreme Court settled his estate in favor of his daughter. It was the twelfth time the nation's top justices had ruled on the case, which over the course of more than half the nineteenth century grew so voluminous that the legal documents had to be hauled around in two large trunks. By the end, Myra Clark Gaines, in pursuit of her father's fortune, had employed more than thirty lawyers—seventeen of whom died while working for her. Called by one Supreme Court justice "the most remarkable case in the records" of jurisprudence, the dispute so threatened the city of New Orleans that for more than a generation its residents referred to it bitterly as "the Gaines case."

It all boiled down to whether or not Myra Clark Gaines was a bastard. Her father was a wealthy Irish real estate speculator who, after helping secure the

Louisiana Territory for the United States, became its first territorial representative in Congress. In 1801 Clark took up with Zulime Des Granges, the beautiful French wife of a New Orleans confectioner. Years later, testifying on behalf of Myra, two of Zulime's sisters said Clark and Zulime had married secretly in Philadelphia in 1802.

In 1805 Zulime had a child by Clark. The baby girl was turned over to Samuel Davis, a sea captain friend of Clark's, who named the child Myra. She grew up believing she was Davis's daughter, though Clark visited her often. Myra moved with the family to an elegant Delaware mansion in 1812 and attended an elite school for girls in Philadelphia. It wasn't until Myra got married in 1832 that she was told of her true parentage. She was also told that her real father had died in 1813. Zulime had moved back to France.

In 1833 Myra and her husband visited New Orleans and discovered that Clark had left an enormously wealthy estate. Besides several large plantations in Louisiana and Mississippi, Clark had owned vast tracts of land in the city of New Orleans. When he was alive the land was on the outskirts of town, but by the 1830s it had become some of the most valuable property in the city, including its most prestigious shopping squares.

Although Clark had left it all to his widowed mother in Philadelphia, and although the parcels had long since been sold off to other owners, Myra believed the land belonged to her. And in fact, under Louisiana law she was entitled to four-fifths of the estate *if* she could prove that she was Clark's legitimate daughter. The trouble was, her parents' marital history was muddy at best. She claimed Clark and Zulime had indeed married secretly, although there was no record of it. And Zulime had been free to marry, Myra claimed, because she had not been legally married to the confectioner since he was already married to somebody else.

In 1835 she sued the executors of Clark's estate and then sued twenty-five people who held title to the various parcels. The next year she sued another one hundred people who lived on the disputed land. Over the next four decades she would sue hundreds more. Her action quickly made her a public pariah. "By and large," wrote one historian, "the whole population of the city came to feel itself in jeopardy as long as Myra Clark roamed at will through the halls of justice."

Much of the land she wanted had been sold and resold several times. Also, she was laying claim to the heart of the city, land that in the 1860s would be valued at $32 million when the entire city was assessed at $100 million. The first response of New Orleans city officials was to throw her husband in jail for libeling the executors of Clark's estate. Myra's husband developed yellow fever and died soon after he was released. In the North, however, Myra received much favorable publicity, portrayed in magazines and newspapers as a lone widow battling against backward slave-owners. She was featured in dime novels and was on the cover of *Harper's Weekly*.

Meanwhile, Myra drove her case through the courts. A wiry woman under five feet tall, with bright red hair curled around her forehead, she occasionally argued her own case. After she remarried in 1839, she appeared in court backed by her husband, a sixty-two-year-old widowed military hero who always wore his dress uniform. By the time General Edmund Gaines died in 1849, she had exhausted his entire fortune for her legal claims.

In 1848 Myra appeared to be vindicated when the U.S. Supreme Court upheld her claim in one of her many lawsuits. But then, three years later, the justices reversed themselves on another of her cases. In 1855 she suddenly claimed that her father had in fact written a second will, since lost, that left everything to her. Amazingly, the Supreme Court ruled in her favor in 1861. Her victory was postponed by the Civil War but in 1867 the justices again supported her claim.

Despised in New Orleans, Myra became a regular character in Washington, where she visited frequently to press her appeals. "Don't you know who I am?" she asked one stranger in front of the Capitol. "I am Myra Clark Gaines. I have suits all the way from that building to the Gulf." Nearly bankrupt by legal debts, she lived in tawdry boardinghouses to save money. But Myra never had trouble attracting attorneys—including many of the most prominent in the state—who looked forward to a fortune if she won. Over the years she won some settlements—totaling some $250,000—but that money, too, was applied to her larger battle.

Eventually, the case focused on one large tract of the Clark estate that had become the site of the city's water works. Clark's estate had sold the land in 1821 for $4,760. When the Supreme Court justices issued their final ruling on the matter in 1891—after admitting that they couldn't possibly read the entire case history—Myra's share was deemed to be worth $576,707.92.

But for Myra it was too late. Impoverished, she had died of a bronchial condition in 1885 at the age of seventy-nine. Her winnings, coming fifty-six years after she filed her first lawsuit, were awarded to her six grandchildren. They promptly sued each other over how to divide the estate.

SOPHIE GERMAIN

A FOUNDER OF MATHEMATICAL PHYSICS

In the study of mathematics, the name of Sophie Germain appears only in the most complete and complex studies of the subject. She is considered a founder of mathematical physics, but her contributions to the science were, for the most part, esoteric. Nevertheless, if we consider when she lived, her accomplishments are nothing short of amazing.

Born in Paris in 1776, Germain was the daughter of a wealthy merchant who played a small role in the French Revolution. It was the turmoil in the streets, in fact, that Germain said caused her to study geometry. In her father's library, she read about Archimedes, the Greek mathematician who was so absorbed in a geometry problem that he ignored invading Carthaginian soldiers and was killed. Germain decided that any subject that was so engrossing was right for her. While the Reign of Terror raged outside, Germain studied calculus. She taught herself basic math, as well as Latin and Greek, and read the works of Isaac Newton and the early, great mathematicians in Latin.

Her parents, alarmed that their daughter was not preparing herself for marriage, tried to prevent her studies. When they found her reading in her room at night, they began sending her to bed with no clothes and a bare fireplace. Germain would wrap herself in blankets, light her secreted candles, and study until morning even though her inkwell was frozen.

Her parents finally relented, but French scholars were no more receptive initially. As a woman, she could not be admitted to the Ecole Polytechnique. So instead, Germain collected professors' lecture notes from other students. She submitted a paper to the famous mathematician, Joseph Lagrange, under a pseudonym. Lagrange was so impressed that he sought her out, and ultimately became her mentor. Germain carried on a correspondence with another noted mathematician, Karl Gauss, for years before he discovered her identity.

Still, they were not so supportive in 1811, when the Académie Française sponsored a competition to apply mathematical laws to study the vibrations of elastic surfaces. Even though the competition was ordered by Napoléon, most leading French mathematicians declined to participate because they believed the extremely complicated subject was impossible to solve. Germain, having faced nothing but impossible conditions throughout her studies, submitted a paper. It did not win, but neither did the Académie award the prize to anyone else.

After withholding it a second time in 1813, the Académie finally awarded Germain the grand prize in 1816. The public acclaim she received made her name famous throughout France, and she became the first woman invited to attend sessions at the prestigious Institut de France. Wrote one mathematician on her winning paper, "It is a work which few men are able to read and which only one woman was able to write."

She continued to publish papers on mathematics and elasticity until she died of cancer in 1831 at the age of fifty-five. Some accounts say that Germain's discoveries on the elasticity of materials were used more than a half-century later by Gustave Eiffel in designing his famous tower. Her name was not among the seventy-two scientists and scholars engraved on the Eiffel Tower. But given the resistance she faced while she was alive, that may not mean a thing.

IRENE LANGHORNE GIBSON

THE ORIGINAL "GIBSON GIRL"

Today, men and women dress and cut their hair like movie stars, or models in a magazine. But in the 1890s, American women fashioned themselves after a series of ink drawings. With simple, fine black lines, illustrator Charles Dana Gibson created the "Gibson Girl," a woman whose sweeping hair, upturned nose, and aloof expression came to define American beauty until World War I.

More than that, the "Helen of Troy and Cleopatra of her day," as Sinclair Lewis called her, embodied an attitude. Gibson's girl—who first appeared on the pages of *Life*, *Collier's Weekly*, and other popular magazines—was a woman who thought for herself. Gibson drew her as the bored young wife of an elderly millionaire, or the object of a gentleman's passionate courtings, with her mind clearly elsewhere. She was, in one sketch, a sullen woman who had begun a letter with the words "Dear Tom" in a cartoon entitled "Yes or No." The Gibson Girl was, said *Time* magazine, "the gaslight era's symbol of genteel femininity, [who] influenced the dress, manner and flirtations of a generation of U.S. girls."

The woman who personified the Gibson Girl, and who modeled for Gibson more than anyone else, was his wife. Some historians insist that there was no real live Gibson Girl, and in fact Gibson had sketched hundreds of society girls before he met Irene Langhorne. But she was clearly the model for his art, the woman who inspired the artist.

Irene Langhorne was a Southern belle, one of four beautiful daughters of Colonel Chiswell Dabney Langhorne (another would become Lady Astor). Born in 1873 and raised at Mirador, the Virginia family home, Irene was in finishing school in New York when she met Gibson, who already was a successful illustrator. They married soon after, in 1895, and Gibson began to sketch his wife regularly.

For a while, it must have seemed like the Gibson Girl was everywhere. In 1904 *Collier's* proclaimed, "We find the Girl burnt on leather, printed on plates, stenciled on hardwood easels, woven in silk handkerchiefs, exploited in the cast of vaudeville shows, and giving her name to a variety of shirtwaist, a pompadour, and a riding stock." In 1906 there was even a hit song, "Why Do They Call Me a Gibson Girl?"

Irene Gibson, herself, never sought to capitalize on her fame once removed. Instead she lived the life of a wealthy wife. The mother of two, she founded the Protestant Big Sisters and for twenty-five years was chairman of the Child Placing and Adoption Committee of the New York State Charities Aid Association, hosting annual Gibson Girl charity balls for the organization. She toured the South in 1928 to campaign for the Democratic presidential nominee, Al Smith, and she was a delegate to the party's convention that year and in 1932.

Her husband died in 1944, but Irene Gibson remained, said *The New York Times*, "one of the last symbols of elegance in New York in the Gay Nineties." On her death in 1956 at the age of eighty-three, the newspaper said, "Her famous Gibson Girl profile retained its pure line until four or five years ago. Even at the age of eighty, she presented a queenly figure, beautifully dressed."

MARY KATHERINE GODDARD

SHE PUBLISHED THE FIRST OFFICIAL COPIES OF THE DECLARATION OF INDEPENDENCE

The Declaration of Independence is so indelible a document that most of us probably can get a fairly clear picture of it in our minds. But if you look closely at some early copies of the paper, beyond the flourished signature of John Hancock and the other fifty-five men who signed it, you will also find the name of one woman, Mary Katherine Goddard. It was she, a Baltimore printer, who published the first official copies of the Declaration, the first copies that included the names of its signers and therefore heralded the support of all thirteen colonies.

Mary got into printing by being a good sister. Her twenty-two-year-old brother had used the money left by their late father, a Connecticut doctor, to open a printing shop in Providence, Rhode Island, in 1762, and twenty-four-year-old Mary and her mother went along to help. William proceeded to get into trouble with his business partners and his creditors, so it was Mary and her mother who were left to run the shop. In 1765 they began publishing the *Providence Gazette*, a weekly newspaper. William, meanwhile, moved on to Philadelphia to start the *Pennsylvania Chronicle*. Again, he had business problems, and Mary moved down to smooth things over.

Their pattern continued in Baltimore, where in 1773 William started the city's first newspaper, the *Maryland Journal*, and then brought Mary in to run it. As the American Revolution approached, William went broke trying to organize a colonial postal service independent from the British system. While he was in debtor's prison, Mary's name went on the newspaper's masthead for the first time. She also ran the printing shop completely on her own, operating the presses by herself.

Mary was in fact Baltimore's only printer, so after the Continental Congress fled there from Philadelphia in December 1776, it commissioned her to print the first official version of the Declaration of Independence in January 1777. The first copies of the document, of course, had been circulated just hours after the delegates approved it on July 4. But those copies, besides containing several errors, only carried the names of John Hancock and the Congress's secretary. After Mary printed her official copies, she herself paid the post riders to deliver the Declaration throughout the colonies.

During the Revolution, Mary continued to publish Baltimore's only newspaper, which one historian called "second to none among the newspapers of the colonies." She also was the city's postmaster from 1775 to 1789—appointed by Benjamin Franklin—and is considered to be the first woman to hold a federal position. When President Washington awarded the job to someone else as a political favor, hundreds of Baltimore residents signed petitions in protest, but to no avail.

By then Mary also had lost her newspaper after her

brother forced her to sell her share back to him in 1784. He soon got the newspaper in financial trouble again, but Mary never returned to printing. She ran a bookstore until 1809 and died at the age of seventy-eight in 1816.

MOTHER GOOSE

WAS SHE FOR REAL? SEVERAL POSSIBILITIES

Most children have two mothers—their own and Mother Goose. But was Mother Goose ever anyone's real mother? Believe it or not, it's possible, though just as scholars have dug deeply to find hidden meanings in her nursery rhymes—Humpty Dumpty really was Richard III, and "Sing a Song of Sixpence" was about Henry VIII—they also have uncovered several theories about her own origins.

According to one tradition, Mother Goose was a Bostonian. Her name was Elizabeth Foster, born in 1665, who in 1692 married a fifty-five-year-old man named Isaac Vergoose. He already had ten children and she gave him six more, though the tale about the old woman who lived in a shoe and had so many children she didn't know what to do didn't become a part of the Mother Goose collection until sometime later.

Mrs. Vergoose told tales to her broad brood, and in turn they were passed on to her grandchild by her oldest daughter. That daughter was married to Thomas Fleet, who ran a printing shop on Pudding Lane, now Devonshire Street, in Boston. Fleet, so the story goes, published his mother-in-law's *Mother Goose's Melodies* in 1719. The only trouble is, no copies of that book still exist.

There is also a French tradition that Mother Goose was "Goose-Footed Bertha," the mother of Charlemagne, who would sit at a spinning wheel, spinning tales for children who gathered around her. It is most likely, however, that Mother Goose is fictional, though French. The first printed use of the name has been traced to Charles Perrault, who in 1697 published *Contes de Ma Mère L'Oye*—"Tales of My Mother Goose." It was a collection of popular tales of the day, including those of Little Red Riding Hood, Sleeping Beauty, and Cinderella. The term "Mother Goose" was simply a popular expression which referred to fanciful stories to amuse children.

But while the name is probably French, most of the tales of Mother Goose are English. Many of the rhymes were part of the folklore of England, created as a form of political satire. So it may well be that "Mary, Mary, Quite Contrary" was about Mary, Queen of Scots, and "Yankee Doodle" celebrated the victories of Prince Rupert in the British civil wars in the seventeenth century.

The rhymes were first collected and published in the late 1700s by John Newbery, a London publisher. Author Oliver Goldsmith worked for Newbery at the time, so it is likely that he had a hand in that first edition, which included the tales of Jack and Jill, Little Jack Horner, and "Hickery Dickery Dock." The first American edition appeared in 1785.

In 1824 another Boston publisher issued a collection by "Jemima Goose." And nine years later, another American edition was billed as "The whole compared, revised and sanctioned by one of the annotators of the

Goose family." Since then, "Mother Goose" has become a catch-all for children's nursery rhymes.

Fortunately, whoever she was—if ever she was—makes no difference to her delighted little listeners.

REBECCA GRATZ

THE MODEL FOR SIR WALTER SCOTT'S HEROINE IN *IVANHOE*

At the moral center of Sir Walter Scott's turbulent classic novel, *Ivanhoe*, there is Rebecca. A Jewish woman of almost angelic goodness who saves Ivanhoe, though her love remains unrequited, she is the conscience of Scott's medieval fable, published in 1819. William Makepeace Thackeray called her "the sweetest character in the whole range of fiction."

But like many fictional characters, Rebecca may not have been entirely made up. Though Scott didn't know her directly, he may have used as his model Rebecca Gratz, a generous Philadelphian who was called "the foremost American Jewess of her day." Born in 1781, Gratz was the seventh of twelve children of a prominent fur trader and shipper whose home was a social center for the city's young, talented elite, including artist Thomas Sully, actress Fanny Kemble, and writer Washington Irving. Gratz and Irving became very close in 1809 when she nursed his dying eighteen-year-old fiancée, who was also her friend.

By then, Gratz already had begun a lifetime of charitable works. At the age of twenty she had helped found one of the city's first aid societies, the "Female Association for the Relief of Women and Children in Reduced Circumstances." Reputedly a beautiful woman who remained a spinster all her life (like her fictional counterpart, Gratz's love was unrequited because her beloved wasn't Jewish), she went on to help start the Female Hebrew Benevolent Society, the Fuel Society, the Sewing Society, and an orphanage.

In 1817, Irving was in England visiting his brother when he met Scott at his large country estate. Irving apparently talked about his admired friend, Gratz, at the time when Scott was working on his medieval tale. And though he never specifically confirmed that Gratz was his Rebecca, Scott sent Irving a copy of his completed *Ivanhoe* in 1819 with a letter that said, "How do you like your Rebecca? Does the Rebecca I have pictured compare well with the pattern given?"

Gratz, herself, was aware of the connection. To her sister-in-law she wrote of the book, "I am glad you admire Rebecca, for she is just such a representation of a good girl as I think human nature can reach . . . You may believe I feel grateful for the justification of the Jewish character." But when people would ask whether she was Ivanhoe's Rebecca, she would merely say, "They say so, my dear."

But the achievement she cherished more, the one she called "the crowning happiness of my life," was her Hebrew Sunday School. Begun in 1838 when Gratz was fifty-seven, the school was the first of its kind, patterned "to follow the example of other religious communities" in educating the congregation's children. Gratz wrote prayers and taught classes, and within a few years other Hebrew schools had sprung up in New York, Charleston, and Richmond. She continued as president of the school until 1864 when she was eighty-three. Gratz died five years later, leaving a record that Ivanhoe's Rebecca would have admired.

HETTY GREEN

"THE WITCH OF WALL STREET"

In the days when John D. Rockefeller and J. P. Morgan could be seen striding through Wall Street in their top hats and tails, there was also a pathetic-looking little woman scurrying about New York's financial district. In her moth-eaten cape and frayed bonnet, carrying a black bag that contained unwrapped food for her lunch, Hetty Green only betrayed her true status by the great clump of safety-deposit box keys she strung around her waist.

Considered the richest woman in the world in the late nineteenth century, Green never had her name linked with oil or railroads the way her well-dressed counterparts did. But she had millions of dollars invested or loaned in many of their deals. She was, said *The New York Times*, "the recognized 'ready money' lender on Wall Street." She was also eccentric beyond endearing, and as the weird tales about her grew, she became known as "the Witch of Wall Street."

As the only child of a wealthy Quaker whaling fortune of New Bedford, Massachusetts, Henrietta Howland Robinson might well have become one of the great society matrons of her day. But ignoring her flighty mother, she grew up reading the financial pages to her dim-sighted grandfather and accompanying her father, "Black Hawk" Robinson, on his daily rounds to collect money and dicker over new deals. "I was forced into business," Green said later. "I was the only child of two rich families, and I was taught from the time I was six years old that I would have to look after my property."

After her parents died in the early 1860s, Hetty, a good-looking woman with beautiful brown hair, inherited a $1 million–plus income from a $4 million trust, plenty in that day to keep her lavishly comfortable for the rest of her life. But when her spinster Aunt Sylvia died and left her a trust with income of $65,000 a year, Hetty sued to get the entire estate, claiming that her aunt had dictated to her a second will before she died. The case, which she lost after a five-year legal battle, erupted into a sensational trial where handwriting experts testified that Aunt Sylvia's signature on Hetty's copy of the will was a badly executed forgery.

Meanwhile, in 1867, thirty-two-year-old Hetty married Edward Green, a forty-six-year-old Vermont millionaire who made his money trading in the Philippines. Though her husband was hardly poor, Hetty insisted they sign a prenuptial contract keeping their fortunes separate. That proved to be wise when Edward's rash speculations caused him to go bankrupt in 1885. To prevent her funds from being used to pay her husband's debts, Hetty pulled her money out of a New York bank, causing it to fail.

Green compounded her fortune in workmanlike fashion. While she and her husband lived in London during the Civil War, Green bought depressed U.S. bonds and after the war made millions—two hundred thousand dollars in one day—when the bonds soared in value. She invested in the new railroads and her name occasionally was linked with the market raids of Cornelius Vanderbilt. Green also bought real estate in booming cities from coast to coast. At her death it was estimated she owned some eight thousand parcels of land. She had a knack for getting out of the market before a panic—she was accused of causing some—and then she lent her money at 6 percent interest to strapped investors.

Green left a fortune of more than $125 million, but what made her legendary was how she handled it. "I wasn't raised to be arrogant and haughty like the little lordlings you see now," she said, but that hardly explained it. Besides wearing worn clothes, Green conducted her business with smudged hands and face, covered with dirt from her office at Chemical National Bank where she would sit on the floor and shuffle her bonds and mortgage notes. She believed in saving money by having only the bottom layer of her petticoats laundered. Dressed that way, Green would ride in public stagecoaches carrying bonds worth thousands of dollars.

Those habits were a little weird, but Green gained the wrath of the public when it was exposed that she went to doctors at charity medical clinics. In fact, after her fourteen-year-old son, Ned, dislocated his knee, Green first tried to cure it herself, then took him to a free clinic, where doctors said it was too late for the boy's leg to heal properly. Five years later, complications forced Ned's leg to be amputated.

Green also spent years living in tawdry boardinghouses to escape paying taxes in New York City. She claimed residence in her husband's less-taxing home state of Vermont, and avoided tax collectors by living under a variety of false names with her son and daughter in cold-water flats in Brooklyn, Harlem, and Far Rockaway, and in Hoboken, New Jersey. In her later years she came to believe that her parents, her Aunt Sylvia, and her late husband had all been murdered, and she began sleeping next to a string that was rigged to fire a revolver that she had aimed at the door.

After suffering a series of paralytic strokes in 1916, Green died in the comfort of her son's Manhattan townhouse at the age of eighty-one. She left her son and daughter each some $60 million. Ned, whose false leg supported his six-foot four-inch, three-hundred-pound frame, became a yachtsman, bought one of the first cars in Dallas, and blew most of his fortune. Green's daughter, Sylvia, married a distant Astor heir and left her mother's fortune to a wide range of charities.

Despite her infamy as "the Witch of Wall Street," Green seemed to have a wry sense about her status. In one of her many interviews with reporters, she said, "My life is written for me down in Wall Street by people who, I assume, do not care to know one iota of the real Hetty Green. I am in earnest, therefore they picture me as heartless. I go my own way. I take no partners, risk nobody else's fortune, therefore I am Madame Ishmael, set against every man."

Indeed, though Green had many transgressions, *The New York Times* offered an interesting perspective on this lone female financier shortly after she died. "If a man had lived as did Mrs. Hetty Green," the newspaper said, "devoting the greater part of his time and mind to the increasing of an inherited fortune that even at the start was far larger than is needed for the satisfaction of all such human needs as money can satisfy, nobody would have seen him as very peculiar."

CATHERINE GREENE

CO-INVENTOR OF THE COTTON GIN

To say that the cotton gin revolutionized the South is no exaggeration. It was the cotton gin that gave the region its greatest crop, producing one-third of the world's supply by 1820. It was the cotton gin that made large plantations thrive and slaves more vital to owners. And, as we all know from the third grade, it was Eli Whitney who invented the cotton gin.

But if your picture of Whitney is that of some lonely inventor tinkering away in his workshop, forget it. Whitney built his machine in the comfortable mansion of a plantation widow named Catherine Greene, who financed the project and may have gotten it to work properly. In fact, it is also no exaggeration to say that without Kitty Greene, Whitney probably would have become a lawyer and third graders would be reading about somebody else.

Catherine Littlefield was the daughter of a prominent Rhode Island family. She married Nathanael Greene, one of George Washington's most trusted and able generals during the Revolution. Kitty, a captivating, even flirtatious woman, had left her own impression on Washington when, while staying with her husband during the long winter at Valley Forge, she danced with the future president and cheered his beleaguered troops. After the war, General Greene was rewarded with a loyalist estate in Georgia, the prize of which was the beautiful Mulberry Grove plantation on the Savannah River. But soon after the Greenes and their five children moved south in 1785, the general died, leaving Kitty with the debt-ridden lands.

It was while she was summering in Newport in 1792 that Greene met Whitney. Fresh out of Yale, Whitney was planning to travel to a plantation near Mulberry Grove to tutor the owner's children and study law on the side. The teaching assignment had been arranged by his friend, Phineas Miller, who was Greene's plantation manager, so Whitney ended up joining the widow on her journey south. By the time they reached Mulberry Grove, the tutoring job had fallen through, but Greene invited Whitney to stay.

Whitney was a born tinkerer. He grew up spending hours in his father's workshop, fixing watches and crafting a violin. During the Revolution he made nails, which sold so well that at the age of sixteen Whitney hired an assistant. So during his stay at Greene's plantation, the twenty-seven-year-old Whitney was eager to offer his talents however he could. When Greene complained that her embroidery frame didn't fit right, Whitney devised a new tambour that delighted her. He also made toys for her children.

The fatefulness of their relationship became evident that winter. Greene's cheerful hospitality had made Mulberry Grove a gathering place for many local planters. One day a group of them was discussing the sorry state of southern agriculture, and they agreed that the answer lay in cotton. The problem was that cleaning the seeds out of the fiber was a tedious process, one that required a full day for a slavewoman to produce one pound of clean cotton. What was needed was a machine to speed the process. "Gentlemen," said Mrs. Greene, "apply to my young friend Mr. Whitney. He can make anything."

The Yankee didn't know a thing about cotton, but ten days after discussing the project with the planters,

Whitney had devised a model of what would become his cotton gin. For the next six months he worked in a locked room (they were concerned about patent rights) in the basement of the Mulberry Grove mansion. Whitney later wrote about how important Greene's encouragement was to his work, though he never mentioned what may have been her essential contribution. Apparently Whitney's first working model was flawed because even though the gin pulled the seeds from the cotton, the loose seeds got clogged in the rollers. Many accounts say it was Greene who, after Whitney explained the problem, handed him a brush from the hearth, which Whitney installed in the cotton gin to sweep away the seeds.

The machine was indeed a breakthrough. One person turning the crank could clean as much cotton as fifty working by hand. The trouble was, the machine was so simple that, as word of it got out, copycat gins were quickly built on other plantations. Whitney sailed to New York to get his patent from Secretary of State Thomas Jefferson, but it was too late. His partnership with Miller, Greene's plantation manager, almost went bankrupt as they fought to prevent others from using their machine. It was Greene who provided the funds for them to stay in business, ultimately selling Mulberry Grove in 1800 to pay the cost of their many patent lawsuits.

Eventually Greene, who had married Miller in 1796, and Whitney, who was jealous of the marriage, went their separate ways. After Miller died in 1803, Greene invited Whitney to return from the North and visit her, but he kept putting her off. She died of a fever in 1814 at the age of fifty-nine. Whitney, meanwhile, finally had won full title to the cotton gin in 1807, but by then the patent was ready to expire. Neither he nor his important backer ever saw much profit from their revolutionary machine.

ROSE O'NEAL GREENHOW

HER SPYING HELPED THE CONFEDERATES WIN AT BULL RUN

With its vastly superior forces, the Union army that marched against Confederate troops at Bull Run in the early days of the Civil War was counting on an easy rout that might lead to a quick end to the war. The thirty thousand Union soldiers, after all, would face a much smaller Confederate army which was scattered over several locations. So entertaining did the whole affair promise to be that women and children rode out in their carriages from nearby Washington, D.C., to watch the battle. But by the end of the day—July 21, 1861—it was the Union troops and their well-dressed spectators who were driven into a panicked stampede back to the capital.

The Confederate troops, aided by timely reinforcements, had met the enemy at every turn. It was as if they knew in advance where the Union army planned to attack. In fact, that was exactly the case. Said Confederate General Pierre G. T. Beauregard, "I was almost as well advised of the strength of the hostile army in my front as its commander."

He had gotten the information from Rose O'Neal Greenhow, one of Washington's most delightful and well-connected hostesses who charmed her way into becoming one of the Confederacy's most useful spies. The daughter of a wealthy Maryland planter who had died when she was an infant, Rose was raised by an aunt who ran a fashionable Washington boardinghouse where many politicians lived when Congress was in session. With black eyes and hair, olive skin, and great allure, she was called "the Wild Rose" during the populist days of the Jackson presidency.

Rose came into her own as a Washington hostess in 1835 when she married Robert Greenhow, a lawyer, doctor, and friend of Lord Byron's, who worked in the State Department. As a hostess, Rose was less interested in her social status than her political connections. She mingled with diplomats and government leaders like John C. Calhoun, the staunch states' rights advocate whom she called "the best and wisest man of this century," and James Buchanan, who later as president was romantically linked to the then-widowed Rose.

By the time of the Civil War, Rose Greenhow was one of the most politically significant hostesses in Washington, "a bright and shining light," said the *New York Herald*. Like most in the divided capital, she had many friends on both sides of the battlefield—her brother-in-law held a high position in the Treasury Department; her niece was the wife of Senator Stephen Douglas. But unlike most, who either supported the Union or moved south, Greenhow decided to ply her Union friends to help the Confederacy.

Her home on Sixteenth Street became the center of much activity, with everyone from soldiers to senators seen coming and going at all hours. Wrote one Union officer, "Although I was never in the least danger of being diverted from my purpose, yet I well remember how often I was lured to the brink of the precipice." Greenhow was not the only Washington hostess who sympathized with the South. But federal officials had chosen to ignore their activity because they didn't believe that women could cause much trouble, and to arrest them would seem unchivalrous.

That changed after Bull Run. Greenhow had sent three messages to Confederate officers informing them specifically as to how many Union troops they would face and when the attack would commence. Union General George McClellan said, "She knows my plans better than Lincoln or the Cabinet, and has four times compelled me to change them."

McClellan created a Union secret service and he put detective Allan Pinkerton in charge of it. After observing the activity at Greenhow's home, Pinkerton arrested her on her doorstep on August 23 as she tried to swallow a coded message. At first Greenhow and one of her four daughters were placed under house arrest in her home. But after she managed to continue slipping information to Confederate agents she was sent to the Old Capitol Prison, where she waved a Confederate flag from her window. "I am a Southern woman," she later wrote, "born with revolutionary blood in my veins."

In the spring of 1862 Greenhow was released to Confederate officials in the South on the condition that she not return to Union territory. Jefferson Davis, who awarded her $2,500 for her services, greeted her with the words, "But for you there would have been no battle of Bull Run." In August 1863 Greenhow sailed to Europe to raise funds for the Confederacy. Her book, *My Imprisonment and the First Year of Abolition Rule at Washington*, sold well abroad, and she was presented at the French and British courts, including a private audience with Napoléon III.

A year later, with a pending marriage proposal from a British lord, Greenhow set sail on a British steamship to return to the Confederacy and report to Davis. But on the night of September 30, after dodging Union gunboats, the ship was grounded near Wilmington, North Carolina, by a violent storm. Greenhow, afraid of being captured, demanded that the captain allow her to sail for shore in a small boat. With a crew of three, the tiny vessel quickly capsized in high waves. The forty-nine-year-old Greenhow, who was carrying around her neck a leather bag loaded with gold pieces from her book royalties, sank immediately. Her body eventually washed ashore, and she was buried with full military honors in Wilmington.

PEGGY GUGGENHEIM

PATRON OF MODERN ART

When Peggy Guggenheim published her memoirs, *Out of This Century*, which detailed not only her career as a vital avant-garde art patron, but also her many, many lovers, her scandalized relatives called the book "Out of My Mind." Guggenheim undoubtedly was not upset by their reaction. The granddaughter of nineteenth-century mining magnate Meyer Guggenheim spent her life trying to shock, and she succeeded.

Along the way, she built one of the world's greatest

collections of modern art and was instrumental in introducing the Abstract Expressionist movement, which after World War II turned the eyes of the art world away from Europe and toward New York. But even then, she specifically distanced herself from her family's more famous modern art museum founded by Solomon Guggenheim, a museum she referred to as "my uncle's garage, that Frank Lloyd Wright thing on Fifth Avenue."

Peggy Guggenheim was never so much attracted to contemporary art itself as she was to the bohemian art world that was so different from her aristocratic roots. "My childhood was excessively unhappy," recalled Guggenheim, born Marguerite. "I have no pleasant memories of any kind." She spent summers in Europe, attended finishing school in Paris, and made her debut in 1916. Guggenheim lost her father on the *Titanic*, and although it was generally assumed that he left her a huge fortune, she actually inherited less than $1 million, as Benjamin had left the family partnership before the real money was made.

After whiling away the 1920s at European cafés with a husband she called "the King of Bohemia," Guggenheim took an interest in art at the suggestion of one of her lovers, writer Samuel Beckett. Her knowledge of paintings had ended with those of the Italian Renaissance, but with the close supervision of Marcel Duchamp—the early modernist master who painted *Nude Descending a Staircase*—she opened the Guggenheim Jeune gallery in London in 1938. Her gallery was one of a few devoted to the fledgling Surrealists, but so few works sold that she began buying paintings herself to encourage unknown talents like Kandinsky and Miró.

As her collection grew, her motto became "Buy a

picture a day," and she made some of her best deals in Paris in the desperate last days before the Nazis invaded. Ultimately, Guggenheim would spend less than $500,000 to acquire some 260 works of art. In 1986 her collection was valued at $50 million, and that was before the more recent price boom.

Guggenheim's real impact on the art world came with her second gallery, which she opened in New York in 1942. Displaying her own avant-garde collection as well as works by young American artists, Art of This Century was unlike any art gallery ever before. It featured curved walls and turquoise floors, paintings mounted on baseball bat–shaped projectiles and others fastened to spinning wheels. "My eyes have never bulged further from their sockets than at this show," one critic said of the first exhibition, and though not everyone was so enthusiastic, Guggenheim's gallery drew crowds that lined up around the block.

Ironically, Guggenheim—who at the time was married to the painter Max Ernst—often didn't understand what she was showing. When she first saw a painting that Jackson Pollock had submitted for her exhibition of new artists, she said, "Pretty awful, isn't it?" Piet Mondrian convinced her otherwise, and Guggenheim ended up supporting Pollock for four years until his paintings began to catch on. She gave many Abstract Expressionists, including Pollock, Mark Rothko, and Robert Motherwell, their first one-man shows.

"I took advice from none but the best," Guggenheim said later. "Many people buy the best advice, but they don't heed it. I listened, how I listened! That's how I finally became my own expert—at least, I knew enough to manage on my own." Composer John Cage, who stayed at Guggenheim's and Ernst's home in New York during that period, recalled, "It was like Grand Central Station for artists. People enjoyed Peggy, enjoyed the affluence in the environment. She was not reticent about having ideas. Peggy had the keys to the whole art world."

Guggenheim's reputation was not entirely artistic. Once asked "How many husbands have you had?" she replied, "My own, or other people's?" Her stream of affairs between and during her two marriages flowed continuously, and often involved the artists she supported. "Just a question of being oversexed, probably," dismissed Guggenheim, who called herself "Mrs. Guggenheim" throughout her life. The mother of two children by her first husband, she lost custody of her son when they divorced. Her daughter, Pegeen, died in 1966 of an overdose of alcohol and tranquilizers.

After her second marriage, to Ernst, ended in 1946, Guggenheim closed Art of This Century and took her collection to Venice. In 1951 she opened a gallery in an eighteenth-century white stone palace on the Grand Canal. Her paintings and sculptures were displayed in the garden, the cellar, and the servants' quarters while she lived in the other rooms, sleeping on a sterling silver bed designed by Alexander Calder.

The gallery became one of Venice's most popular tourist attractions—the Venetians called her *L'Ultima Dogaressa,* "the Last Duchess"—but it was far from the vibrant New York art world she had helped create. "I gathered Pollock was becoming very important in America," she wrote in one letter. "It certainly is due to me and Lee [Krasner, his wife], but he is so ungrateful that they never even answer my letters."

As the price of paintings soared, Guggenheim bought less and less, decrying the commercialization of art and calling the next movement, Pop Art, "phooey." Finally in 1969, her collection was exhibited at the Guggenheim Museum in New York. "I have spent most of my life trying not to be square," the seventy-one-year-old patron told one interviewer. "Then I loved being official and loved being shown in museums. And now I'm at another stage: blasé."

Guggenheim spent her last years almost a recluse, venturing out only each evening for a ride in her gondola with her pair of Lhasa apso dogs. She died of a stroke in 1979 at the age of eighty-one, leaving her entire collection to the care of her "uncle's garage"—but only, she insisted, if her art remained in Venice.

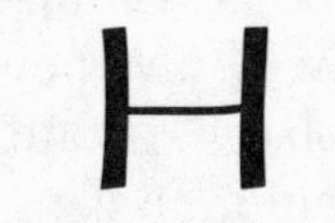

HELENA

MOTHER OF CONSTANTINE AND OF CHRISTIANITY

It has often been said that if you collected all of the relics cherished by churches as part of the true Holy Cross, there would be enough wood to build a ship. In fact, there's not even enough to create the cross (somebody measured it). A better question is whether any of those relics actually could have been part of the cross on which Christ was crucified.

To answer that, we must rely on Helena. The mother of the Roman Emperor Constantine, Helena is credited with finding the pieces of wood in the fourth century to which nearly all of the relics can be traced. While it is her son who is known for transforming Christianity from a persecuted sect into the religion that would dominate the Western world, it was Helena who accomplished some of the most concrete legacies of Constantine's Christian rule. Helena sometimes is even credited with converting her son to Christianity. But so little is certain about most of her life that it isn't clear which of them converted first.

It is generally accepted that Helena was the daughter of an innkeeper and grew up on the Turkish coast, though there is a British tradition that says she was the daughter of one of their kings. She met the Roman Emperor Constantius I during one of his military conquests, and although some sources say they were married, her lowly background probably meant that Helena was the emperor's concubine, making their son, Constantine, illegitimate. After nineteen years together, Constantius banished Helena in 293 when he married another woman to consolidate his power.

When Constantine gained the throne after his father died in 306, he recalled his mother to the capital of Rome (which he later moved to Constantinople, now Istanbul). He named Helena empress and put a likeness of her face on coins. Some historians say that by the time Helena joined her son, she already had become a Christian, and it was her influence that converted Constantine. But it is more generally accepted that Constantine converted in 312 when the ruler believed he saw a Christian symbol in the sky just before he won a major battle. The following year Constantine issued his Edict of Milan, which ended the persecution of Christians.

Meanwhile, Helena became, according to the historian Eusebius, "such a devout servant of God, that one might believe her to have been from her childhood a disciple of the Redeemer of mankind." In 324, when she was nearly seventy, Helena made one of the first pilgrimages to the Holy Land. Jerusalem lay in rubble after centuries of neglect, but Helena marshaled her experts to search for the true cross.

They believed they had found the location on a site covered by a pagan temple. Helena destroyed the temple and supervised the excavation which uncovered what she claimed to be the cross. On the site, she built the Church of the Holy Sepulchre. In Bethlehem, Helena claimed to locate the site of the manger, and there she built the Church of the Nativity. Both locations were guesses at best, but the churches still stand, and they draw thousands of pilgrims each year.

Helena's good works undoubtedly encouraged Constantine's church-building program, which included the original St. Peter's in Rome. The emperor also appointed Christians to high government posts and adopted the Christian calendar. But whereas Constantine was not entirely successful in turning the Roman Empire towards Christianity—and indeed, some of the theological issues have never been resolved—his mother's legacy has survived intact. Writing in this century, Evelyn Waugh described Helena (long-since anointed a saint) as "a lonely, resolute woman with a single concrete, practical task clear before her; to turn the eyes of the world back to the planks of wood on which their salvation hung."

ANNE HUTCHINSON

PURITAN HERETIC

If Martin Luther is the father of religious freedom in the Old World, then Anne Hutchinson is its mother in the New World. At a time when the fledgling colony of Massachusetts was governed by its Puritan religious leaders, Hutchinson preached her own ideas. It cost her dearly, but history has repaid her by recognizing that hers was the first important protest in the development of religious tolerance in America.

Born in England in 1591, Anne Marbury took after her father, an Anglican clergyman who was imprisoned twice for criticizing his superiors and was finally stripped of his church. In 1612 she married a prosperous businessman, and over the next twenty-four years she bore him fifteen children, twelve of whom survived.

Along the way, Hutchinson became a follower of Joseph Cotton, a Puritan who preached that one's personal acceptance of God—not a moral life—was the essential act of salvation. For his heresy, Cotton was forced to flee from England to Boston in 1633. Hutchinson, saying she had had a divine revelation, prompted her family to follow the next year.

Hutchinson was in trouble from the time her family arrived in Boston. Reports of her religious discussions on the crossing ship nearly got her banned from the church, but Cotton smoothed her acceptance. Then, while her husband became a successful cloth trader—he was chosen a Boston selectman—Hutchinson began holding religious discussions in their home.

At first, the meetings involved only women, many of whom Hutchinson had tended during their time of childbirth. But soon men began joining the sessions, including many of Boston's most prominent citizens and even the colony's governor. Indeed, at her later trial, one of her prosecutors said, "She had more resort to her for counsel about matters of conscience, and clearing up men's spiritual estates, than any minister in the country."

The trouble was, Hutchinson went further than Cotton, believing that since one's personal relationship with God was most important, obeying church laws was not. In those days, that was not just the subject of a theological debate. The church controlled the social and business life of the colony. Just how gravely Hutchinson's views might threaten the colony became apparent when one of her followers refused to join a military expedition against some Indians. Merchants supported Hutchinson because they wanted a freer business climate.

By 1637, Hutchinson's views had become so widespread that her supporters were preparing to remove the more conservative religious leaders from power. But the conservative side acted first. They purged Hutchinson's followers from the General Court and elected an orthodox governor, John Winthrop. Hutchinson herself was put on trial for "traducing the ministers and their ministry."

At her trial, Hutchinson tried to debate her religious differences with her prosecutors. She was more than holding her own until Winthrop cut her off. "We do not mean to discourse with those of your sex," he said. The pressure and taunting finally caused Hutchinson to lose her temper. "I bless the Lord, he hath let me see which was the clear ministry and which the wrong," she said, claiming that God directly had told her who would be saved and who would not. She told her prosecutors they would all, literally, go to hell.

With that, Hutchinson's support fell away and she was ordered banished from the colony. So threatening was she perceived to be that the judges also ordered seventy-five of her supporters to turn in their guns. In the spring of 1638, Hutchinson and her family moved to a new colony established by her husband on the island of Aquidneck, now Portsmouth, Rhode Island.

After her husband died in 1642, Hutchinson and

her six youngest children moved to the Dutch colony of New Netherland, to what is now Pelham Bay Park in the Bronx. There, in August 1643, Hutchinson and all but her youngest daughter were massacred by Indians. Her foes in Massachusetts greeted the news as divine evidence from God. Said one minister, "And therefore God's hand is the more apparently seene herein, to pick out this wofull woman, to make her and those belonging to her, an unheard of heavie example of their cruelty above al others."

Hutchinson's challenge to the religious order did not die with her. Some of her followers joined the new Quaker movement. And the Puritans, of course, exist today only in history books.

HYPATIA

EARLY GREEK MATHEMATICIAN

Hypatia may not have been the first female mathematician, but she is the first about whom we know very much. At the least, the ancient Greek woman's life was important as a symbol. But in some ways, the more significant symbol was her death.

Living in the late fourth century, at a time when Alexandria was the mecca of learning, Hypatia was the daughter of the director of the city's university. Her father raised her the way most men raised their first-born sons; she received the best education, she was given an exercise regimen, she traveled abroad and was sent to study in Athens under Plutarch the Younger.

None of her works have survived the ages, but among her writings on astronomy, philosophy, and mathematics was a thirteen-volume compilation on the new subject of algebra that was said to carry the study as far as it got until the Renaissance. Hypatia also invented an astrolabe, which measured the positions of the stars, and a hydroscope to measure the specific gravity of liquids.

At her father's university, she taught mathematics and philosophy. Her lectures were extremely popular. It was said that students traveled from all over Europe as well as Asia and Africa to hear her speak. Hypatia was considered an oracle, and legend has it that letters addressed to "the Muse" or "the Philosopher" were delivered to her. Poets called her "the Virgin of Heaven" and "the spotless star."

Her overwhelming popularity—combined with her emphasis on science as a rational study—greatly disturbed Cyril, the patriarch of Alexandria and the city's top Christian official. The university was seen as a hotbed of the city's paganism, and Hypatia was its brightest ember.

In 415 a mob of men, incited by Cyril, pulled Hypatia from her chariot as she rode to class one morning. She was, according to one historian, "stripped naked, dragged to the Church, and inhumanly butchered by the hands of Peter the Reader [Cyril's assistant] and a troop of savage and merciless fanatics; her flesh was scraped from her bones with sharp oyster shells, and her quivering limbs were delivered to the flames."

Not the first or the last scholar to be persecuted during that time, Hypatia and her brutal demise signaled that the age of learning was ending and the Dark Ages were about to begin.

I

THE ANONYMOUS WOMAN WHO INVENTED THE ICE CREAM CONE

Ice cream without a cone is like a hot dog without a bun. But although Marco Polo returned from China in the thirteenth century with news of fruit ices, the ice cream cone was born less than one hundred years ago. Several men have claimed to have invented the cone, but it took a woman to show them what to do with it.

It happened in 1904 at the World's Fair in St. Louis. There were several ice cream vendors at the fair grounds, as well as several who were selling thin waffles coated with sugar or jelly. A Syrian immigrant named Ernest Hamwi is credited by the International Ice Cream Association with inventing the ice cream cone because he sold his waffles rolled.

But if Hamwi was the first to put ice cream in his waffles, he didn't come up with the idea on his own. The story goes that an ice cream salesman named Charles Menches was at the fair one day with a young lady whose name has been lost to the ages. Menches, gentleman that he was, bought his date a bouquet of flowers and also an ice cream sandwich. The young lady was having trouble holding both her gifts at the same time without making a mess. So to prevent the ice cream from dripping, she wrapped the biscuits from the ice cream sandwich around the ice cream into the shape of a cone.

This masterful act apparently was witnessed by Abe Doumar, a souvenir salesman. He told Hamwi to give it a try, and Hamwi's ice cream–filled waffles were so successful that he gave Doumar a waffle iron at the end of the fair. Doumar later began a successful business selling ice cream cones at Coney Island in New York. Hamwi founded the Cornucopia Waffle Company in Missouri. Ice cream production, meanwhile, increased more than a hundredfold from 1900 to 1950. And today, Americans consume more than twenty quarts per capita per year—most of it on top of cones. The ice cream cone industry can turn out 150,000 cones an hour.

As for the young lady, we don't even know if she liked her date.

J

ANNA JARVIS

CREATOR OF MOTHER'S DAY

While the rest of us are thinking of Mom on Mother's Day, the greeting card makers, florists, and phone companies ought to be thinking of Anna Jarvis. To her they owe their best business day of the year, even if she did lessen the favor by calling them "charlatans, pirates, racketeers, kidnappers and other termites."

For Jarvis, Mother's Day began as a way to remember her own mother, the wife of a Methodist minister in Grafton, West Virginia, who in the late 1800s had promoted "Mother's Friendship Days" to try to heal the scars in the border state after the Civil War. Jarvis, who herself never married, lived with her mother and blind younger sister in Grafton and in Philadelphia, where she taught school and later became a librarian for an insurance company.

Two years after her mother died in 1905, Jarvis held a memorial service for her in Grafton on the second Sunday in May, the day she had died. She decorated the church with five hundred carnations, her mother's favorite flower. Jarvis was so moved by the ceremony that she began a massive letter-writing campaign, urging congressmen, state legislators, governors, business leaders, and newspaper editors, among others, to adopt a formal holiday honoring mothers. The next year churches in Grafton and Philadelphia held special observances for mothers, and everyone wore carnations as a symbol of motherhood.

In 1910 West Virginia became the first state to recognize Mother's Day. A year later, amidst Jarvis's flurry of letters, nearly every state had followed. Legislators may not have been ready to grant women the vote, but Mother's Day had few enemies. In 1915, President Wilson signed the law making Mother's Day, the second Sunday in May, a national holiday.

But Jarvis was not finished. She incorporated herself as the Mother's Day International Association and began addressing her letters to foreign leaders. Her correspondence became so voluminous that she bought the three-story brick house next door to store her letters. It was believed that by the time Jarvis died in 1948, forty-three nations had created Mother's Day observances.

Meanwhile, in this country, the holiday soon enraged its founder. The carnations that Jarvis had urged everyone to wear were in such demand that florists raised their price. Greeting card makers and candy companies, too, profited from the new holiday. "A printed card means nothing except that you are too lazy to write to the woman who has done more for you than anyone in the world," Jarvis snapped. "And candy! You take a box to Mother—and then eat most of it yourself. A pretty sentiment."

In 1923 Jarvis threatened to sue New York Governor Al Smith to stop a planned Mother's Day festival at a New York City stadium. And in 1925 the sixty-one-year-old woman was arrested for disturbing the peace at a Philadelphia convention of war mothers, where the women were selling Mother's Day white carnations to raise money. "They are commercializing *my* Mother's Day!" charged Jarvis, who was further insulted when a florist's association offered to give her a commission on each carnation its members sold for the holiday. "This is not what I intended. I wanted it to be a day of sentiment, not profit!"

But as easy as it had been for the mother-loving spinster to create the holiday, Jarvis found it impossible to turn back the tide of its sales appeal. To replace carnations, she tried to get people to wear white buttons, and she paid to ship thousands of them to schools and churches but to little avail. Eventually her campaign against the commercialization of her holiday had cost her the appreciable estate she had inherited from her own mother.

By her seventies, Jarvis and her sister were recluses in their Philadelphia home, where a sign on the window said "Warning—Stay Away," and only those who knocked in code could bring her to the door. In her parlor she kept a shrine to her mother, with palms from her funeral and a bowl of china roses in front of her large portrait. One account said Jarvis, who grew blind and partly deaf, would sit listening to the radio, expecting to hear her mother's voice.

In 1943, impoverished and ailing, Jarvis was put in a nursing home by a group of friends who formed a committee to raise funds for her care. She was never told that a florists' trade publication had donated $1,580. Shortly before Jarvis died at the age of eighty-four, a reporter visited her at the nursing home, where every Mother's Day her room had been flooded with cards from all over the world. "She told me with great bitterness," said the writer, "that she was sorry she had ever started Mother's Day."

POPE JOAN

THE LEGENDARY FEMALE POPE

If you look in the Catalogue of Popes, you will see that after Leo IV died in 855, he was succeeded by Benedict III. But according to some medieval writings, the catalogue is incomplete. Recorded one monk in the eleventh century, "Leo the Pope died on the first of August. To him succeeded John, who was a woman, and sat for two years, five months and four days."

The legend of Pope Joan, or John VIII, has annoyed the Catholic Church for centuries. While there is no evidence dating to the ninth century that would prove that a female pope ever existed at that time, her story so proliferated during later centuries that in 1601 Pope Clement VIII felt it necessary to officially declare the entire tale false. And even in 1886, a novel about Pope Joan got its Greek author, Emmanuel Roydis, excommunicated.

The first written record of Pope Joan was the two simple sentences set down by that eleventh-century monk. By the thirteenth century, she had a whole life to be told. It was said she was the daughter of an English priest. She fell in love with a monk and—dressed as a man for disguise—she followed him to Athens. There, maintaining her costume, she became a noted scholar and "made such progress in various sciences that there was nobody equal to her." She later traveled to Rome, where her accomplishments got her appointed a cardinal. When Leo IV died, she was unanimously elected to replace him.

Then apparently Pope Joan had a fling, and according to one thirteenth-century document, "On a certain day, when he was riding, he gave birth to a child, and straightway in accordance with Roman justice, his feet were tied together and he was dragged for half a league at a horse's tail while the people stoned him." Another monk said it was during a papal procession that "while going from St. Peter's to the Lateran, being taken in labour, she brought forth a child between the Coliseum and St. Clement's Church." Some say Pope Joan was not stoned but died, along with her baby, from shock.

The legend of Pope Joan was so prevalent that there was said to have been a statue of a woman and a suckling child that used to stand on a narrow street where Joan allegedly gave birth. Also, it was said, papal processions were rerouted away from that street. Still, Pope Joan was not given her place in the catalogue "as well on account of her female sex as on account of the foul nature of the transaction."

The question, of course, is how did such a tale ever get started? Some historians trace it to the real female patriarch of Constantinople at about the same time, or a series of powerful women in the tenth century who largely controlled, but did not occupy, the papacy. Whatever, the story, once created, was too good to ignore. Said one modern historian, "Evidently the element of extravagance and coarseness in the Pope Joan fable appealed to the medieval imagination, and copyists of a later date, who were troubled with few scruples on the grounds of textual accuracy, considered it a pity that in any general history this spicy incident should not find a place."

More recently, two feminist authors say the tale served another purpose. In *A History of Their Own*, Bonnie Anderson and Judith Zinsser say the legend of pregnant Pope Joan was designed to prove that women couldn't be trusted to run the church. "A salacious, cautionary fable," they say, "displaced the memory of the lives and writings of the great abbesses and their women scholars."

MOTHER JONES

THE STALWART UNION ORGANIZER

Today she is better known as the title of a magazine, but in her day, Mother Jones was a cantankerous crusader who could make company officials quake when she showed up to rally striking workers. "You goddamned cowards are losing this strike because you haven't got the guts to go out and fight and win it. Why the hell don't you take your high-powered rifles and blow the goddamned scabs out of the mines!" When she riled that particular group of West Virginia miners in 1917, Jones was eighty-seven.

If she sounds like an angry old woman, she had every reason to be. The immigrant daughter of an Irish railroad construction worker, Mary Jones saw her husband and four children die in a matter of weeks during the yellow fever epidemic of 1867 in

Memphis. She started over with a dress-making business in Chicago, only to be burned out by the Great Chicago Fire in 1871. After that loss, Jones sought solace at meetings of the Knights of Labor.

At a time when workers were on the job fourteen hours a day and were paid a pittance that they could spend only in the high-priced company store, Jones found plenty of outlets for her anger. In 1877 she helped organize her first strike, which turned out to be a bloody struggle by Pittsburgh railroad workers. And for almost the next forty years, though she was nearly fifty when she began, Jones traveled among the coal mines of Appalachia, the copper mines of Colorado, and the cotton mills in the South organizing workers. She lived with striking families and moved on when the battle was over. "My address is like my shoes," she said. "It travels with me."

Nicknamed by workers for her matronly appearance, Mother Jones cut all the more striking a figure because she stomped around at a time when workers were regularly gunned down simply for attempting to organize. But though she was barely five feet tall and weighed less than a hundred pounds, Jones, in her widow's black and wire-rimmed glasses, was not intimidated. "Pray for the dead," she said, "and fight like hell for the living."

In a series of coal strikes in 1900, after striking miners had been replaced by other workers, Jones led a brigade of women swinging mops and pounding dishpans to scare the mules and disrupt work. Her critics said she incited violence, and Jones did not disagree. "The militant, not the meek, shall inherit the earth," she said.

It would be wrong to say that Jones led the charge in the strikes in which she participated. But her rallying cry could be crucial. Remembered one worker, "With one speech, she often threw a whole community on strike, and she could keep the strikers loyal month after month, on empty stomachs and behind prison bars." Jones herself was jailed many times, but eventually local officials came to realize that the publicity only fueled her campaign.

And Jones was an expert at getting attention. To highlight the abuses of child labor, she once led young textile workers on a twenty-two-day march from their mills in Pennsylvania to President Theodore Roosevelt's home on Long Island. On the way, she took one ten-year-old boy with her when she spoke to a class at Princeton. "Here's a textbook in economics," she said. "He gets three dollars a week and his sister, who is fourteen, gets six. They work in a carpet factory ten hours a day, while the children of the rich are getting their higher education."

Perhaps one of the reasons Jones hasn't made a bigger appearance in the history books as a great labor leader is because she frequently turned her wrath on the union leaders. She had begun by working for the United Mine Workers, but she quit when union president John Mitchell tried to prevent her from organizing workers in Colorado. Jones criticized Mitchell for staying in expensive hotels. After she helped found the Social Democratic Party, she turned around and accused one of its leaders of "drunkenness and immoral conduct." Said Clarence Darrow, "Mother Jones was always doubtful of the good of organized institutions. Those require compromise. To her there was but one side. Right and wrong were forever distinct."

Jones continued her crusade well into her nineties, rallying Chicago dressmakers to strike in 1924. She spent her last years in the home of a retired miner and his wife outside Washington, D.C. Her one-hundredth birthday in 1930 drew greetings from prominent officials across the country, including one from John D. Rockefeller, Jr., whose father had owned some of the Colorado copper mines where Jones had fought decades before. "He's a damn good sport," Jones said. "I've licked him many times, but we've made peace. This telegram rather squares things."

Seven months later, Jones died. She was buried in a miner's cemetery in southern Illinois. Since then, the memory of Mother Jones has faded compared to the established labor leaders of the period, though perhaps their reputations would not have been what they were without her. Said one of her biographers, "Mother Jones was a . . . folk heroine whose inspiration reached down to those people who were unimportant in name or wealth or title, but all-important in numbers."

K

DR. FRANCES KELSEY

THE FDA OFFICIAL WHO BLOCKED THALIDOMIDE FROM THE U.S.

It was called "Europe's favorite sleeping pill." Beginning in 1958, thalidomide was taken by millions of people—to go to sleep, to calm down, to ease morning sickness—and some countries didn't even require a doctor's prescription for it. Unlike other tranquilizers, thalidomide didn't cause hangovers, and doctors thought it was impossible to take an overdose. But the fad ended tragically in 1961, when it became clear that thalidomide was causing thousands of babies to be born with severe birth defects—babies with no arms and flipper-like hands attached to their shoulders, others with no legs or deformed internal organs.

While the fate of thalidomide babies has been a continuing legacy in Europe and many other countries around the world, it is a rare topic in the United States. That is primarily because of Dr. Frances Kelsey, a mid-level bureaucrat in the Food and Drug Administration who stared down a major drug company and refused to approve thalidomide for sale here. Said

The Washington Post, "She saw her duty in sternly simple terms, and she carried it out, living the while with insinuations that she was a bureaucratic nit-picker, unreasonable—even stupid." President Kennedy said Kelsey "prevented a major tragedy."

The woman who was hailed as a hero of American medicine was born in Vancouver, Canada. The daughter of a retired British officer, "Frankie" Oldham came to the University of Chicago in 1938 to get a Ph.D. in pharmacology, a new field which studied how the body reacts to drugs. In 1943 she married a colleague, Fremont Kelsey, and they had two children while Frances went through medical school. She followed her husband to the University of South Dakota and then to Washington, D.C., in 1960 when he got a job at the National Institutes of Health.

Frances Kelsey was hired as a medical officer at the Food and Drug Administration. Her job was to evaluate applications by pharmaceutical companies wanting to market new drugs. Her first major assignment, it turned out, was to study thalidomide, in September 1960. "It was deemed to be a simple application," she said later, "and since I had just reported to work, it was assigned to me."

By then, thalidomide, which was first sold in West Germany in 1958, was being marketed throughout Europe as well as the Middle East and Canada. The American marketer, the esteemed, century-old William S. Merrell Company, plainly thought FDA approval was a pro-forma matter. Officials told Kelsey they were merely waiting to print the bottle labels. But Kelsey, described by one magazine as "a tall, severe-looking woman in sensible tweeds and low oxfords," was not convinced. "I was bothered by the fact that thalidomide would not put a horse to sleep," she said.

"It was a very unusual kind of drug and we had no idea how it worked."

While Kelsey was waiting for more information from Merrell, in February 1961 she read a report in a British medical journal that thalidomide was causing some users to develop a tingling or numbness in their arms and legs. In the worst cases, some got cramps, became unbalanced, and developed uncontrollable twitching muscles. The report led Kelsey to question whether thalidomide would affect unborn babies when the drug was taken by pregnant women. That seems like an obvious concern today, but it was a new idea at the time. In fact, it was Kelsey and her husband, in a ground-breaking study in 1943, who had demonstrated that rabbit fetuses could be harmed by drugs even when the mother showed no ill effects.

Kelsey again sought more information from Merrell officials, who by this time had become impatient and angry over delays in approving what was likely to be a very profitable drug. When Kelsey refused to ease up, company officials took their case to her bosses, even to the head of the FDA. They all supported their medical officer. Kelsey later recalled, "If this drug were a cancer treatment or helpful in really dread diseases, I wouldn't have worried about minor side effects. But I could anticipate the results of an enthusiastic sales effort. Everybody—sick and well, old and young—would be taking it. That's why I had to be completely sure."

Kelsey was facing a stack of Merrell medical reports the size of four telephone books when, in November 1961, a West German scientist linked a peculiar spate of birth deformities to pregnant women who had taken thalidomide. Merrell quietly withdrew its application, as the number of thalidomide babies grew wherever the drug had been sold. Some five thousand deformed infants were born in West Germany, as well as hundreds in England—an estimated ten thousand worldwide. In the United States, nine cases were reported, caused by the wide distribution of the drug to doctors for what Merrell said were testing purposes.

Most Americans were oblivious to the thalidomide controversy at the FDA until the toll from Europe became clear. Then, in 1962, Kennedy presented Kelsey with the President's Award for Distinguished Federal Civilian Service, the highest honor for a U.S. Government employee. Kelsey received a flood of mail from American mothers thanking her, some enclosing pictures of their healthy newborn babies.

As a result of the thalidomide episode, the FDA was given new powers to limit the testing of new drugs. Kelsey was put in charge of a new department to monitor the research that pharmaceutical companies produce to support their applications. It is a job she was still performing in 1990, at the age of seventy-six.

KHADIJA

WIFE OF MUHAMMAD, AND HIS FINANCIAL BACKER

As with most great forces in the world, the Islamic Empire began with one person. Muhammad, a seventh-century Arabian businessman, saw a vision on a mountain and returned to found the Muslim religion which, within a generation of his death, defeated the powerful Byzantine and Persian empires and continues to command a potent position in the world today.

But also like most great forces in the world, Muhammad did not do it alone. Historians—and the Koran, the Muslim bible, itself—agree that the most important element that allowed Muhammad to become one of the world's most influential religious leaders was his wife. "A perfect woman," the Koran calls Khadija, "the mother of those that believe."

Muhammad, born in 570 in the town of Mecca in what is now southern Saudi Arabia, was orphaned when he was six. He was raised by a struggling uncle who took the boy on trading caravans to Syria. It was this uncle who introduced Muhammad to Khadija, a wealthy woman, twice widowed, with substantial holdings. Khadija, believed to be about forty, fifteen years older than Muhammad, hired him to manage a caravan of her goods to Syria. He did well, and when he returned, she proposed marriage. According to one story, she got her uncle drunk so he would approve the union.

The marriage was the turning point of Muhammad's life. Whereas before he had no property and therefore no prospects for wives or advancement, Khadija gave him an entrée into the commerce of Mecca, a prosperous trading town ruled by a few wealthy families. Khadija's fortune was apparently large enough that Muhammad didn't have to work very hard. He began spending much time meditating. He would wander into the mountains overlooking Mecca and sit in an isolated cave for days at a time. Then he would return and discuss his thoughts with his wife.

In 610, in the cave, Muhammad had a vision telling him he was a messenger of God. Muhammad was so terrified that he almost threw himself off the mountain, but instead he returned to his wife. "I went in to Khadija and sat by her thigh and drew close to her," he said. She became Muhammad's first convert, telling him, "You will be the Prophet of the People." Khadija's support—and her fortune—were crucial to Muhammad in the early years when he was scorned for his preachings.

Muhammad and Khadija were unusually devoted to each other. At a time when polygamy was common, Muhammad took no other wives until she died. He later married twelve women, many for political reasons, and is said to have told one of them about Khadija, "She believed in me when no one else did. She was my first disciple, and she honoured and protected me when I was poor and forsaken." Khadija bore him two sons, who died in infancy, and four daughters.

When Khadija died in 619, Muhammad's religion had yet to spread beyond a devoted few. But his loyal converts followed Muhammad out of Mecca, where they were persecuted, to the distant town of Medina. There Muhammad consolidated his forces and in 630 reentered Mecca with ten thousand men. Besides being a religious leader, he had become the most powerful military ruler in Arabia by the time of his death in 632. Within twenty years, Muslims ruled from Libya to Persia, and that was only the beginning.

Khadija's tomb remains a point of pilgrimage for Muslims. But the irony—that a woman and her fortune helped launch a religion that would severely restrict the role of future women—is not apparent at the shrine.

MARY KINGSLEY

AFRICAN EXPLORER

Once, in a dark jungle in West Africa, Mary Kingsley rescued a leopard from a snare. Instead of being grateful, the beast began circling her. She stared right back and said, "Go home, you fool." It did. This and other adventures prompted Rudyard Kipling to remark, "Being human, she must have been afraid of something. But one never found out what it was."

It is ironic that at a time when most proper Victorian ladies were too stifled to wield more than calling cards, Mary Kingsley was employing her umbrella to whack an encroaching alligator on its snout. She was not alone. Victorian England produced a sorority of intrepid women who climbed mountains, sought the source of the Nile, and trekked through Tibet, to name just a few of their feats. But few trudged deeper, and perhaps none had greater impact, than Kingsley. Her ventures into the jungles of West Africa produced many new discoveries and, said a Nigerian historian, "helped to change in a profound way the attitude of European colonial administrators towards their African subjects."

Kingsley was not raised to be a world-beater. While her father spent years abroad, including time in West Africa collecting specimens for the British Museum, Kingsley stayed home to care for her mother, who took to her bed whenever her husband was away. She educated herself by reading in her father's library, and when he became ill she helped him prepare his travel notes for publication. She took care of both her parents until they died, six weeks apart, in 1892. Herself thirty, Kingsley was a pale, thin, and melancholy woman.

"Dead tired and feeling no one had need of me anymore, I went down to West Africa to die," she wrote in a letter. Actually, her purpose was to finish some research that her father had begun, but her death was not unlikely. Called the "white man's grave," the Sierra Leone region of West Africa was a land of wild animals and cannibal tribes, largely unexplored except by David Livingstone and very few others.

Into Africa Kingsley went, by herself, with one portmanteau and a waterproof bag. She carried cloth and tobacco to trade, and a wardrobe of proper Victorian attire because, she said, "one would never want to go about in Africa in a way that would embarrass one to be seen in Piccadilly." So it was that a woman in a long black skirt could be seen trudging through swamps up to her neck. The wardrobe came in handy when Kingsley once found herself facing a tribe of cannibals with nothing to trade but her twelve blouses. They looked very interesting, she reported, "when worn by a brawny warrior with *nothing* else but red paint and a bunch of leopard tails."

For a woman to venture into Africa was so bizarre that many European traders and African tribesmen alike couldn't believe Kingsley wasn't traveling with her husband. She got so tired of explaining, she finally began telling them, "I am looking for him."

After two trips that spanned seventeen months from 1893 to 1895, Kingsley returned to England with a variety of insects and plants as well as eighteen species of reptiles and sixty-five fish—including two that were new and named for her. Her achievements spread further when she published two best-selling books and began lecturing on her travels. The formerly meek, awkward young woman enthralled audiences with her mildly racy language and tales of gorillas and near-drownings on the Ogooué River in the French Congo. "One appalling corner I shall not forget, for I had to jump at a rock wall, and hang on to it in a manner more befitting an insect than an insect-hunter."

In her lectures, Kingsley also told what she had learned about the native customs of African tribes. Missionaries, she said, ignored long-practiced, rich tribal religions in favor of a level of Christianity that even the English didn't fully follow. She put forth the idea that Africans didn't need white patrons and that the British only belonged in Africa as traders, not as rulers. Although by today's standards Kingsley still had a very colonial view, she was way ahead of her time. Her opinions were sought by British colonial administrators, and while she didn't always convince them, she is credited with making them at least consider how their policies would affect the Africans.

In 1900, tired of lecturing, Kingsley returned to Africa. This time she went to South Africa to serve as a nurse in the Boer War. She had survived much on her previous journeys, but in Cape Town she caught typhoid fever and died three months after she arrived. She was buried at sea. Her career had lasted only eight years, but her influence lived much longer.

MARGARET KNIGHT

SHE INVENTED THE GROCERY STORE BAG, AMONG MANY OTHER THINGS

"I'm not surprised at what I've done," nineteenth-century inventor Margaret Knight once said. "I'm only sorry I couldn't have had as good a chance as a boy, and have been put to my trade regularly."

We should share her lament. For although obituaries hailing her as the "Woman Edison" were overly enthusiastic, this barely educated woman received patents on more than two dozen inventions, some of which remain quite useful. Next time you're carrying groceries home from the store, thank "Mattie" Knight.

"As a child I never cared for the things that girls usually do," Knight, born in Maine in 1838, wrote in a letter. "Dolls never had any charms for me. I couldn't see the sense of coddling bits of porcelain with senseless faces. The only things I wanted were a jackknife, a gimlet and pieces of wood. My friends were horrified. I was called a tomboy, but that made very little impression on me. I sighed sometimes because I was not like other girls, but wisely concluded that I couldn't help it, and sought further consolation from my tools."

After making sleds and kites for her brothers, Knight is credited with dreaming up her first invention when she was just twelve years old. While visiting her brothers in a cotton mill in Manchester, New Hampshire, she saw a worker injured when a steel-tipped shuttle fell off the machine. Knight, it is told, devised a way to secure the shuttles.

It was while she was working in a paper bag factory in Springfield, Massachusetts, in 1870 that the thirty-two-year-old Knight got her first patent. She came up with an attachment for the bag-folding machine and produced the first square-bottom bags. Now universally used, square-bottom bags didn't make a fortune for their inventor. As with most of her patents, Knight sold it to her employer to earn some extra cash.

Over the next thirty years Knight was awarded a total of twenty-seven patents, some of which came out of the factories where she was working. Some were household items: a dress and skirt shield, a spit, a clasp for holding robes, and a window frame. But what was particularly unusual was that Knight made innovations in heavy machinery, a most unladylike nineteenth-century pursuit. She invented and improved a shoe-cutting machine in the 1890s. In 1902 she got a patent on a rotary engine and later invented several motor components.

When she died in 1914 at the age of seventy-six, Knight, for all of her inventions, left an estate of just $275. She was no Edison, but she might have been.

ROSE KNOX

"AMERICA'S FOREMOST WOMAN INDUSTRIALIST"

Rose Knox didn't change the world, but her Knox gelatine did change the kitchen. Formerly involving a laborious process of boiling cow bones that limited its use to special occasions, gelatine, in Knox's orange box, became "as familiar a bit of kitchen Americana as the arm and hammer on the baking soda label," said one magazine. It also, according to *Collier's Weekly*, made Knox "America's foremost woman industrialist."

Born in 1857, Rosetta Markward was the daughter of an Ohio druggist. After high school, she got a job sewing gloves and in 1883 married one of the glove salesmen, Charles Knox. In 1890 the Knoxes took their savings of five thousand dollars and bought a gelatine manufacturing company in Johnstown, New York.

Rose and Charles had very different ideas about how to get more people to buy gelatine. Charles did a lot to draw attention to the company. He bought a stable of race horses, "the Gelatine String," and covered one of the first motor cars with Knox banners. He did the same with a hot-air balloon. During the 1896 presidential campaign, Charles strung a banner across Herald Square that said "Bryan Wants to Win, McKinley Wants to Win, Knox Gelatine *Always* Wins!" For such antics, Charles Knox was called "the Napoleon of Advertising."

But it was his wife who sold more gelatine. Charles's stunts got the attention of men, but Rose realized it was women who would buy their product. In her kitchen, she began developing new recipes using gelatine, and in 1896 she published a booklet called *Dainty Desserts*. The company distributed one million booklets annually, and sales soared.

In 1908, Charles died. Rose, then fifty-one, wanted to keep the business until her two teenage sons were old enough to run it. "I either had to run the business myself, or employ a manager," she said. "If I did the latter, I figured that by the time my boys came of age the business would belong to the manager."

So Rose took over, selling off her husband's other business investments, and concentrating on her female customers. She published a second book of recipes and began writing a newspaper column called "Mrs. Knox Says." She established an experimental kitchen at the plant, which developed hundreds of recipes, and she sponsored fellowships at the Mellon

Institute to create new uses for gelatine. By 1915, the value of the Knox Gelatine Company had tripled, and the firm was easily the industry leader. (Later, Knox did miss the boat on flavored gelatine and was surpassed by Jell-O.)

As a boss, Knox was described as "benign but brisk." On her first day as head of the company, she closed the rear door of the plant, where the workers had entered. "We are all ladies and gentlemen working here," she announced. "We'll all come in through the front door." She reduced the work week to five days from five-and-a-half, removed the time clock, and granted two weeks of vacation. In 1935 it was reported that her employees were loyal—a majority had worked for the company for at least twenty-five years—but "all of them are terrified of crossing her will."

Knox herself continued to arrive for work at 9:30 A.M. until she was eighty-eight, when arthritis forced her to work at home. At ninety, she finally made her son president, but she remained chairman of the board until she died two years later in 1950.

The year before, confined to a wheelchair, she had told one magazine, "What I'd really like to do is write an article of advice for men, and have it printed in a men's magazine. 'Take your business home with you,' I'd tell them. 'Talk it over with your wife. Keep her informed. You'll broaden the base of mutual understanding, and if your wife is ever left alone, as I was, she won't be stranded.' "

BARONESS PANNONICA DE KOENIGSWARTER

ROTHSCHILD HEIRESS TURNED JAZZ PATRON

When jazz great Charlie Parker died in 1955, the New York *Daily Mirror* headlined, "Bop King Dies in Heiress's Flat." It was an attempt to sensationalize the fact that Parker, a black saxophone player who was also a drug addict, had died in the tony hotel suite of the Baroness Pannonica de Koenigswarter, daughter of a Rothschild and wife of a French diplomat. But the real story was far less scandalous. In fact, it was fitting that Parker found his final haven in the home of the woman who was called the "Baroness of Jazz" or the "Bebop Baroness." Said one musician, "Most of the jazz people could count on her. She was their one regular customer."

The baroness had traveled a long way from her roots. Kathleen Annie Pannonica Rothschild was born into the English branch of the world's wealthiest banking family; her brother would become the third Baron Rothschild. She attended finishing school in Paris and made her debut in London, where her mother was a close friend of Queen Mary. "I was moved from one great country house to another in the germless immunity of reserved Pullman coaches while being guarded night and day by a regiment of nurses, governesses, tutors, footmen, valets, chauffeurs, and grooms," she said later.

She took up flying, and it was on a French airfield where she met Jules de Koenigswarter, a French mining engineer whom she married in 1934 when she was twenty-one. She spent World War II as a decoder for

General de Gaulle and as a private in the Free French Army. After the war, she settled into life as the wife of a French diplomat, but became so bored that she began making trips to New York. The baroness had loved jazz since she was a teenager, and in New York she met pianist Thelonious Monk, sax players Charlie Parker and Coleman Hawkins, and other musicians who were the vanguard of the hottest new sound, "bebop."

In 1951 the baroness—by then the mother of five—left her husband at the French Embassy in Mexico City and moved into the Hotel Stanhope on upper Fifth Avenue. She became a regular at New York's most avant-garde jazz clubs, like the Five Spot, the Village Vanguard, Birdland on 52nd Street, and Small's in Harlem. Said *Time* magazine, "Seeing her pull up in her Bentley with purse crammed with Chivas Regal, the musicians took enormous pride in her friendship." But it was more than her money. Said drummer Art Blakey, "I was never able to keep a band together until I met her. I learned a lot just from sitting down and talking to her. She taught me about using diplomacy with people and how to carry myself."

The baroness became especially close to Parker and Monk. "Bird" Parker had become one of the most popular progressive jazz musicians, but he had also suffered terribly, developing a heroin addiction that had cost him his precious cabaret card, preventing him from performing in New York. He had tried to commit suicide, spent time in a mental hospital, and generally had wrecked his body so severely that after he died the doctor estimated he was fifty-three years old when in fact he was only thirty-four.

For Parker, the baroness's home was a refuge. She

said, "We did have a wonderful friendship going, nothing romantic. He always dropped in unexpectedly anytime during the day or night. He was a relaxed type of person, and you sometimes hardly knew he was around. He liked to play peggity with my daughter."

Monk found the same comfort from the European heiress. An eccentric figure—he never spoke to his audiences and always wore a Chinese coolie cap or some other hat—Monk had been slower to gain popularity, though later he would be called the most serious jazz composer next to Duke Ellington. Monk and the baroness had been friends since the early 1950s, and in 1957 she helped him regain his cabaret card that he had lost six years earlier on a heroin charge. She gave Monk rooms to work in, and they were frequently seen around town, the baroness in her mink, Monk slouched in his bohemian garb.

The people who were most shocked by the strange pair were the other residents and management at the Hotel Stanhope. Monk often sat in the hotel lobby wearing dark glasses and holding a white cane, and residents also complained about his late-night jam sessions. After the hotel doubled her rent, the baroness eventually moved out, but ran into the same trouble at other hotels. "I had lots of bread then," she said, "but wasn't welcome after a while, mainly because of my musician visitors. They couldn't actually *throw* me out, but whenever I'd leave for a little while, they'd always be full up when I tried to come back."

In 1958 Monk convinced the baroness to buy a large house in Weehawken, New Jersey, just across the Hudson River from Manhattan. He lived with her off and on, and spent the last twelve years of his life there until he died of a stroke in 1982 at the age of sixty-four. Meanwhile, Monk had remained married to his childhood sweetheart, Nellie, and occasionally she and their two children moved in with the baroness, too. After the baroness died, Nellie said, "She's been a very sincere friend, and we've had very few. She's been exactly what we needed."

Monk wrote a composition for the baroness entitled "Pannonica," and her influence in the jazz world could be seen and heard through many other performers. Pianist Horace Silver wrote "Nica's Dream," and others composed "Nica Steps Out," "Tonica," "Nica's Tempo," and "Blues for Nica."

After Monk died, the baroness became fairly reclusive, living in her Weehawken house with many, many cats. She died in December 1988 during heart bypass surgery, a week before her seventy-fifth birthday. In 1960, she had tried to explain to a writer for *Esquire* magazine how an aristocratic heiress became a patron of bohemian jazz musicians. "The music," she said, "the music is what moves me. It's everything that really matters, everything worth digging. It's a desire for freedom."

L

MARGARET GETCHELL LAFORGE

SHE RAN MACY'S DEPARTMENT STORE

When Rowland Hussey Macy, a former Nantucket whaler, opened his first dry goods store in Massachusetts, he went bankrupt. His second attempt, in New York, fared better, growing into what remains the world's largest department store, in Herald Square. The difference, even he admitted, to a large degree was Margaret Getchell. It was she who transformed the small fancy-goods shop into a full-fledged department store, and it was she who began the Macy's tradition of eye-grabbing gimmicks to draw customers inside. "Miss Getchell lived before Mickey Mouse and helium gas," said one magazine, "but she had the right idea."

Like many girls in her time, Getchell became a schoolteacher when she was still a teenager, at the age of sixteen in 1857. But three years later, after she was forced to wear a glass eye due to a childhood injury, Getchell decided to seek a less vigorous job. She left her native Nantucket for New York and called on Macy, her distant cousin, who in 1858 had opened a fancy-goods store on Sixth Avenue just south of Fourteenth Street.

Macy hired Getchell to be a cashier at the store, which at the time sold a limited variety of ribbons, laces, and other accessories. But although her position was limited, Getchell took her job very seriously. Living in a room across the street, she regularly stayed late to help balance accounts. And she began making suggestions to Macy—"putting a bug in his ear," she called it—to improve operations. It was her idea to expand the merchandise to include specialty clothes, toiletries, and hats. Later, she would add jewelry, china, silver, home furnishings, books, and most successfully, groceries.

In 1863, when Getchell was twenty-two, Macy promoted her to bookkeeper, the third-highest position in the store behind the superintendent and Macy himself. Three years later, he named her superintendent. The only woman in the city in charge of what by then was becoming a major store, Getchell oversaw its expansion as Macy's tripled in size, occupying the entire blockfront between Thirteenth and Fourteenth streets. Macy's, which sold ninety thousand dollars worth of goods its first year, by 1869 had sales of more than $1 million and employed two hundred people.

Getchell was a talented administrator, but she also proved to be a great salesman. She put two cats, dressed in doll clothes, in a store window, where they would sleep for hours in twin cribs. The display drew crowds, and Getchell further capitalized on it by selling photographs of the cute cats. She also installed a soda fountain deep inside the store to attract thirsty customers past the merchandise.

Getchell had gone to live with Macy's family in 1863, and when she took an interest in Abiel LaForge, a friend of Macy's son, Macy helped move things along by seeing to it that the Civil War captain frequently was invited to dinner. Getchell and LaForge were married in 1869, and soon after, Macy hired him as a lace buyer. The couple moved into a five-room apartment directly above the store so Getchell could continue to work nights on inventory and accounts.

Over the next eight years, as she gave birth to six children including twins, Getchell's duties at Macy's decreased. Her husband, meanwhile, got more involved, and Macy made him his only partner in 1871. From that point on, Getchell herself received no salary, because Macy considered LaForge's share of the profits to be her compensation, too. Still, Macy continued to consult Getchell daily, and when he and LaForge went to Europe in 1873, she was left in charge.

The happy arrangement was not to last for long. Macy died in 1877, leaving LaForge and one of his nephews in control of the store. Then LaForge died of tuberculosis the following year, and Macy's nephew bought out Getchell for $82,500. More suddenly, Getchell died in 1880 of a "flabby heart" and inflamed ovaries. Just thirty-eight years old, she left behind what would become one of the most enduring institutions in New York.

FLORENCE LAWRENCE

THE FIRST MOVIE STAR

America without movie stars would be like ancient Greece without gods. And yet the early moviemakers originally wanted it that way. Movie companies thought their audiences cared more about which studio made the movie than who was in it. The Biograph studio proclaimed that its actors "have their names locked in a big safe and only get them back when they leave." Director D. W. Griffith said he never told the initially nameless Mary Pickford how much fan mail she got because "I didn't want her asking for a raise in salary," which in those early days ranged from five to fifteen dollars a week.

Those days have been gone for a long time, and when America's version of royalty began, Florence Lawrence was its first queen. Raised by her mother in a Canadian traveling tent show, by 1892, at the age of three, she was billed as "Baby Florence, the Child Wonder." Her movie career began in 1907 when she was hired by Thomas Edison's film company for the one-reeler *Daniel Boone*. She got the part because she could ride a horse.

Lawrence became a regular player for the Vitagraph Company, but she was not its leading lady. That role belonged to Florence Turner, whom audiences knew only as "the Vitagraph Girl." In 1908 Griffith hired Lawrence and gave her her own anonymous title, "the Biograph Girl." With her large nose and puffy cheeks, Lawrence wasn't beautiful. But she had a certain all-American-girl quality that movie audiences adored, and she appeared in most of the sixty films that Griffith directed that year. One early review said, "Of course, the chief honors of the picture are borne by the now famous Biograph Girl, who must be gratified by the silent celebrity she has achieved." Lawrence was not. In an early demonstration of her budding star quality, she demanded a separate dressing table and more money for playing leading roles.

In 1909 Biograph fired its "Biograph Girl" after Lawrence tried to get work at another film company. Biograph officials simply replaced Lawrence with another nameless "Biograph Girl," and they assumed moviegoers would go along. Instead, Biograph received hundreds of hostile letters like this: "The leading lady isn't 'the Biograph Girl' at all. Whoever she is, she is all right, very pretty, a superb and charming actress, and in every way adorable, but she is not 'the Biograph Girl.' " But Biograph did not bring Lawrence back, and in fact the company got her blacklisted from the other major movie companies, which in those early days had formed a trust to prevent outsiders from breaking into the movie business.

It was a happy coincidence for Carl Laemmle, who had formed his own Independent Motion Picture Company (IMP) to battle the trust and later would start Universal. Laemmle quickly hired the extremely popular Lawrence and made her "the IMP Girl." Movie audiences followed, and Lawrence proved it was her they wanted to see, not the studios.

The best evidence came on March 21, 1910, in St. Louis. The previous month, a story had appeared in several newspapers around the country reporting that Lawrence had been killed in a street car accident in St. Louis. It has been debated whether Biograph officials had planted the story to ruin its lost star—or whether Laemmle spread the tale to drum up some publicity. Whichever, Laemmle took advantage of the opportunity. He announced that Lawrence would appear personally in St. Louis to prove that she was alive, "will continue to appear in 'IMP' films, and very shortly some of the best work in her career is to be released."

What happened in St. Louis is straight out of Nathanael West's *The Day of the Locust*. When her train arrived at Union Station, reported a St. Louis newspaper, "Suddenly the throng broke into wild tumultuous shouts as a remarkably pretty young woman appeared at the gate. The crowd surged toward her like a wave, and for a moment it looked as if the young woman would be drowned in the human sea." The crowd, which was bigger than the one for President Taft the previous week, tore the buttons from Lawrence's coat and grabbed her hat. She fainted, and the first star was born.

Lawrence made fifty films for Laemmle's company in eleven months, and she was largely responsible for keeping IMP in business. She later staked out further territory for future stars by arranging her own independent production deal with Laemmle, one that gave her complete artistic control and an unheard-of five hundred dollars a week. She shot her movies at a studio in Fort Lee, New Jersey, and went home to a fifty-acre estate in Westwood.

In 1915, filming a scene for a movie called *Pawns of Destiny*, Lawrence was supposed to carry her leading man, Matt Moore, down a burning staircase. But the flames got out of control, and Lawrence, instead of jumping to safety, went back into the building to rescue Moore. She suffered a bad fall, injuring her back and burning her face. When she tried to return to the set a month later, she collapsed and was partially paralyzed for four months.

Lawrence made no films for six years. By the time she attempted her comeback in 1921, the movie business was radically different. There was a new movie town, Hollywood, with its own stars like Mary Pickford and Charlie Chaplin, and new movie studios run by men who didn't remember Florence Lawrence. She got her nose bobbed, but got little work. She married a car salesman (her first marriage to her costar and director Harry Salter had ended after her accident), and they opened a cosmetics shop in Hollywood. Her third marriage ended after five months because he beat her.

In 1936 the long-forgotten star, who shared a West Hollywood apartment with two other women, signed with M-G-M as a bit player for seventy-five dollars a week. On December 27, 1938, Lawrence called the studio to say she was ill and couldn't report for her 1 P.M. call. She then drank a mixture of poison ant paste and cough syrup. A neighbor heard her scream and called an ambulance, but Lawrence died before she arrived at a Beverly Hills hospital. The first movie star to be known by her own name is buried in an unmarked grave in Hollywood Memorial Park Cemetery.

IDA LEWIS

LIGHTHOUSE KEEPER; SHE SAVED EIGHTEEN LIVES

"Are we to believe that it is 'feminine' for young women to row boats in storms?" asked *Harper's Magazine* in 1869. "Is it 'womanly' to tug and strain through a tempest, and then pull half-drowned men into a skiff?" After considering the quandary at some length, *Harper's* soberly concluded, "No man will be such an—let us say donkey—as to insist that it was unfeminine in Ida Lewis to pull off in her boat to save men from drowning."

They called Ida Lewis "the American Grace Darling" after the British woman who had rescued nine people from a steamer wreck in the 1830s. But actually, Darling should have been called "the British

Ida Lewis," because Lewis saved twice as many people. And, as the keeper of the light for more than half a century at the Lime Rock Lighthouse off Newport, Rhode Island, she did it over and over again.

Idawalley Zoradia Lewis was the eldest of four children of Captain Hosea Lewis, who became the first keeper of the light in Narragansett Bay in 1853. Four years later, he suffered a stroke, and Ida, just fifteen years old, took over. Her main job was to maintain the red beam in the lighthouse, which guided the great yachts of the social elite who summered in Newport each year. But she also was responsible—besides caring for her ailing parents—for taking her three younger brothers and sisters to school, which meant rowing a small skiff to and from the mainland—a distance of some three hundred yards—twice a day no matter what the weather.

That proved to be good practice. She made her first rescue in 1859 when four Newport boys, sons of wealthy families, were roughhousing in a small sailboat in the bay and capsized. None of the boys could swim and all would have drowned had not seventeen-year-old Lewis rowed out and scooped them up. In 1866, she pulled out a drunken soldier whose skiff had overturned. And the next year, she saved three Irish sheepherders who had capsized while they were trying to rescue a valuable sheep (belonging to prominent banker August Belmont) that had escaped from the herd along the shore. After she put the shepherds on dry land, Lewis went back and got the sheep.

It was a rescue in 1869 that made Lewis famous. On a raw, snowy March afternoon, two soldiers who had hired a fourteen-year-old boy to row them from the mainland to Fort Adams capsized in the raging sea. Lewis, who was suffering from a bad cold, was wrapped in a blanket with her feet in the oven when she heard their cries. Barefoot, with no hat or coat, she rowed a half-mile to reach them. With the help of her younger brother, she hauled the two soldiers—one unconscious—onto her small boat (their young rower had drowned). Back at the lighthouse she worked for an hour to revive the soldier.

After so many previous rescues, this one captured the attention of the national press. *Harper's* described Lewis as "slender, blue-eyed, with light brown hair, frank and hearty, and likely to be more famous next summer than any Newport belle." Indeed she was. Newport residents presented her with a new boat, christened the *Rescue*, and the boisterous speculator James Fisk built a shelter for it.

She received so many famous visitors and tourists that it became a nuisance. "They bother dreadfully when I have washing or cooking to do," she said. Lewis also received many marriage offers, some by mail. In 1870 she accepted the in-person proposal of a Connecticut fisherman. It didn't last long, and she continued to be called "Miss Lewis."

In 1877 she rescued another three soldiers and in 1881 two more. In 1879 Congress gave her a gold medal, and the same year—seven years after her father died—she finally was granted the official title of keeper of the light. In 1906, at the age of sixty-four, Lewis made her eighteenth and final rescue, when a woman coming to visit her fell out of the boat.

Lewis, who lived in the modest, two-story lighthouse with her brother, Rudolph, a cocker spaniel, and six cats, never stepped down from her post. She suffered a stroke while on duty on a Friday night in October 1911 and never regained consciousness before she died the following Tuesday.

Two years before, at the age of sixty-seven, she had been asked why she was willing to risk her life so often.

"If there were some people out there who needed my help, I would go to them even if I knew I couldn't get back. Wouldn't you?" she replied, then repeated, "Wouldn't you? We have only one life to live, and when our time comes we've got to go; so it doesn't matter how."

ANN LOHMAN ("MADAME RESTELL")

INFAMOUS NINETEENTH-CENTURY ABORTIONIST

Though it seems an issue very much of modern times, abortion stirred just as much controversy more than a century ago. In the early 1800s, many doctors, as well as a broad class of unlicensed practitioners, mostly women, offered a variety of drugs, herbs, and surgical techniques to end pregnancies. Initially, abortions were sought mostly by single women to protect their reputations. But by mid-century, the practice was far from uncommon among respectable, middle-class housewives who wanted to limit the size of their families. Most states had no law against it, and by one estimate, one abortion was performed for every five or six live births in the 1850s and 1860s.

Like today, as the practice of abortion spread in the nineteenth century, so did opposition to it. And at the forefront of that early battle was Ann Lohman, a woman whose career as an abortionist mirrored the rise and fall of the practice. She had been a poor English immigrant working as a seamstress in New York until 1836, when she married Charles Lohman, a newspaper typesetter who worked as an unlicensed doctor on the side. She soon joined him in selling medications—concocted by her brother—that were supposed to prevent pregnancies or induce abortions.

Soon Ann Lohman took over the business, advertising herself as "Madame Restell, female physician and professor of midwifery," which included an adoption service. At the time, abortionists advertised openly in newspapers and magazines, offering their services for "female complaints." And while Lohman was hardly the only one, she became the most successful and therefore the most visible. As her clinic grew on Greenwich Street in lower Manhattan, public pressure led to her arrest in 1841. She was charged, under a rarely enforced law, with aborting a "quickened" fetus—one that had developed enough to show signs of movement.

It was a sensational trial, with the prosecutor declaring that if Lohman were allowed to continue her practice, "lust, licentiousness, seduction and abortion would be the inevitable occurrences of every day." Lohman was found guilty of two minor offenses. But instead of reducing her activities, she used the publicity to expand, opening clinics in Boston and Philadelphia, and sending salesmen on the road to peddle her pills.

In 1845 Lohman was arrested for performing an abortion in which the mother died. The number of botched abortions had increased with the growing practice, and the press covered Lohman's trial like none before. Stories recounted the medical testimony in detail that was shocking for the times. "Restellism" became synonymous with abortion. This time, Lohman was convicted and sent to prison for one year, though she received such lenient treatment that public outcry forced the warden to resign.

After her conviction, one doctor said, "Restell is to be looked upon as an effect, rather than a cause. The legislature must go to the root of the evil, of which this abomination is the fruit." New York legislators responded by strengthening the law, making all abortions manslaughter and making the pregnant woman herself liable for prosecution.

But those were the days when New York City was ruled by Boss Tweed, who chose to look the other way while Lohman and many others carried on their business. She continued to advertise and developed a sizable mail-order business as well. Because of her success, Lohman's clientele was largely middle-class or even wealthy women, and not a few daughters of prominent families. She opened a larger facility on Chambers Street and in 1864 built a lavish, four-story brownstone at Fifty-second Street and Fifth Avenue, where she lived with her husband, stepdaughter, and two grandchildren.

It is said that she chose the location to rile the Catholic archbishop, who was building St. Patrick's Cathedral two blocks away. But her home—as well as the sight of her fancy carriage parading through the streets—angered far more than the archbishop. The lots on either side of her brownstone remained vacant as long as she lived. *The New York Times*, in her obituary, wrote that she had "ostentatiously flaunted her wealth before the community and made an attractive part of the finest avenue in the city odious by her constant presence."

After her husband died in 1876, Lohman finally reduced, but did not end, her practice. In 1878 she threw an extravagant wedding in her home for her beloved granddaughter. Soon after, she sold some contraceptive pills to a man who turned out to be

Anthony Comstock, an anti-obscenity crusader who had pushed Congress to pass a law against possessing or selling articles for "immoral use."

The sixty-six-year-old woman was scheduled to go on trial April 1. But after years of maintaining her composure against rising public disdain, Lohman this time lost control. She rambled around her mansion saying, "What shall I do? What shall I do? I have never injured anybody. Why should they bring this trouble upon me?" The morning of her trial, a chambermaid found Lohman in her bathtub, where she had slit her throat with a carving knife. She left her estate of $1 million to her two grandchildren. There was no funeral.

Lohman's suicide was the lead story in *The New York Times*, which quoted Comstock, who had caused her arrest, as proclaiming it "a bloody ending to a bloody life." And while her demise did signal a turning point in the nation's tolerance toward abortion—the practice eventually became outlawed later in the century and remained so until *Roe v. Wade*—the hostility against Lohman also reflected society's deep conflict with itself. Said one historian, "She flourished in a society which, having failed to live up to its own rigid sexual code, resolved the dilemma by outlawing—but then tolerating—the troubling forms of behavior."

MABEL DODGE LUHAN

HOSTESS OF THE MOST NOTABLE SALON IN AMERICAN HISTORY

"I have always been myself and at the same time someone else; always able to be the other person, feel with him, think his thoughts, see from the angle in which he has found himself," wrote Mabel Dodge in one of her memoirs. "It is the only genius that I have ever had, but it has been enough."

As with many of the great salon hostesses, Mabel Dodge is best remembered not for what she did, but for what she inspired others to do. In the years before World War I, her brownstone on lower Fifth Avenue became the most famous salon in American history, the nerve center for the definitive Who's Who of pre-war artists and intellectuals. From Lincoln Steffens and Margaret Sanger to John Reed and Emma Goldman, New York's best minds found a fertile gathering place—and many a hot meal—in the home of a woman who spent her life searching for her identity through others, and found it everywhere.

One reporter called Dodge "the most peculiar common denominator that society, literature, art and radical revolutionaries ever found in New York and Europe." Part of the peculiarity was that she had begun her life as just another middling Victorian debutante. The daughter of inherited wealth in Buffalo, in 1900 at the age of twenty-one she had a proper marriage to a man who died in a hunting accident three years later. To recuperate from a nervous breakdown, she sailed to Europe, where she married a man she had met on the crossing ship. She and Edwin Dodge lived in a villa in Florence, where Mabel dressed in Renaissance clothes, entertained American artists, and twice attempted suicide.

She returned to New York alone in 1912 and settled in a brownstone at 23 Fifth Avenue, in the heart of Greenwich Village. It was Steffens who encouraged her to open her home to New York's intelligentsia. "You have a centralizing, magnetic, social faculty," he told her. "You attract, stimulate, and soothe people, and men like to sit with you and talk to themselves. You make them think more fluently, and they feel enhanced."

Soon, Wednesday evenings at "the Salon Dodge" became the hottest spot in the city. Besides the well-known—which also included Alfred Stieglitz, Gertrude Stein, and Walter Lippmann—Dodge invited radical labor leaders and suffragists, as well as stuffy society women and conservative ministers. From the jumble emerged debates about anarchism, Freud, abstract art, and whatever other subjects drew the most attention. Some nights, which always included a midnight buffet, focused on special topics. Margaret Sanger hosted Birth Control Night; Reed and Lippmann led Socialism Night.

Said Steffens, "Mabel Dodge managed her evenings and no one felt that they were managed. She sat quietly [in a long white dress] in a great armchair and rarely said a word; her guests did the talking. Practiced hostesses in society could not keep even a small table of guests together; Mabel Dodge did this better with a crowd of one hundred or more people of all classes."

Amidst the clutter of ideas, Dodge embraced it all. She freely spent her inherited fortune on a wide variety of social and political causes. She patronized artists, fed hungry poets, and bailed radicals out of jail. Writer Max Eastman called her the "Mother Postulate." Dodge also plunged into psychoanalysis and astrology. For a year she wrote a weekly column for Hearst newspapers that helped popularize Freudian psychology. And she clung to a tempestuous two-year affair with radical John Reed. When she finally realized he wouldn't commit himself to her, Dodge again attempted suicide.

For all its notoriety, Dodge's salon lasted just three

years. In 1916 she moved north of New York to Croton-on-Hudson, where she met and married post-impressionist painter Maurice Stern. It was Stern who introduced her to her next passion, the community of Taos, New Mexico. Mabel embraced the southwestern landscape and the Indian culture, especially after she fell in love with a Pueblo Indian named Tony Lujan, who became her fourth husband in 1923.

Mabel Luhan (she changed the spelling) became convinced that Taos was "the beating heart of the universe." She saw the Pueblo culture as the answer for America's dying spirit, and she saw herself and Tony as messiahs who would spread the message. Mabel attempted to recreate her New York salon in New Mexico by inviting everyone to visit her. Several did, including, most notably, artist Georgia O'Keeffe.

She also drew British writer D. H. Lawrence to Taos, which sparked a major feud between Luhan and Lawrence's wife, Frieda. "I wanted to seduce his spirit so that I could make him carry out certain things," Mabel wrote. "I did not want, particularly, to touch him." It was never clear how far their relationship went. Nevertheless, as *The New York Times* said in her obituary, "Her literary friends discussed it in books numerous enough to form a small library."

Mabel's dream for Taos, of course, never unfolded. She remained interested in Indian affairs until she died of a heart attack in 1962 at the age of eighty-three. Her biographer, Lois Rudnick, summed up: "The outstanding fact of Mabel's life is that she never found a clear and coherent direction for herself." But considering the many lives she touched and nurtured, perhaps that wasn't such a bad thing.

CLARA MAASS

VICTIM OF THE YELLOW FEVER IMMUNITY EXPERIMENTS

Advances in medical science nearly always are credited to the doctors, not to the patients on whom the breakthrough experiments were performed. Who, for example, received the first heart transplant from Dr. Christian Barnard? And whom did Dr. Jonas Salk first inject with his polio vaccine? At the turn of the century, it was Dr. Walter Reed who made his career by proving that yellow fever was transmitted through the bite of a mosquito. His name was bestowed on one of the army's most prominent medical centers in Washington, D.C.

But almost forgotten was the single American who died in the yellow fever experiments, a hard-working army nurse named Clara Maass. The oldest of nine children of a German immigrant mill worker in East Orange, New Jersey, Maass had to quit school at the age of fifteen so she could earn money for her family. She sent her mother five dollars a month—half her wages—while she trained at the Newark German Hospital School of Nursing, then joined the Army Nursing Corps during the Spanish-American War.

Many of the soldiers she treated in Florida and Cuba were not injured in the fighting. More than twenty thousand American soldiers came down with yellow fever, an agonizing illness marked by high fever, vomiting, and liver complications that cause the skin to turn yellow. The disease, which occasionally reached epidemic levels in marshy southern cities, killed some fifteen hundred soldiers—more than the number who died in battle.

At the time, doctors didn't know what caused yellow fever, and Maass was praised for her willingness to be exposed to the disease during her work. A couple of years later, working in the Philippines, she contracted dengue fever—which causes severe joint pain—and almost died. But after she was sent home to recover, she volunteered to return to Havana in 1901.

The year before, Reed had proven that yellow fever was spread through mosquitoes by having them bite twenty-two volunteer soldiers. All came down with mild cases of the disease and none died. But in 1901, doctors still weren't sure how to control the spread of the disease. They planned to destroy much of the mosquito population, but they also wanted to develop a program of purposely infecting people to make them immune. The doctors believed that with proper medical care, their patients would only develop mild cases of the fever.

Maass, partly attracted by the offer of one hundred dollars for volunteers, immediately signed up for the immunity experiments along with about twenty others. She wrote to her mother, "Do not worry, Mother, if you hear that I have yellow fever. Now is a good time of the year to catch it if one has to. Most of the cases are mild, and then I should be an immune and not be afraid of the disease anymore." She was bitten by an infected mosquito on August 4 and soon she developed a mild case of yellow fever. But doctors decided her case had been too mild to render her immune, so she was bitten a second time on August 14. She died ten days later at the age of twenty-five.

Maass's death ended the immunity experiment. And while those tests were less important than the earlier ones conducted by Reed, one of the doctors said, "they had much more effect in the city of Havana in convincing the physicians and people generally that yellow fever was conveyed by the mosquito than did the work of the army board."

Maass was largely forgotten for half a century. Then in 1951, Cuba issued a commemorative stamp in her honor. In 1957, Newark Memorial Hospital became Clara Maass Memorial Hospital. And in 1976, the U.S. Postal Service issued a commemorative stamp for her, the first to honor an individual nurse. Said the pastor of the East Orange church who led the campaign for the stamp, "Here we have a martyr and no one has ever heard of her."

MOLLY MAGUIRE

THE WOMAN BEHIND THE FAMOUS "MOLLY MAGUIRES"

Though dozens of murders were alleged to have been committed in her name, Molly Maguire may never have really existed. In fact, there is even some debate as to whether the "Molly Maguires"—the band of Irish coal miners who reputedly terrorized the coal fields of eastern Pennsylvania in the 1860s and 1870s—ever lived up to their legend.

But let's start with the woman herself. History has left no actual evidence of Molly Maguire, but tales about her abound. She may have been a large Irish woman who packed two pistols and led raids against English landlords. Or, by some accounts, she was a crazy woman who fantasized that she controlled vast armies. But the most popular story is that she was an aging widow who in 1839 was evicted by her English landlord from the land she tilled.

According to one account, "The widow was old, and as the constabulary and bailiffs led the aged woman out of her cabin, her feeble and helpless appearance produced a great impression upon the spectators. Next came her little grandchildren and their mother in tears. The bailiffs cast their bed and bedding, with what little furniture they possessed, into the road and leveled the house to the ground. This eviction made such a sensation that the name quickly became famous."

Whether a woman named Molly Maguire really suffered this fate or not, the story found a sympathetic audience in Ireland, where such evictions were common and antagonism with the English dated back centuries. By the 1840s, a popular song included the chorus,

So let the toast go merrily round,
Each Irish heart conspire.
Those tyrant hounds will be crushed down
By matchless Molly Maguire!

The name wasn't identified with any single group but emerged as the general mark of Irish gangs who battled their English landlords. One letter threatened a landlord, "Molly Maguire and her children have been watching you."

When Irishmen, suffering evictions and famine, immigrated to the United States, many found themselves working for English descendants who owned the abundant coal mines in Schuylkill County, Pennsylvania. Conditions were abysmal and wages were low. As acts of sabotage occurred, there were rumors that some of the Irish gangs had regrouped in America. When a mine supervisor was murdered in 1862, the "Mollies" were blamed.

In the next three years in Schuylkill, forty mine managers and owners were killed. And although none of the murders were solved, the Molly Maguires were blamed for all of them. The name became the catchall for mine violence, as newspapers reported on a "Molly Beating" or "Molly Coffin Notice."

In 1873, Frank Gowen, the president of the Philadelphia & Reading Railroad, hired detective Allan Pinkerton to root out the Molly Maguires. Pinkerton—who made his name on the case—sent James McParlan, a native Irishman, to infiltrate the mines. McParlan returned with information that launched a series of sensational trials from 1875 to 1877. He testified that there was, indeed, a central, secret circle of men—the Molly Maguires—who directed the violence. McParlan's testimony was never corroborated, and some historians since have cast doubt on how far the Mollies actually reached.

But Gowen made the most of it. He branded the leaders of a growing union movement as Mollies. The public, fed up with the violence, supported him, and the union effort failed. The trials, meanwhile, ended with twenty men sent to the gallows, ten in one day. It was a far cry from the tale of a poor widow in Ireland.

MALINCHE

GUIDE FOR—AND MISTRESS OF—HERNANDO CORTÉS, THE CONQUEROR OF MEXICO

Of all of the European conquests of the New World, none is more awesome than that of Hernando Cortés. With just a few hundred men, the sixteenth-century Spanish explorer defeated tens of thousands of soldiers to conquer the centuries-old Aztec Empire of Mexico. He did have some advantages—cannons, for example, and the Indians' belief that the white-skinned Spaniards might be gods. But historians agree that what gave Cortés the edge was an Aztec woman who was first his slave and later his mistress. Malinche, according to Bernal Díaz, who chronicled Cortés's expedition, was "the principle of our conquest. Cortés kept her always by his side."

Cortés, an adventurous Spaniard who with Diego Velázquez had conquered Cuba and enjoyed success there in business and politics, was named to lead the first expedition to colonize Mexico after other explorers returned with reports of the land's great wealth. With eleven ships, seven hundred men, and sixteen horses, Cortés landed in February 1519 near the village of Tabasco, on the Gulf Coast west of the Yucatan Peninsula. He and his men immediately encountered the enemy and fought their first battle, killing eight hundred Indians before the Tabascans fled at the sight of the Spaniards' horses—animals they had never seen before.

As a peace offering the Tabascans presented Cortés and his men with food, gold, and twenty women. Among them was Malinche. Not a native of the Tabascan tribe, she had been sold by her widowed mother to slave traders so that her mother's son by her second marriage could inherit the family's estate. The slave traders later sold her to the Tabascans. Malinche has gone down in many Mexican history books as an evil woman who betrayed her people, but given her past, it isn't clear to whom she should have been loyal.

Initially, Malinche was taken as a mistress by one of Cortés's aides. But since she spoke the language of the Aztecs, as well as the ancient Mayan language that was also spoken by a member of Cortés's party, Malinche quickly became a vital member of the expedition. As Cortés marched toward the inland Aztec capital of Tenochtitlán (now Mexico City), Malinche provided information on the local customs of the various tribes he faced. As he defeated each of them, she spoke to the Indians and helped Cortés make alliances against Montezuma, the Aztec emperor. In fact, since the Indians conversed only with her, they called Cortés "Captain Malinche."

In one instance, Malinche saved Cortés's life. His last major hurdle before reaching the capital was the holy city of Cholula. The Cholulans appeared to be friendly and invited Cortés and his men into the city. But an old woman, who wanted to save the life of a fellow Indian, told Malinche that the Cholulans planned to ambush the Spaniards. Malinche warned

Cortés, and his men attacked first, slaying six thousand Cholulans. Montezuma was so worried by the loss that he sent gold and other valuable gifts to try to persuade Cortés to turn back. Instead, the display of wealth only encouraged the explorer to press on.

Cortés and his men faced no resistance as they marched into Tenochtitlán in November 1519. Montezuma treated them as guests, but when the guests invited him to visit their quarters, he hesitated. According to Díaz, Malinche told him: "Lord Montezuma, please accompany them immediately to their quarters and make no protest. I know they will treat you very honorably as befits your station. But if you stay here, you will die." Cortés then imprisoned his host, who later was beaten to death by his people for betraying them. After a final, bloody battle in 1521, Cortés was made governor of Mexico.

At some point during his conquest, Cortés took Malinche as his mistress. He had, conveniently, sent the aide who had originally chosen her back to Spain with some dispatches. Malinche converted to Catholicism, and some history books call her Doña Marina. She had a son by Cortés, and though the boy was ten years older than Cortés's only legitimate son—by his second Spanish wife—he inherited none of the explorer's wealth back in Spain. Some accounts say they also had a daughter.

In 1523, Cortés had Malinche marry another of his aides, Juan Jaramillo, and he gave her an estate north of Mexico City. Cortés, meanwhile, continued to explore Mexico and the territory that became the southwestern United States. After some bureaucratic disputes, he returned to Spain in 1540 and died, out of the crown's favor, in 1547.

Malinche's final fate is less certain. Most accounts

say she died in Mexico sometime after 1537. But her legacy has lived far longer. In Mexican folklore, she is La Llorana, the Weeping Woman of Mexico. She is also Matlalciuatl, the goddess of a volcano near the site of one of Cortés's major victories. But her name is best remembered in a less exalted fashion. The Mexicans have a word, used derogatorily, that refers to someone who wants to open Mexico to the outside world: *malinchista*.

MARY MALLON

OR "TYPHOID MARY"

In 1906, 23,000 people died of typhoid fever in the United States. New York City alone had some 3,500 cases and 639 deaths from the wrenching disease marked by a high fever and diarrhea. Scientists had isolated the typhoid bacteria in 1884, and they knew that the disease could be spread through unsanitary water and food. But because they didn't know how to stop it, fear of typhoid ran nothing short of hysteria.

What scientists didn't yet know was that typhoid also could be spread by human carriers, people who themselves weren't sick but who could infect others. They made that discovery because of Mary Mallon, a blonde, blue-eyed, plump cook who unknowingly risked infecting people every time she made a meal.

Although no one is sure, her doctors believed Mallon had been born about 1870 in Ireland. She apparently survived a case of typhoid—making her immune to the disease—and after her parents died she immigrated and found work as a cook in wealthy homes. The families she worked for always were delighted with her meals, but her tenure was usually short. Each time she began cooking for a new family, typhoid broke out in the household, and Mallon, eventually aware that something was wrong, abruptly left.

Scientists later traced her career through a series of outbreaks of the disease. It included a summer home in Mamaroneck on Long Island in 1900, a vacation home in Dark Harbor, Maine, in 1902 (where nine of the eleven people in the household got sick and two died), and a job in Ithaca, New York, in 1904, the year that 1,000 of the city's 13,000 residents got typhoid and 100 died. It was an outbreak in 1905 at a home in Oyster Bay on Long Island that led George Soper, a sanitary engineer for the New York City Department of Health, to begin looking for the only variable in the family's daily life—its cook.

Through the employment agency that placed Mallon in many of her homes, Soper in 1907 finally tracked her to a brownstone on Park Avenue in the sixties. When he arrived, already the laundress and a daughter of the family were ill with typhoid. Soper found Mallon in the kitchen, where he explained to her his theory that she might be infecting people through the meals she prepared. He told her he needed to get samples of her blood, urine, and feces. At that point Mallon, terrified by the unbelievable things she was hearing, picked up a carving fork and chased Soper out of the house.

After Soper visited the home again with no success, several days later a female doctor showed up with three police officers and some ambulance workers. Confronted, Mallon ran out of the back of the house and hid in an alley for two hours before she was caught. "I literally sat on her all the way to the hospital," the doctor said. "It was like being in a cage with an angry lion."

Tests proved Soper was correct. So rife was Mary Mallon's body with typhoid bacteria that some doctors called her "the human culture tube." It was then, reporting the discovery for the first time, that newspapers dubbed her "Typhoid Mary." Mallon, meanwhile, believed none of it. And because she refused to cooperate with doctors' demands that she give up cooking, she was committed to Riverside Hospital, located on the small, isolated North Brother Island in the East River.

Although her legal appeals failed, Mallon at first won public sympathy for her plight. It wasn't her fault, after all, that she was infected with this strange bacteria. Finally in 1910 Mallon was released after she promised to find work that didn't involve handling food. She also was supposed to check in with the Health Department regularly.

A few months later, Mallon vanished. Unable to find work through the regular agencies, Mallon assumed false names and began cooking in restaurants, hospitals, and other institutions. Once again, typhoid followed her. This time, the newspapers considered Typhoid Mary a killer. One cartoonist portrayed her dropping human skulls into a skillet. It wasn't until 1915 that the authorities tracked her down again, working in a Manhattan maternity hospital where twenty-five employees had come down with the disease.

Mallon was returned to North Brother Island, where she stayed for the rest of her life—twenty-three more years. For a few years, Mallon was a bitter, withdrawn woman who yelled at her doctors. But eventually she became friends with the hospital staff and was given a job in a laboratory. In 1923 the city built her a cottage on the island, a one-story house with a porch, a lawn, and an elm tree.

Over the years, hundreds of other typhoid carriers were identified, and they were allowed to remain free as long as they cooperated with health officials. But Mallon remained on the island in her cottage, where she entertained her friends from the hospital. When it was time to eat, they left. She read a lot, sewed curtains, and converted to Catholicism. Occasionally, Mallon was allowed to go into Manhattan for a few hours on her own. On Christmas Day in 1932 Mallon suffered a stroke that left her partially paralyzed. She was moved to an invalid ward, where she died six years later at about the age of sixty-eight.

Today, *Webster's Dictionary* defines Typhoid Mary as "one that is by force of circumstances a center from which something undesirable spreads."

MARIA MARTIN

AN IMPORTANT ASSISTANT TO JOHN JAMES AUDUBON

In *The Birds of America*, John James Audubon painted a portrait of this new nation that in some ways was just as revealing as the maps drawn by explorers or the paintings of the landscape artists. Lush with the diverse wildlife of the still undocumented continent,

Audubon's collection of 435 portraits of birds, completed in 1838, captured not only the life-size scientific detail of his creatures, but also their dramatic actions—a marsh bird catching a lizard or a hummingbird flitting above a delicate flower. Famed French naturalist Georges Cuvier called Audubon's work "the most magnificent monument which has yet been raised to ornithology."

What is interesting is that some of the paintings of the man known for his birds are in fact dominated by other elements—colorful flowers, or a bold branch of leaves laden with finely detailed insects. Audubon left that work to his assistants, the most enduring and perhaps most able of which was a spinster from Charleston, South Carolina, named Maria Martin. Though only briefly referred to in Audubon's original text—and then only as "my friend's sister"—Audubon later granted her credit in his stilted fashion. "I feel bound," he wrote, "to make some ornithological acknowledgment for the aid she has on several occasions afforded me in embellishing my drawings of birds by adding to them beautiful and accurate representations of plants and flowers."

Called by Audubon expert Alice Ford perhaps "the most influential woman on the American nineteenth-century natural history horizon," Martin became so quite by accident. The daughter of a well-off Charleston family, Martin was thirty-one in 1827 when she moved in with the family of her sister, Harriet, who was in poor health from the births of nine children, though she was to have five more. Harriet's husband, John Bachman, was a Lutheran minister with a deep interest in natural history. Martin joined Bachman in his avocation and showed quite a talent for painting plants and insects.

Both were thrilled to learn that Audubon—already distinguished for his early bird portraits in the 1820s—was to visit Charleston in 1831. Bachman met the famed naturalist the day he arrived and invited him to stay at Bachman's large house. Eventually, Bachman, Martin, and Audubon converted the basement into their studio, stuffed with freshly killed birds and the wire that would pose them. Audubon encouraged Martin to paint birds, which he found so impressive that he asked her to paint backgrounds for him.

Her work was in some ways more difficult than Audubon's. Martin's flowers, insects, and branches had to be every bit as detailed as Audubon's birds—which he usually painted on a little branch or in mid-air—and they also had to complement the birds in scale and coloring. Sometimes Martin would paint around Audubon's work, but often she worked separately and the two paintings were combined by the printer.

Audubon clearly was enamored with Martin's work. In one letter to Bachman he wrote, "I much wish that your Dear Sister, our Sweetheart, would draw plants and branches of trees for me to the number of fifteen or twenty drawings for small plates." He referred to another assistant, "who has drawn plants to some of my birds, although not so successfully as my amiable friend Miss Martin." As a measure of his devotion, Audubon named a subspecies of the hairy woodpecker *Picus Martinae* in her honor.

It is not clear exactly how many backgrounds Martin contributed to Audubon's *Birds*. Art scholars have definitely identified more than thirty, but they are uncertain of many others which may be her work, or his work, or a combination. It's possible that even some of the birds attributed to Audubon actually were painted by Martin, or at least were based on her work.

Besides working on *Birds*, which was published in four volumes in England, Martin also helped Audubon prepare his smaller American edition in 1844. She and Bachman also compiled and edited the text for Audubon's *Ornithological Biography*, completed in 1839, and his *Viviparous Quadrupeds of North America*. That was completed, after Audubon had died in 1851, with the help of his two sons, both of whom had married Bachman's daughters. In another interesting twist, Martin married Bachman in 1848, two years after her sister died.

Aside from Audubon's few references, Martin received no attention for her work during her lifetime. After her last project with Audubon, she continued to paint on her own. When her right arm failed her when she was sixty, Martin taught herself to draw left-handed. During the Civil War she fled to Columbia, South Carolina, to escape the shelling. She died there in 1863 at the age of sixty-seven.

MARY THE JEWESS

INVENTOR OF THE STILL

Today if you call somebody an alchemist, you probably mean he's a swindler, because we associate alchemy with the futile effort to turn base metal into gold. But in fact the ancient alchemists sought far more than elusive precious metals. Through a combination of philosophy, magic, and primitive experiments, the alchemists tried to explain the natural world with sound scientific principles. They were the forerunners—by more than a millennium—of the founders of modern chemistry.

All that may sound a little fuzzy, but the early alchemists did leave behind some very real achievements. Next time you have a cocktail, consider that it was the only female alchemist, named Mary the Jewess, who invented the still.

The record of her life, which is believed to date to the first century A.D. in ancient Alexandria in northern Egypt, is sketchy at best. The few references to her are as mystical as her work. "Of the race of Palestine, sister of Moses, behold Miriam equally rejoices and triumphs in the Chymic choir," says a book published in 1624 based on original, now lost, documents of the alchemists. "She knew the hidden secrets of the great stone."

Many of Mary's discoveries came about as by-products of her attempts to create gold. Alchemists had the idea that by applying chemical vapors to base metals they could create the precious metal. They usually tried sulphur, because it was yellow. Mary built an apparatus that would heat the materials, blend their vapors, and then capture the cooled mixture in another tube. Called a *tribikos* by the Greeks, it was the first distillation device.

According to one translation, here is how Mary described the process, albeit puzzlingly. "If the two do not become one, i.e., if the volatile does not combine with the fixed, nothing will take place which is expected . . . But when one yellows, three becomes four, for one yellows with yellow sulphur. At the end, when one tints into violet, all things combine into violet!"

Mary also invented the *kerotakis*, a cylindrical device that allows metals to be treated with chemical vapors. Instead of producing gold in the contraption, the procedure produces a lead-copper alloy that is still called "Mary's Black." She also invented a water bath —a double boiler—that the French still call a *bain-marie*.

Antoine Lavoisier, an eighteenth-century Frenchman, is considered the father of modern chemistry. No swindler, Mary the Jewess was its ancient grandmother.

ELSA MAXWELL

INTERNATIONAL HOSTESS WITHOUT PORTFOLIO

"To get fifty people to a cocktail party in New York, you ask one hundred. In Hollywood, you invite twenty." Some people considered her brash, crass, and even "a dangerous fool," but give Elsa Maxwell credit: she knew about parties. Probably the world's supreme party-giver between the world wars, Maxwell entertained one evening's guests with Serge Diaghilev and his entire Ballet Russe. For music at another party she recruited Vladimir Horowitz. It was not unusual to see titled Europeans sitting on the floor of her apartment giggling over the antics of Noel Coward and Beatrice Lillie.

George Bernard Shaw called Maxwell "the eighth wonder of the world," and part of the wonderment came from the fact that she did it all—down to the gowns she wore—with other people's money. But exactly *how* she was able to do it remained so puzzling that even at her death *The New York Times* summed up, "Miss Maxwell was neither beautiful nor wealthy nor socially prominent, and it was a great mystery how she got to the position of social prominence she reached and held for more than forty years."

The *Times* understated on all three counts. Of her lack of beauty, the sharp-tongued Maxwell herself said, "I'm fat, dingy and oversized, but I don't care." Her wealth was so far below that of those who attended her parties that at her death she left behind a scant few thousand dollars. And as for social prominence, the only position in society open to Elsie Maxwell, the unmarried daughter of an insurance salesman from Keokuk, Iowa, was the one she invented for herself.

Maxwell later claimed that her schooling had included the Sorbonne, but in fact her education ended in 1897 when she was fourteen. She began working as a piano player in a vaudeville theater in San Francisco (where her family had moved) and then left the city in 1905 to join a Shakespearean troupe. She also wrote songs, publishing eighty that have long been forgotten.

It was when her vaudeville talent took her to Europe that her real career began. Maxwell hooked into European high society, and by the end of World War I her rich friends were asking her to plan their parties. She was known for dreaming up novel entertainment. "Anything, so long as it's different," Maxwell said. "Down with boredom!" At one party she brought live seals into the ballroom, and at a charity function she had debutantes milking cows. Hardly earth-shattering stuff, but it gave Europe's bored royalty something to do, and it thrilled America's bored rich who were enraptured by all those titles.

Maxwell did not get rich off her parties, though her friends did provide her with enough cash to live comfortably. Still, when one grateful wealthy American gave her a five-thousand-dollar account at Cartier, Maxwell spent it to hire violinist Fritz Kreisler for her next bash. Eventually, hotels offered Maxwell their ballrooms free of charge for the publicity she would bring. At the end of her frequent dinner parties at Maxim's in Paris, the headwaiter traditionally would report to her that her check had been lost. And designers donated their gowns to her, though her figure was charitably described as "roly-poly."

Maxwell claimed credit for much more than throwing great parties—and some of it she deserved. She said she invented the game of "scavenger hunt," and if she did not, she at least popularized it. (Her version was likely to require her guests to retrieve a black swan from the Bois de Boulogne or a pompon off the cap of a French sailor.) She also did much to put Monte Carlo on the social circuit, working with the Prince of Monaco to publicize his gambling resorts. Beyond that, Maxwell claimed she brought jazz to Europe, that she introduced Rita Hayworth to Prince Aly Khan, and that she convinced David Niven to become an actor.

Armed with her gala reputation, Maxwell returned to the United States during World War II. She failed to make it in Hollywood, but found her niche as a gossip columnist, both in newspapers and on the radio. In 1957 she made a splash on television as a regular guest on Jack Paar's "Tonight Show." The always outspoken Maxwell would appear each Tuesday night wearing some outlandish gown which she would model for the audience, then sit down and say, "Now Jack, let's go after things."

And she meant it as no idle threat. Once invited to

a party given by King Farouk of Egypt, Maxwell had replied by telegram, "I do not associate with clowns, monkeys, or corrupt gangsters." But she was as willing to accept her barbs as give them. "I've been compared to a whale, a charwoman at daybreak, and an Eskimo igloo during the summer thaw," she said. "I can respect the person who gives me a darned good crack, if it's well-worded and well-aimed." Of her harshest critics, Maxwell maintained, "Important enemies to me are the *sauce piquante* to my dish of life."

Maxwell never married, claiming, "The world is my husband." She spent her last years in an apartment at New York's Waldorf-Astoria Towers, for which she said the management wouldn't accept her rent check. In late October 1963, Maxwell attended her last party—the April in Paris Ball—in a wheelchair. A week later, the day after she entered the hospital with a heart ailment, she died at the age of eighty, leaving less than ten thousand dollars, a Persian rug, and a portrait of herself. In the last of her many memoirs, *The Celebrity Circus*, Maxwell said of her life, "I've always been laughed at, but I've never been ignored."

KATHARINE McCORMICK

FINANCIAL BACKER OF THE PILL

What the steam engine was to the Industrial Revolution of the mid-1800s, the birth control pill was to the sexual revolution of the 1960s. Affecting more than just sexual behavior, the Pill transformed the nature of family planning and the entire concept of world population control.

It is interesting that the device—which put complete contraceptive control into the hands of the women who took it—was developed by a group of male scientists. But their work may not have occurred, or at least may not have proceeded as rapidly, without the money of an impatient widow.

Katharine McCormick had tried before to use her money to get what she wanted. Born in 1875 to a wealthy Chicago family, she was one of very few women to graduate from the Massachusetts Institute of Technology in 1904, earning a degree in biology. The same year, she married Stanley McCormick, comptroller of the International Harvester Corporation and an heir to that fortune. But soon after, Stanley developed a progressive mental illness such that by 1909 he was declared incompetent.

With her science background, McCormick fought with her husband's psychiatrists to determine what was wrong and how to cure it. She came to believe Stanley was schizophrenic, and she funded a research foundation at Harvard Medical School to pursue a cure. The scientists never did solve her husband's problems, and he lived in seclusion until he died in 1947.

McCormick, meanwhile, became active in the women's rights movement, working with Carrie Chapman Catt and others to organize demonstrations in Massachusetts. Through that work during the time of World War I, she met Margaret Sanger, the controversial advocate of birth control. McCormick became devoted to Sanger's cause. In 1927, McCormick opened her mother's Swiss chateau for a conference on world population, and throughout the decade, she was one of several European travelers who smuggled diaphragms into the United States for Sanger's research.

McCormick began to give money for contraceptive studies, and her letters to Sanger demonstrate her concern on the subject for more than twenty years. With knowledge gained from her biology studies and dealing with her husband's illness, she was particularly adept at determining where best to donate her money. Still, progress was slow, and in 1952 she wrote Sanger that she was "feeling pretty desperate" about the lack of a female oral contraceptive. She had been giving money to research sponsored by the Planned Parenthood Federation, "but it does not make me feel any better about the vitally constructive effort necessary to achieve a fool-proof contraceptive, which is the main end I hold in view at present, and over which I chafe constantly."

The following year, Sanger introduced McCormick to Dr. Gregory Pincus, research director at the Worcester Foundation for Experimental Biology outside Boston. Pincus was researching the new idea of suppressing ovulation with synthetic hormones, and at Sanger's suggestion he had applied to Planned Parenthood for grants. He had been awarded $3,100 in 1951 and $3,400 in 1952, not nearly enough to pursue his research.

McCormick was familiar with the Worcester Foundation, which had been involved in the schizophrenia studies concerning her husband. When she met Pincus, she immediately pledged $10,000. Nearly seventy-eight years old by then, McCormick ended up donating $150,000 that year and every year for the rest of her life. The effect was dramatic. Said James Reed, author of a book about the history of the birth control movement, "She provided the funds that turned a desultory Planned Parenthood Federation of America project into a crash program to develop an oral contraceptive."

The money worked. Using synthetic steroids supplied by the G. D. Searle Company, Pincus successfully produced the first birth control pill by 1956. It went on the market in 1960 as Enovid, but quickly was joined by other brands and became known simply as "the Pill." By 1967, the year that both Pincus and McCormick died (she at ninety-two), it was estimated that one in five American women of child-bearing age used the Pill.

Earlier, Sanger had written to her patron, "You must, indeed, feel a certain pride in your judgment . . . You came along with your fine interest and enthusiasm and with your faith, things began to happen, and at last the reports are now out and the conspiracy of silence has been broken."

JANE McCREA

HER MURDER TURNED MANY AMERICANS AGAINST THE BRITISH DURING THE REVOLUTION

Often it's the events off the battlefield that change the course of a war. For example, early in the American Revolution, British troops appeared poised to strike a near-fatal blow when General John Burgoyne invaded the Hudson River valley from Canada and threatened to isolate New England. Marching through an area dominated by Tory sympathizers, Burgoyne easily forced the Americans to abandon Fort Ticonderoga early in July 1777. With the rebels demoralized and ill-trained, it seemed the British might reach Albany by late summer.

That is, until they discovered the massacred body of Jane McCrea. The orphaned daughter of a Presbyterian minister, Jane—by that time in her early twenties—was living with her oldest brother near the frontier outpost of Fort Edward, which was down the Hudson River from Fort Ticonderoga. Jane had two brothers in the American army, but she was hardly an enemy of the British. Two of her half-brothers were loyalists, and she was being courted by a lieutenant in Burgoyne's army, David Jones, whom she had known since childhood.

When American troops decided to give up Fort Edward and try to make their stand farther south, most rebel sympathizers quickly fled to Albany. More than the threat of the British, they feared the Indians, whom Burgoyne had bribed to support him. In the late 1700s, Indian attacks on frontier homes were still fresh in the minds of upstate New Yorkers, as Burgoyne well knew. That summer, he issued an order to the Indians—which he made sure American settlers saw—stating, "In conformity and indulgence of your customs, which have affixed an idea of honour to such badges of victory, you shall be allowed to take the scalps of the dead, when killed by your fire in fair opposition."

Despite her brother's pleas, Jane decided to stay behind. She had just received a letter from Jones which said, "In a few days we will march to Fort Edward, where I shall have the happiness to meet you after a long absence." Jane believed they were to marry when he arrived, so on the morning of July 27 she was wearing a formal bonnet over her long blond hair when she went to the home of her friend, Mrs. Sarah McNeil. She found Mrs. McNeil frantically packing to flee to Albany.

Sometime after noon, a band of Indians arrived. The two women had tried to hide in the cellar, but Mrs. McNeil was too fat to fit through the trap door and Jane was found hiding below. What happened after that has never been clear. The women were led from the house and apparently were to be presented to Burgoyne for a reward. But along the way, Mrs. McNeil and Jane became separated. The Indians later handed over Mrs. McNeil to the British. Jane was found dead. Naked and covered with leaves on a hill not far from Fort Edward, she had been scalped, shot four times, and stabbed many more.

The most accepted story is that the Indians, while they were on their way to the British camp, had been accosted by a second group of Indians who wanted to take one of the women so they could claim their own reward. The two bands quarreled and Jane was killed during the fight. Another version is that one of the bands of Indians had been sent by her suitor, Jones, to protect her. Indeed, after the Indians proudly presented her beautiful three-foot long scalp of hair to the British army, Jones is said to have bought it and fled to Canada.

Whatever actually happened, the blame fell directly on Burgoyne. He claimed the Indians had violated their orders not to hurt innocent residents. But he had enlisted them in the first place, and even his own nation was shocked. In the House of Commons, Edmund Burke called for the British army to stop using Indians as its agents. London's *Annual Register* said, "Every circumstance of this horrid transaction served to render it more calamitous and afflicting. The young lady is represented to have been in all the innocence of youth, and bloom of beauty . . . and to wind up the catastrophe of this odious tragedy, she was to have been married to a British officer on the very day that she was massacred."

Instead of prompting Americans to seek British protection, the Indian massacre sent thousands of wavering colonists to the side of the rebels. American military leaders made sure that the tragedy was well-publicized, and immediately new recruits showed up to join the army. Said one historian, "The preservation of their families was now become an object of immediate concern. They flocked in multitudes to General [Benedict] Arnold's camp, and he soon found himself at the head of an army, which, though composed of militia, and undisciplined men, was animated with that spirit of indignation and revenge which so often supplies all military deficiencies."

Indeed, the American army, which started with six thousand men, burgeoned to nearly twenty thousand by September, when it finally faced Burgoyne's brigade of five thousand at Bemis Heights, near Saratoga. Depleted and demoralized by rebel snipers, Burgoyne's army surrendered on October 17, less than three months after Jane McCrea was killed.

There were, of course, several military factors that gave the Americans their first major victory of the Revolution, including some well-timed reinforcements. But it was the death of Jane McCrea that kindled the flame. Said her biographer, "In the history of the Revolutionary War, perhaps no single incident is recorded which, at the time of its occurrence, created more intense sympathy, or aroused a spirit of more bitter indignation, than the massacre of Jane McCrea."

FANNY MENDELSSOHN

PERHAPS A BETTER COMPOSER THAN HER BROTHER, FELIX

Felix Mendelssohn has gone down in history as one of the great German classical composers, but he may not have been the best that his family had to offer. From a very young age, Felix was praised for his talent, but it was, according to one visitor, "still inferior to that of his elder sister, Fanny." Writer Johann Wolfgang von Goethe called her "your equally gifted sister." And even Felix himself admitted when he finished a performance in London, "But you should hear my sister Fanny."

The Mendelssohn household was fertile ground for cultivating talent. Through their father, Abraham, a wealthy banker and the son of the famous Enlightenment philosopher Moses Mendelssohn, the four children grew up among Berlin's elite artists and intellectuals. In their early years, the children were educated by their parents, starting right after breakfast at 5 A.M. Fanny, the oldest, and Felix, three years younger, received their first piano lessons from their mother, who had remarked when Fanny was born that she had "Bach-fugue fingers."

As they got older, both Fanny and Felix studied piano with famous teachers, living for a time in Paris to receive advanced instruction. Fanny surprised her father when she was thirteen by playing twenty-four Bach Preludes from memory. But although Fanny was by all reports at least as talented as her brother, her parents made it clear that she was not to take it too seriously. Her father wrote her when she was fourteen, "Music will perhaps become Felix's profession, while for *you* it can and must be only an ornament, never the root of your being and doing . . . and your very joy at the praise he earns proves that you might, in his place, have merited equal approval."

Fanny played at her family's fortnightly Sunday musicales at their home, but she was not allowed to give public concerts, as her brother began doing to great acclaim even as a teenager. She also composed many choral and piano pieces, but was not allowed to publish them. Felix, too, discouraged his sister from publishing her works, writing in a letter to their mother, "Nothing but annoyance is to be looked for from publishing, where one or two works alone are in question . . . and from my knowledge of Fanny, I should say she has neither inclination nor vocation for authorship. She is too much all that a woman ought to be for this."

That didn't stop Felix from publishing six of Fanny's works under his own name. Though it wasn't generally known at the time, one music critic did write, "Three of the best [of twelve published songs by Felix at age fifteen] are by his sister, a young lady of great talents and accomplishments." One of Fanny's songs became a favorite of Queen Victoria, who sang it for Felix in 1842. Felix wrote to his sister, "It was really charming . . . then I was obliged to confess that Fanny had written the song (which I found very hard, but pride must have a fall), and beg her to sing one of mine also."

Felix relied heavily on Fanny in his own compositions. He consulted her constantly on his new works, and after she arranged private performances of his pieces before their public premieres, she helped him make revisions. Early in Felix's career, Fanny wrote, "He never writes down a thought before submitting it to my judgment. For instance, I have known his operas by heart before a note was written."

Fanny and Felix grew apart somewhat after they each married. In 1846, after their parents had died, Fanny finally published a few of her songs under her own name. She died of a stroke in May 1847 while she was conducting a rehearsal of her brother's "Walpurgisnacht" for one of the Mendelssohn Sunday concerts, leaving unpublished nearly all of the four hundred musical compositions she is believed to have written. Though the works still exist in several private collections, music historians say that too few are available to evaluate her standing as a composer.

Her influence on her brother is more clear. Felix was destroyed by his sister's sudden death. His last great work, a string quartet in F minor, was titled "Requiem for Fanny." He became ill while visiting her grave in Berlin in October 1847. He suffered a stroke at the end of the month and died a week later. He was buried near his sister.

PERLE MESTA

"THE HOSTESS WITH THE MOSTES' "

"When the orchestra seemed to wilt," *New York Times* reporter Flora Lewis wrote of party-giver Perle Mesta in her prime, "she rushed over to whisper tensely, 'Pep it up, make it lively, don't let it die.' When the fun approached the other extreme, she temporarily closed the well-stocked bar. And just before the first yawn, she signaled 'Good Night, Sweetheart' to the orchestra and posted herself at the door."

Dubbed "the Hostess with the Mostes' " by Irving Berlin, Perle Mesta was truly the maestra of merriment in the nation's capital during the 1940s and '50s. It was common knowledge that the food she served was mediocre, and her guest list was so unexclusive that Lady Astor once sniffed, "Nobody who's anybody ought to go." But where else could you hear President Truman play the piano, President Eisenhower sing "Drink to Me Only with Thine Eyes," and Mrs. Cornelius Vanderbilt whistle? Said one devotee, "She could give you a good time if she had only a five-cent beer."

Unlike most Washington hostesses, Mesta did not make her parties mandatory events because of being married to a senator or Cabinet member. She arrived in 1941 already a widow, well-endowed with her father's Texas oil fortune and her late husband George's stake in Pittsburgh's Mesta Machine Company. Active in Oklahoma politics and the women's rights movement in the 1930s after her husband died, Mesta switched from the Republican to Democratic party and, with uncanny foresight, attached herself to the fastest-rising star in Washington—a little-known senator from Missouri named Harry Truman.

Said *Time* magazine in 1949, "Perle Mesta won her position not by prestige and not alone by wealth. She won by 303 electoral votes—those that elected Harry Truman." She campaigned for him, threw parties for him when he was vice president, and hosted an affair for his daughter, Margaret, when she sang. When Truman inherited the White House in 1945, Mesta became his unofficial First Lady at many parties because Bess hated the role.

But well beyond these social ties, Mesta had a knack for throwing parties. A Christian Scientist who didn't drink and whose figure was graciously described as "Rubenesque," Mesta kept her affairs informal and relaxed. Said one guest, "You go to a great many beautiful formal houses in Washington where people barely speak above a whisper. You go to Perle's and you know it's going to be fun." She sent out invitations based on the headlines. "I like to have guests who are in the thick of things," she said in her 1960 memoir. "Whether or not they are in *The Social Register* means nothing to me."

Her parties fit no schedule except whatever political issue she was pushing at the time. "In an atmosphere of good food, music, and gracious women, differences sometimes can be settled or important matters of policy worked out," she wrote. "A Cabinet member who might not want to be seen going to call on a senator at his office may be able to settle a problem with him off in a quiet corner at a party. Or a legislator can say to a colleague over a demitasse, 'What's wrong with my bill?' "

After Truman won his own election to the White House in 1948, Mesta got the chance to ply her talents officially. Truman named her Envoy Extraordinary and Minister Plenipotentiary to Luxembourg, a job that previously had been handled by the ambassador to Belgium. The press cracked that the president had given Mesta an embarrassingly large party favor. But in fact, Mesta had raised vast sums of money for the struggling Democrats in 1948 and, through her husband's business dealings, was quite familiar with European affairs.

It was an incident during her first morning on the job that made her legendary. A staff member asked her how she wished to be addressed, and Mesta said, "You can call me Madame Minister." Her reply was reported as "Call me Madam," which a year later became the title of the smash Broadway musical based on her life, starring Ethel Merman. Mesta, meanwhile, was a hit in Luxembourg, where her frequent visitors from Washington and Hollywood thrilled the locals.

After Truman left office, Mesta returned to her exalted social position in Washington. She began to fade during the Kennedy years, partly because the couple set their own style, but also because Mesta had supported Nixon. By the end of the sixties, when her parties were out of vogue, Mesta was described as "a gray-haired lady in a fringed mini-skirt . . . the essence of mod, like Auntie Mame come to life."

Mesta gave her last party in 1972. Two years later, after she broke her hip, she moved to Oklahoma City to be near her brother. She died of anemia there in 1975 at the age of eighty-five. After a life of parties, Mesta's funeral was private.

JULIA MORGAN

ARCHITECT OF WILLIAM RANDOLPH HEARST'S SAN SIMEON

Perched high on a hill overlooking the Pacific Ocean, William Randolph Hearst's castle at San Simeon is the perfect monument to the publishing lord. With a total of fifty-eight bedrooms, forty-nine bathrooms, and a gold-leafed indoor swimming pool, the castle's arrogant splendor seems inseparable from Hearst's audacious ego. Funny, then, that although it clearly was built to Hearst's taste, San Simeon in fact was crafted by a frail-looking spinster who appeared more like a librarian than one of the finest architects in the nation. Hearst told her he wanted a "Jappo-Swisso bungalow," and Julia Morgan built him one of the most breathtaking palaces in the twentieth century.

The daughter of a family that lived off her mother's inheritance, Morgan was the first woman admitted to the College of Engineering at the University of California at Berkeley and in 1898 was the first woman to study architecture at the prestigious Ecole des Beaux-Arts in Paris. It was while she was at Berkeley that Morgan met Hearst's mother, Phoebe, who often opened her nearby home to the few women on campus. After Morgan returned from Paris, Mrs. Hearst encouraged her to open her own architectural office and helped her win some of her first commissions.

Morgan gained early recognition when she was hired to rebuild San Francisco's Fairmont Hotel which had been devastated in the 1906 earthquake. She remained busy for the next forty years, designing more than seven hundred buildings, mostly in California, including schools, churches, private homes, and several YWCAs. But despite her prolific career, Morgan remains less known than most of her colleagues, partly because she didn't promote her work through articles or competitions. Never granting interviews, Morgan said she didn't want to be a "talking architect."

In addition to creating all of this other work, Morgan built her and Hearst's crown jewel, a project that lasted more than twenty years. They met while she was completing his mother's estate at Pleasanton, east of Berkeley. In 1915 he hired her to build offices for his Los Angeles *Examiner.* And four years later he commissioned Morgan to design San Simeon, located on his family's vast oceanside ranch midway between Los Angeles and San Francisco. Hearst told Morgan he was "tired of camping out and wanted something more comfortable on the Hill." He actually was far more specific than merely suggesting a "Jappo-Swisso bungalow." He wanted his castle to incorporate his eclectic collection of art and pieces of buildings—medieval tapestries, Renaissance ceilings, choir stalls—that he had acquired in Europe.

It was, of course, up to Morgan to make it all fit together. "Mrs. Hearst and I feel that each bedroom should have its own bath. Divide up the baths or figure out something," Hearst said in one of hundreds of letters to Morgan that were the basis of their communication. Hearst could be frustratingly specific—he wanted a tree moved because a branch was too low—and maddeningly whimsical—he ordered a fireplace to be rebuilt on the other side of the room, then decided he wanted it put back in the original place. And yet Hearst, so notorious for his ego, was uncharacteristically accommodating with his architect. "I do not want you to do anything you do not like," he wrote her. Morgan, with painstaking diplomacy, would either find a way to comply or tactfully convince Hearst that he didn't really want what he said he wanted.

To keep up with the massive project, Morgan rode the train from her office in San Francisco to San Simeon—two hundred miles each way—about three weekends a month for eighteen years, from 1920 until 1938. Barely five feet tall, wearing round, wire-rimmed glasses, a silk blouse, and a man-tailored jacket, Morgan clambered over the rocky hills to determine the structural specifications of the castle, and in later years climbed around ladders and scaffolds to inspect the progress. Morgan built herself her own room in the main castle, and although she didn't join in Hearst's famous Hollywood-studded parties, at dinner she always was placed across the table from the publishing mogul so they could go over building plans.

San Simeon—which grew to include three guest houses, a second swimming pool, and a zoo—was never considered a finished project, though construction wound down as Hearst's publishing empire retrenched in the early 1940s. By then it was estimated Hearst had spent some $5 million on his castle, perhaps one-tenth of what it would cost today. For all of her efforts over twenty years, Morgan was paid some seventy thousand dollars.

Also the architect of a group of fantastical homes on Hearst's Wyntoon estate in northern California, Morgan retired in 1946. She suffered a series of strokes in 1951—the year Hearst died—and she died in 1957 at the age of eighty-five. The following year, San Simeon was donated to the state of California, and it remains one of the state's most popular tourist attractions.

BELLE MOSKOWITZ

THE POWER BEHIND AL SMITH

As with many women throughout history, you have to wonder where Belle Moskowitz would have ended up if she'd had all the opportunities that men had. As it was, she became the power behind the throne of Al Smith, the boisterous reform governor of New York in the 1920s and the Democratic candidate for President in 1928. Without titles or elections of her own, Moskowitz during Smith's tenure "wielded more political power than any other woman in the United States," said *The New York Times* at her death; "She came nearer than any woman had come before to being the maker of a President." Said one reformer, "Mrs. Moskowitz was Al Smith's tent pole."

Moskowitz was part of a generation of social reformers. Born Belle Lindner in 1877, she was the daughter of a Polish immigrant watchmaker and grew up in Harlem, which at the time was an affluent Jewish suburb. She went to work in settlement houses, and in 1911 she and her first husband spearheaded a successful state campaign to license dance halls so single girls would have a respectable place to meet men. After her husband died, she got a job settling labor grievances for the Dress and Waist Manufacturers Association. In four years she resolved more than ten thousand disputes.

As a member of the new Progressive Party—her second husband, Henry Moskowitz, was a party candidate for local offices—Moskowitz hardly seemed a likely supporter for Al Smith. A rough-edged, cigar-smoking, Irish-Catholic politician, Smith was a product of the thoroughly corrupt Tammany Hall political machine, which stood for everything Moskowitz and other Jewish reformers fought against. But when he became the Democratic nominee for governor in 1918, though officially still a Tammany candidate, Smith showed signs of reform. Moskowitz convinced Smith to make a special appeal to women, who were voting for the first time.

Smith won, and from then on he never made a move without consulting "Mrs. M," as he called her. It was Moskowitz who pushed Smith to create his Reconstruction Board that set the governor's reform agenda: low-cost housing to relieve the post–World War I shortage, better health care, and a modernized state government. It was also Moskowitz who kept a careful list of everyone the governor had helped, and pressed them to return the favor when Smith pushed his reforms through the legislature. And it was Moskowitz who helped execute the reforms by hiring a young, unknown bureaucrat named Robert Moses, who later would change the face of New York with his massive building programs.

Moskowitz did most of this behind the scenes. Her title was never more than executive secretary or publicity director. "It's the best way I can be of service," the small, low-voiced woman said demurely, rejecting bigger titles. A profile in *The New Yorker* sized it up better: "To modesty her friends attribute her comparative obscurity. Her critics call it shrewdness." It was indeed. Government officials and reporters knew to see her before they saw the governor. And if they didn't, when they returned empty-handed, Moskowitz would smile and say, "Well, it's too bad. I'm sorry. You should have seen me first. I think I could have arranged it." To cooperative reporters she offered tips and chicken soup.

Her office actually was in New York City, where she lived with her husband and two children. But she was on the phone constantly with the governor, and every Friday night she took the train to the state capital in Albany, where she would sit in Smith's office, knitting in a corner and waiting for him to ask for her advice, which he always did. One of Smith's reformers,

Frances Perkins, who later was President Roosevelt's Secretary of Labor, recalled, "Almost as soon as an idea was broached, she could think clear through to the end to see what the possibilities were, what the hazards were and how you could do it."

As Smith's most devoted supporter—she called him "a man of destiny"—Moskowitz was thrilled by the possibility that her reformer might become president. In Smith's first attempt in 1924, his campaign manager died a few months before the Democratic nominating convention. Moskowitz took over and rallied enough support to deadlock the convention before Smith lost on the 103rd ballot. She immediately began planning for 1928, and when Smith refused to start campaigning early, Moskowitz sent thousands of copies of his speeches to political groups and newspapers throughout the country. She kept an index of state and local party leaders and was always able to provide the best answer by far as to how Smith stood anywhere in the country. At the 1928 convention, Smith was nominated on the first ballot.

Though she was the only woman on the Democratic National Committee's advisory committee, Moskowitz was never an official member of Smith's closet council, his "War Board." She did not enter the all-male preserve, she said, because "I had so much respect for the political pride of the men leaders of the party." Nevertheless, Smith consulted Moskowitz before and after each meeting.

But for all her efforts, Moskowitz couldn't change the fact that she was supporting a rough-edged Catholic candidate in a nation that at the time was content with its Republican prosperity. In the general election, Smith lost to Herbert Hoover, 21 million votes to 15 million. After that, Smith's career declined and so did hers. Franklin Delano Roosevelt, New York's new governor, refused to offer her a job. She tried to mount another presidential bid for Smith, but with little success. "Politics is a strange game," she said late in her life, "and I confess part of it is a sad disillusionment to me."

On December 8, 1932, Moskowitz fell down the front steps of her home on the Upper West Side of Manhattan, breaking her right arm and her left wrist. She seemed to be recovering until she suffered a heart attack three weeks later. She died of a second attack on January 2 at the age of fifty-five. Smith, who was in Albany for the inauguration of the new governor, wept when he heard the news by phone. "Belle Moskowitz is dead. I'm going to New York," he said, later telling reporters, "She had the greatest brain of anybody I ever knew."

MARY MURRAY

HER HOSPITALITY SAVED THE AMERICAN ARMY EARLY IN THE REVOLUTION

Mary Murray may be the most reluctant heroine of the American Revolution. Honored for her patriotic aid to the American rebels, Mrs. Murray perhaps thought her actions entitled her to be recognized for loyal service to the Crown.

Mrs. Murray played her part early in the revolution. After the Americans declared their independence in July 1776, British General William Howe began amassing a fleet of ships in New York harbor. By late August, thirty thousand British and German troops were prepared to come ashore and quash some twenty thousand loosely organized, untrained rebel troops. The British handily won the first battle on Long Island, and they almost cornered nearly nine thousand American soldiers, which could have brought a quick end to the revolution. The Americans managed to escape into Manhattan, but it was essential that they flee north to the Harlem Heights to avoid another disastrous confrontation.

Most of the American troops headed safely northward, but when General Howe's army reached Manhattan, there were still 3,500 rebels under the command of General Israel Putnam located south of where the British troops landed. Guided by the general's aide, Aaron Burr, the troops began marching north off the main route.

Howe, meanwhile, apparently was unaware of how close he was to the American troops—and a crippling victory. After landing at Kip's Bay, Howe stopped his advance at the home of the prominent Robert Murray and his wife, located on the Heights of Inklenberg—now called Murray Hill. Murray, one of the most successful merchants in the colonies, apparently was pro-British, or at least he wasn't very patriotic. After New York merchants agreed in 1775 not to import British goods, Murray and his brother secretly unloaded a ship from the mother country. The Murrays' leanings during the revolution also may be evident from the fact that British troops never seized the Murrays' elegant home during their long occupation of Manhattan.

The only record of what took place at the Murray home when Howe and his troops paid a visit on September 15 comes from James Thacher, a rebel surgeon who had heard the incident talked about among the troops and described it in his journal. Says Thacher, "Mrs. Murray treated them with cake and wine, and they were induced to tarry two hours or more. By this happy incident General Putnam, by continuing his march, escaped an encounter with a greatly superior force, which (would) have proved fatal to his whole party. One half-hour, it is said, would have been sufficient for the enemy to have secured the road at the turn, and entirely cut off General Putnam's retreat. It has since become almost a common saying among our officers, that Mrs. Murray saved this part of the American army."

Because of Thacher's account, the reputation of Mrs. Murray has been passed down through the years as that of a delightfully devious woman who plied her feminine wiles to outsmart the enemy. Artist E. P. Moran painted a lovely scene called "Mrs. Murray's Strategy" which shows her seated on her front porch next to a table laden with fruit and wine, smiling graciously as she receives General Howe and his aides.

Though it is not at all clear that Mrs. Murray intended to do anything but help the British troops, in 1903 the Daughters of the American Revolution placed a plaque on Park Avenue near Thirty-seventh Street, in the Murray Hill neighborhood. It says, "For services rendered her country during the American Revolution, entertaining at her home, on this site, General Howe and his officers, until the American troops under General Putnam escaped." Mrs. Murray may well be mortified.

N

CAROLINE NORTON

HER BATTLE FOR CUSTODY OF HER CHILDREN CHANGED BRITISH LAW

"Oh, depend upon it. There is no treadmill like the life of a woman of the world, and you see it in the expression of the face. It is the perpetual struggle to be and to do, and the internal and continual dissatisfaction with all one is and does, that eats away the freshness of one's life." Writing in the tightly strictured climate of Victorian England in the mid-1800s, Caroline Norton knew the personal toll of such a life. Charming and vivacious at a time when it was nearly indecent for a woman to be so, Norton lost her children when she separated from her husband. Her battle to regain their custody—and to establish rights for divorced women—didn't kill her, but it nonetheless cost Norton her life.

As a member of England's lesser aristocracy, the daughter of a civil servant, Norton followed her mother's advice to secure her status and married a member of Parliament in 1827 when she was nineteen. Her unfortunate choice, whom she had met only briefly and who had proposed by letter, was George Norton. Whereas she was an attractive, lively conversationalist and popular at parties, her twenty-seven-year-old husband was an unmotivated boor who followed his brief legislative term with an unsuccessful career as a barrister.

Largely because they needed money, Norton began writing. She was successful from the publication of her first poem in 1829, which purposely coincided with the birth of her first child. "The first expenses of my son's life were defrayed from that first creation of my brain," she wrote. And though her work has largely been forgotten, Norton was a very popular writer during the 1830s and 1840s, producing nearly a hundred small volumes of poetry and a few novels. In one year she earned fourteen hundred pounds, far more than her husband.

Norton's career put her in contact with England's greatest writers, including Charles Dickens and Sir Walter Scott, and she often dined in London with them and without her husband. She also made many friends among the nation's leading politicians, and one, Lord Melbourne, a former prime minister and a widower thirty years her senior, was so smitten that he called on her every evening. Norton's husband, not surprisingly, grew jealous, and Norton taunted him for it.

Their marriage deteriorated to the point that George became violent and Norton abruptly moved out in 1836, leaving her three sons behind. At a time when divorce was nearly impossible, George sued Lord Melbourne for "alienating his wife's affections" and sought ten thousand pounds in damages. As a woman, Norton had no standing in the case, but it was presented so weakly that the jury sided against George without even retiring to deliberate.

But because of their separation, Norton had no rights to her children. Under British law at the time, children belonged to their father, and George would not permit his wife to see her sons unless a lawyer was present. Her plight was not unusual, but because of her fame as a writer and her friendship with many politicians, Norton drew much sympathy. She convinced one of her friends in Parliament to introduce the Infant Custody Bill in 1837. While it merely proposed that judges consider the mother's position, the bill was the first women's rights legislation ever put before Parliament.

Norton campaigned tirelessly for the proposal, most notably in her moving essay, "The Natural Claim of a Mother to the Custody of Her Children." She wrote, "You may teach a child to hush his little voice to a whisper when he utters [his mother's] forbidden name . . . but nature's great instinct will remain nevertheless, strong and unchangeable. He will love and honor his mother, he will sometimes wonder at her absence, and sometimes pine for her return."

Largely because of Norton's efforts, Parliament passed the act in 1838. But ironically, the legislation did not help Norton win her own children, who had been sent by their father to school in Scotland, outside the jurisdiction of the new law. George finally relented in 1842 when their youngest son died after he fell off a pony. Norton was able to reestablish her relationship with her other two sons, both of whom died before she did.

But her troubles with her husband were not over. Though they were separated, George still controlled Norton's earnings. He frequently balked at giving her an allowance and delayed her publishing contracts. In 1853 he took Norton to court to try to force her to pay for debts that weren't her own. Norton again published essays supporting her cause, especially "A Letter to the Queen" in 1855.

Her plight happened to come at a time when Parliament was revising England's strict divorce law. In passing the Divorce Act of 1857, the legislators made some changes specifically because of Norton's case. The new law gave divorced and separated women the right to their own earnings. It also granted them the same property rights as single women, and gave judges the right to require a man to support his ex-wife.

But again, her victory rang somewhat hollow. Though she had been legally cleared of adultery in 1836, the mere existence of the charge left her with a scarlet letter that haunted her. Norton grew obsessed with her battles with her husband, and much of her charm gave way to a bitterness that frequently left her nervous, ill, and in her later years, deeply depressed. Some of her later essays focused less on women's rights than on getting even with her husband. Ironically, Norton did not support England's emerging suffragists. In fact, she believed it was precisely because women were inferior that they needed special legal protection.

Norton's husband finally died in 1875. In March 1877 she married an old friend, historian Sir William Stirling Maxwell. It lasted only three months before, at the age of sixty-nine, she died suddenly.

O

MRS. O'LEARY

THE GREAT CHICAGO FIRE STARTED IN HER BARN

Poor Mrs. O'Leary. A working-class wife with five children to look after in a shack of a house on Chicago's Southwest Side, she went to bed one Sunday night in October 1871 only to be rousted with screams that their barn was burning. By morning the fast-spreading fire had swept through downtown Chicago and would not end until it had cut a swath four miles long and two-thirds of a mile wide, destroying more than a quarter of the city's buildings and leaving a hundred thousand people homeless.

And Mrs. O'Leary got the blame. Even after investigations and public hearings fairly well concluded that she, in fact, had not started the fire, it was Mrs. O'Leary—in paintings, poems, and cartoons—who was portrayed milking in the barn as her notorious cow kicked her lighted candle onto some dry hay.

The grain of truth in Mrs. O'Leary's heinous footnote in history is that the fire—one of the most devastating urban blazes in American history—*did* start in the O'Leary barn. Patrick O'Leary, a laborer, and his wife (whose first name has been forgotten) owned a wooden house on DeKoven Street in a shabby neighborhood surrounded by wood mills and lumberyards. Actually the O'Learys lived in an addition on the back of the house and rented out the main house to another family, the McLaughlins.

On that Sunday night, the O'Learys had all gone to bed by 9 P.M. The McLaughlins, meanwhile, were having a party to welcome a relative who had recently immigrated from Ireland. It was a neighbor, Daniel "Pegleg" Sullivan, who on that warm night was sitting on the boardwalk across the street when he spotted flames in the barn behind the O'Leary house. Sullivan later testified he saw no lights on in the O'Leary residence as he yelled "Fire!" and hobbled toward the barn.

Filled with dry hay, the wooden barn was a tinderbox. A fire watchman stationed on the courthouse roof downtown spotted the fire, but he signaled the alarm in the wrong neighborhood. By the time firefighters reached the O'Learys, the barn was engulfed in flames and the fire was quickly spreading to a nearby row of stores. Local residents who were manning a fire hose fled in terror as the fire moved beyond the O'Learys' block.

In fact, all of Chicago was a tinderbox that autumn. The booming city, with 334,000 residents, still resembled a sprawling frontier town. Nearly all buildings were made of wood. There had been six hundred fires the previous year—most starting in barns—and the city had an ordinance against using open lamps or candles in barns unless the flame was enclosed in a lantern. Also, in the month before the O'Learys' barn caught fire on October 8, the city had had only a single inch of rain. Just the night before, a fire had destroyed a four-block area, exhausting half the city's 185 firemen.

Pushed by high winds, the O'Leary fire raced to the northeast, with sparks igniting buildings and raining on fleeing residents, many of whom ran into Lake Michigan to escape. "You couldn't see anything over you but fire," said one fireman. "No clouds, no stars, nothing else but fire." The flames leapt across the south branch of the Chicago River, through downtown Chicago, across the main channel of the river, and up the fashionable North Side, where it consumed the city's finest homes. By the time it burned out early Tuesday morning around Fullerton Street, the fire had killed some 300 people, destroyed 17,500 buildings and caused nearly $200 million in damage, which ultimately would bankrupt 56 insurance companies.

So it is no wonder that the city sought someone to blame for the overwhelming devastation. There never was any evidence that Mrs. O'Leary was out in the barn that night. She testified that she and her family had gone to bed. When the fire began, said one report, "She was so excited in looking after her family and property that she didn't take notice of much else." Mrs. O'Leary managed to rescue a calf, and some cows and a horse also were saved. Though officials never were able to pin the blame on anyone, it is far more likely that the fire was sparked by someone at the McLaughlins' party, or perhaps by one of the O'Learys' children.

Still, it was Mrs. O'Leary who began showing up in cartoons, often portrayed as a witch, milking her cow near an open flame. Soon after the fire, the Chicago *Times* described her as "an old hag, whose very appearance indicated great poverty. She apparently was about seventy years of age and was bent almost double with the weight of many years of toil and trouble and privation." In December, reporting on the fire hearings, the same newspaper said Mrs. O'Leary "is a tall, stout, Irish woman with no intelligence . . . During her testimony, the infant she held kicked its bare legs around and drew nourishment from mammoth reservoirs."

Ironically, as the fire quickly pushed on from the O'Learys', it left one wall of their barn standing, a curiosity that drew many sightseers. The O'Leary house itself was not damaged and a photograph taken soon after the fire shows a cow—allegedly *the* cow—standing out front. The house eventually was replaced with a brownstone, and in this century it became the site of the Chicago Fire Academy, a training school for firefighters.

One of Mrs. O'Leary's sons, "Big Jim" O'Leary, became a millionaire gambling boss who headed a syndicate on Chicago's South Side. But Mrs. O'Leary herself faded into obscurity, even though her legend has not. Said the Chicago *Journal*, "Even if it were an absurd rumor, forty miles wide of the truth, it would be useless to attempt to alter 'the verdict of history.' Mrs. O'Leary has made a sworn statement in refutation of the charge, and it is backed by other affidavits, but to little purpose. She is in for it and no mistake. Fame has seized her and appropriated her, name, barn cows and all. She has won, in spite of herself, what the Ephesian youth panted for."

P

BERTHA PALMER

CHICAGO'S SOCIAL AND CIVIC LEADER

Mrs. Astor and her infamous Four Hundred came to define high society in the late nineteenth century, and it's too bad. Because it gives the impression that the only thing wealthy women did in those days was sit and pray for the next exclusive party invitation. Even in Chicago, the city's grande dame was described in terms of her New York counterpart. Bertha Palmer was called the "Mrs. Astor of the Middle West," but that hardly did her justice. More accurate was Mrs. Palmer's own portrayal of herself. "I am," she said, "the nation's hostess and the nation's head woman servant."

Whereas Mrs. Astor's money was suffocatingly old, Bertha Palmer's wealth was, like her city, much newer. In 1870, when she was twenty-one, she married Chicago's richest bachelor, forty-four-year-old Potter Palmer, who had made his fortune from dry goods and cotton during the Civil War and was getting even richer in Chicago's booming real estate market.

As a wedding gift to his wife, he built her the city's grandest hotel, the $3.5 million Palmer House. When the hotel burned to the ground in Chicago's Great Fire in 1871, it was said that Palmer considered packing up, but it was Bertha who convinced him to stay and help rebuild the charred city.

While Potter built an ever grander Palmer House and many other buildings, Bertha took command of the city's budding society. Like Mrs. Astor, she could regally dominate any affair, dressed always in the most fashionable silk gowns, wearing her characteristic massive plume hats and Parisian stockings. But at least in her domain—unlike Mrs. Astor's—wealth and pedigree alone did not determine social standing.

By her example, Mrs. Palmer made it fashionable, even required, for women to devote their time and money to civic causes and charities. While New York's social climbers had to rely on their ancestors for admission to Mrs. Astor's ballroom, more recent deeds were required to receive the much sought-after prominent placement in the procession that led into Mrs. Palmer's annual charity ball in Chicago.

For her own part, Mrs. Palmer got involved in the Chicago Women's Club, where she met reformers who introduced her to Jane Addams's Hull House. There, amidst the new immigrants at the settlement house, the leader of Chicago society could be seen performing volunteer duties, clad in her furs. She also became active in the Women's Trade Union League and was one of the prime movers in organizing Chicago's millinery workers.

As one historian described her, Mrs. Palmer "was the kind of woman who could look quite at home, in marvelous clothes, during a long multi-course dinner with many wines, served by six men, on damask and plate under sparkling crystal in her house. Yet at big public meetings she could preside with Robert's Rules of Order right at the tips of her glittering fingers."

Critics considered her aloof and domineering, but at least she was there, and her presence was as valuable as her substantial monetary contributions. Often, factory girls would meet in the Palmers' home, a lavish, Norman-style mansion on Lake Shore Drive that was aptly called Palmer Castle. There, in the Louis XVI salon or the forty-foot-high picture gallery, Mrs. Palmer would entertain shop girls one evening and debutantes the next.

Mrs. Palmer hit her peak with Chicago's World Columbian Exhibition in 1893. She organized the "Woman's Building," designed to illustrate the growing role of women and the problems they still faced. Fair officials were astonished when forty-seven nations—many personally recruited by Mrs. Palmer—agreed to set up exhibitions in the Woman's Building. The classical pavilion became the hit of the fair and made Mrs. Palmer a national figure.

She later became vice president of the reform-minded Chicago Civic Federation, and in 1896 was on the platform when William Jennings Bryan made his famous "Cross of Gold" speech at the Democratic National Convention. In 1900, she was the only woman appointed by President McKinley to represent the United States at the Paris Exposition.

By themselves, these are just some more good deeds. But together with the rest of her life, they indicate what a woman in her position could do. After her husband died in 1902, Mrs. Palmer divided her time between Europe and the west coast of Florida, where she developed some of the region's first citrus groves. Shortly before she died of cancer in 1918 at the age of sixty-eight, a British magazine wrote, "When men have diplomacy they are called diplomats; when women have it they are called tactful. If Mrs. Palmer were a man, she would make an ideal ambassador."

FANNY PALMER

ONE OF CURRIER & IVES' MOST PROLIFIC ARTISTS

For a quaint view of nineteenth-century America, there is nothing like a Currier & Ives lithograph. Though at the time they were the closest thing to news photographs—giving many Americans their first views of the West, Indians, and many famous figures—today, on calendars and greeting cards, the prints represent a young, romanticized nation. Adorned with tidy cabins, pristine steam engines, and bountiful farms, Currier & Ives lithographs are pure Americana.

Unfortunately, today's reprints often neglect to indicate that many of those quintessential American portraits were drawn by a cheerful British widow struggling to support her family. Fanny Palmer was the foremost female lithographer of her time, and one of the most prolific of the inner circle who worked for the most famous lithograph company of the century.

Frances Flora Bond was born in 1812 in Leicester, England, the daughter of a successful attorney. Well-educated in London, with strong training in fine arts, in the early 1830s she married Seymour Palmer, a gentleman who proved to be adept only at hunting and drinking. With their fortune dwindling, the Palmers emigrated to New York in 1844.

Palmer and her husband began a lithographic printing business, producing landscapes, sheet music covers, and architectural drawings. She, especially, was praised for her talent, but the firm failed and she joined the staff of Nathaniel Currier. Her first year there, in 1849, Currier published her two famous views of Manhattan, one from Brooklyn Heights, the other from Weehawken, New Jersey.

Over the next two decades, Palmer produced many more famous scenes, particularly landscapes. *American Farm Scenes* (1853), *American Winter Scenes* (1854) and *American Country Life* (1855), all have held their place in the Currier & Ives catalogue. She found many of those scenes on Long Island or up the Hudson River, where she would make quick sketches of farms, cottages, and country lanes before returning to the city.

Palmer also produced broad dramatic scenes—*A Midnight Race on the Mississippi* (1860), *The Rocky Mountains, Emigrants Crossing the Plains* (1861), and *Across the Continent, Westward the Course of Empire* (1868)—though in fact she apparently never left the New York area. She wasn't very good at human figures, and most that appear in her prints were drawn by other artists.

A tiny, frail woman, Palmer did most of her work at home in Brooklyn, supporting her husband, until he fell down the stairs of a hotel and died in 1859, and her equally lazy son, who died of tuberculosis in 1867. One of the few Currier & Ives artists who actually drew on the stones used to make the lithographs, Palmer developed a hunched back from doing her minute work and walked with a pronounced stoop.

After twenty years and a portfolio of some two hundred lithographs, Palmer retired in 1868. She died of tuberculosis, like her son, in 1876, at the age of sixty-four. She did not, for the most part, live the kind of life she portrayed. Still, the tiny letters "F. F. Palmer" in the lower left-hand corner of a Currier & Ives lithograph likely mean it is a classic.

CYNTHIA ANN PARKER

KIDNAPPED BY COMANCHE INDIANS, SHE BECAME THE MOTHER OF THE TRIBE'S GREATEST CHIEF

Of all the major Indian leaders, Quanah, chief of the Comanches, stood out. The tribe's last and greatest war chief, he was the last to surrender after other Comanche bands had been defeated. And though he had led many violent raids against white settlers, Quanah convinced his tribe of four hundred to surrender peacefully in 1875 rather than face the slaughter that other Indians had suffered. But what made Quanah different from all the other Indian chiefs is that he was a half-breed. His father was a tribal chief; his mother was Cynthia Ann Parker, a white woman who as a little girl had been kidnapped and raised as a Comanche.

Parker was the granddaughter of a Baptist preacher who had led his family from Virginia to the edge of the Texas frontier in the early 1830s when it was still Mexican territory. The group of about thirty built their cabins in the shape of a fort in what is now Limestone County, east of Waco. They were out tending their fields one day in May 1836 when a band of Comanches attacked, killing five and taking five others prisoner. Two women eventually were rescued and two boys, including Cynthia Ann's brother, were ransomed in 1843.

But Cynthia Ann, nine years old at the time, was adopted by the Quahadas of the Staked Plains, known as the wildest band of Comanches. She learned to erect a tepee and to preserve buffalo meat and decorate its skins. In time she learned the language of the Comanches and forgot her native English. She married the tribe's chief, Nocona, and bore two sons, Quanah and Pecos, and a daughter, Topsannah.

Because her absence was a constant reminder of the threat of Indians, Parker remained the subject of many searches and became a frontier legend. In 1846, an Army officer reported he had spoken to her, and she had refused his offer to help her escape or be bought back from the Comanches. In 1852, another officer reported, "This woman has adopted all the habits and peculiarities of the Comanches, has an Indian husband and children, and cannot be persuaded to leave them." Her brother was sent to convince her, but, the officer said, "He stated to me that on his arrival she refused to listen to the proposition, saying that her husband, children, and all that she held most dear, were with the Indians, and there she should remain."

That was her last contact with white men until December 1860, when Parker and a group of Indian women were out hunting buffalo. They were attacked by a group of settlers who had been searching for Parker's husband, who had raided a white settlement. Several Comanche women were shot and killed, and

Parker probably would have died, too, except that an officer noticed her blue eyes and fair hair and thought she might be the legendary "White Comanche." Her uncle was brought in to question her through an interpreter, but Parker wouldn't stop crying, and he left convinced that the woman was not his kidnapped niece. Only when she finally heard her name did Parker smile, pat her chest, and say, "Cynthia Ann! Cynthia Ann!"

Parker was returned to her brother, who built her a cabin next to his. The Texas Legislature granted her a pension of a hundred dollars a year. She relearned English and was taught domestic skills such as spinning and weaving. Her daughter, who had been captured with her, was sent to school. According to one contemporary account, "She looked to be stout and weighed about 140 pounds, well-made and liked to work. She had a wild expression and would look down when people looked at her (as Indian etiquette required)." Still, Parker tried to run away several times. After her daughter died in 1864, Parker soon followed.

Quanah, meanwhile, became chief of his tribe. His son, White Parker, said later, "I remember a story he told once of a raid in Texas. They killed the man. Then they saw the woman and children inside the house, and the others wanted to kill them too. But my father said, 'My mother is living somewhere with the white people, and I am not going to hurt any white woman.' "

After he surrendered and led the Comanches onto a reservation near Fort Sill, in Oklahoma, Quanah adapted quickly to his new life. While his tribe continued to live in tepees, Quanah built a twenty-two-room house with separate rooms for each of his five wives. After learning of his mother's death, he adopted her last name and had a painting made from her photograph, which he hung over a reed organ in his parlor.

Quanah became a popular example of an Indian who had converted to the ways of white men. He took part in President Theodore Roosevelt's inauguration in 1905. In 1910 Congress granted him one thousand dollars to move Cynthia Ann Parker's body from Texas to a cemetery near his home. At the ceremony, Quanah said, "Forty years ago my mother died. She captured by Comanche, nine years old. Love Indian and wild life so well no want to go back to white folks. All same people anyway, God say. I love my mother. I like white people. When end come then they all be together again."

Three months later the half-breed Comanche chief died. He was buried next to his mother. In 1957 both graves were moved to make way for a missile range.

HANNAH CALLOWHILL PENN

AFTER HER HUSBAND DIED, SHE KEPT PENNSYLVANIA INTACT

Although most of the American colonies were established in a combined quest for political liberties and commercial profit, few were founded by a man so devoted as William Penn. A persecuted Quaker Englishman who was granted the province of Pennsylvania in 1681 to settle a debt the king owed his late father, Penn guaranteed fundamental rights for his colonial settlers—including freedom of religion and the right to a jury trial—that became cornerstones of the American system.

Penn did not have an easy time with what he called his "Holy Experiment." He was beset by political troubles in England and border disputes in his colony. After he suffered an incapacitating stroke in 1712, Pennsylvania was on the brink of being repossessed by the Crown. That it was not—and that it remained relatively independent until the Revolution—was the no small feat of Penn's wife, Hannah.

Hannah Callowhill was twenty-five in 1696 when she married Penn, a fifty-two-year-old widower with teenage children. The only surviving child of nine offspring, Hannah had been trained by her father to keep accounts at his grocery and trading business in Bristol, England. Hannah was not thrilled with the prospect of traveling to her husband's colony in America, and when they began the three-month sailing journey in 1699, she was four months pregnant with the second of their eight children. When Penn was forced to return to England in 1701 on reports that the Crown was threatening to repossess all proprietary colonies, Hannah insisted on returning with him.

Though Penn had planned on settling in his colony, neither he nor his wife ever returned to Pennsylvania. Penn, the son of a prominent British admiral, frequently was in political trouble depending on who was in power at the royal court. Imprisoned in his youth for his Quaker beliefs, he later was accused of treason for trying to spread his faith. Financial problems in his colony caused him to spend nine months in debtors prison in 1707.

Desperate, Penn began negotiating to sell Pennsylvania back to the Crown. Hannah later wrote that she believed her husband hesitated as long as he did because he was afraid his colony would lose the freedoms he had established, "for the answers I receive from all the great men is that my husband might have long since finished it had he not insisted so much on gaining privileges for the people."

After Penn suffered his massive stroke in 1712, Hannah took over. Although British law would have required that the colony be handed over to Penn's oldest son by his first marriage, or to other men, Hannah skillfully plied her friends at Court and bribed other officials to look the other way while she guided her husband's hand to sign colonial documents. She appointed a new, able governor to preside in Pennsylvania and directed him, "Pray do nothing of consequence without their [Penn's advisers] order, but go upon the old foot. For the people are safe and therefore I would have them think themselves so, and that their comfort is so near interwoven with mine and that my children's whole fortune, my husband's reputation, my own satisfaction and their happiness, being all in a thread together and therefore shall be carefully preserved by me."

Hannah, too, was willing to sell the colony back to the Crown to resolve her husband's financial troubles, but creditors disputed the sale and it never happened. When Penn died in 1718, he passed over the children by his first wife and left the colony to Hannah and their children. Although she was never officially named the proprietor of Pennsylvania, Hannah kept the colony intact for fourteen years, despite pressure from the Crown to surrender it, and pressure from some factions in the colony to abandon it. She stubbornly persuaded royal officials to rule in favor of Pennsylvania over a critical border dispute with Lord Baltimore's Maryland.

She also persevered against Penn's oldest, wayward son by his first marriage who launched a major legal battle to nullify Penn's will and get the colony for himself. When Hannah died of a stroke in 1726 at the age of fifty-five, it was a week after the junior William Penn's claims had finally been dismissed. The proprietorship of Pennsylvania passed to her sons, and the colony remained in the family until the Revolution.

MARY PENNINGTON

SHE DEVELOPED REFRIGERATION

"Ye gods and little fishes!" Mary Pennington would exclaim whenever somebody referred to her as the woman who knew all about refrigerators. "I am an expert in the handling, transportation and storage of perishables and the application of refrigeration." But even that mouthful didn't do her justice. Before Mary Pennington, food spoiled before it could be shipped very far, so what you ate depended on the season and where you lived. Eggs were most available in the summer, chicken in the fall, and fish was always expensive in inland cities. Before Mary Pennington, turkey was not on the Thanksgiving tables of most Americans.

Pennington could pinpoint the moment she decided to pursue a career in which, as it turned out, she would always be the only woman. She was twelve years old, the daughter of a Quaker label manufacturer in Philadelphia, when she read a chapter in a chemistry book about nitrogen and oxygen. "Suddenly, one day I realized, lickity hoop, that although I couldn't touch, taste or smell them, they really existed," she said. "It was a milestone."

She was admitted to the University of Pennsylvania in 1890, but after she completed the requirements for a bachelor of science degree in 1892, the school's trustees refused to grant it because she was a woman. Her professors allowed her to continue her graduate work anyway, and in 1895, at the age of twenty-two, the university awarded Pennington her Ph.D. She became a noted bacteriologist in Philadelphia, where she developed standards for milk inspection that were adopted throughout the nation. Her milk studies were the first ever on preserving perishable foods in cold storage.

Her most significant work began after she took the civil service exam in 1907 to work for the U.S. Department of Agriculture. She applied as M. E. Pennington, and before federal officials realized she was a woman, she was hired. She became head of the department's new Food Research Laboratory, and there she and her staff pioneered methods that revolutionized how food was processed, shipped, and stored. She set standards for everything from the insulation in railroad ice cars to a type of knife that allowed chickens to be killed more cleanly.

Pennington's regulations, which governed the food industry for more than twenty-five years, saved countless tons of food from spoiling. She helped end seasonal and regional scarcities of many meats and produce. What's more, her techniques also made food taste better and greatly reduced the risk—which used to be quite common—of eating spoiled products. She is the reason you can order chicken in February or Pacific salmon in Florida. "There is a thrill," Pennington said, "when a scientific idea suddenly strikes home in the form of a practical solution."

As a bureaucrat, Pennington was not well-known among the general public. But shipping and packaging officials saw her so frequently they called her "Auntie Sam." Her pamphlets—with titles like "Journeys with Refrigerated Food" and "The Romance of Ice"—were so popular in the industry that one and a half million were distributed in one year. She gained some wider notoriety for her research on railroad refrigeration when a story spread that she actually rode thousands of miles in the cold cars to conduct her studies. In fact, she sat in the caboose.

Pennington eventually left the government and became a private consultant, traveling over fifty thousand miles per year well into her seventies. She was the first woman in the American Society of Refrigeration Engineers and the first to be inducted into the Poultry Historical Society's Hall of Fame. According to a profile in *The New Yorker* in 1941, "Her one concession to femininity is to arrange her itinerary so that she can have her severely parted hair waved once a month by her pet beauty-parlor operator in the Stevens Hotel in Chicago."

Pennington never retired, maintaining her office in New York's Woolworth Building until she died at the age of eighty. She would return to her penthouse apartment on Riverside Drive, where her kitchen was described by *The New Yorker* as being "in the Pennsylvania Dutch tradition with overtones of Birds Eye." Indeed, the only canned goods in Pennington's home were likely to be sardines and baked beans. She adored frozen foods and delighted in serving them to dinner guests. "At temperatures above freezing," she said with her customary colorful yet scientific flair, "one is between the Scylla of excessive drying and the Charybdis of molds."

ELIZA LUCAS PINCKNEY

SHE INTRODUCED THE INDIGO CROP TO THE AMERICAN COLONIES

"Wrote my Father a letter consisting of seven sides of paper," Eliza Lucas recorded in her journal in 1739, "about the exchange with Col. Heron, the purchasing of his house at Georgia, the Tyrannical Government at Georgia." It sounds like a somewhat boring bit of correspondence, but what makes it unusual is that Eliza was seventeen at the time. In an era when many girls of her age and wealth were perfecting embroidery or getting married, Eliza Lucas was managing her father's three plantations in South Carolina. A few years later, she would produce a crop that would change the face of the colony's economy.

Eliza, the daughter of a British colonel who was stationed in the British West Indies, was educated in England. She spoke French, played the flute, and could quote Milton. When her father was summoned to war a year after they moved to a plantation near Charleston, South Carolina, in 1738, he left Eliza to run the estate, as well as take care of her ailing mother and younger sister. The main plantation, Wappoo, contained six hundred acres and twenty slaves, and two smaller farms also were planted with rice, the colony's primary crop. Eliza had to record the daily accounts, keep track of shipments and planting, and handle legal matters, "which requires much writing and more business and fatigue of other sorts than you can imagine," she said in one of her many letters that have survived, giving one of the clearest pictures of the era.

The teenager seemed to thrive on her full schedule. "In general," she wrote, "I rise at five o'clock in the morning, read till seven, then take a walk in the garden or field, see that the servants are at their respective business, then to breakfast. The first hour after breakfast is spent at my musick [sic], the next is constantly employed in recollecting something I have learned for want of practise it should be quite lost, such as French or shorthand. After that I devote the rest of the time till I dress for dinner to our little Polly [her younger sister] and two black girls who I teach to read, and if I have my papa's approbation (my Mama's I have got) I intend them for school mistresses for the rest of the Negro children."

In addition, Eliza, at her father's direction, tried to cultivate new crops, since the price of rice was falling. "I have planted a large fig orchard with design to dry and export them," she wrote. Among the seeds she planted—which also included cotton, ginger, and alfalfa—was indigo, a plant which produced a blue dye that was in high demand in England. Charleston planters had tried the crop seventy years earlier and had given up, and Britons grumbled at having to buy it from the French West Indies. Eliza's indigo crop, beset by frosts and worms, was finally successful in 1744.

The impact of her achievement was almost immediate. After she sent seventeen pounds of the dye to London for the merchants' approval, Parliament approved a six-pence bonus on all indigo grown in the colonies. The French, faced with losing their monopoly, made it a capital crime to export indigo seeds from their islands. But it was too late. Eliza distributed seeds from her crop to any South Carolina planter who wanted them. By 1746 the colony exported forty thousand pounds of indigo to England. A year later the total had tripled, and by the 1760s South Carolina was producing more than one million pounds of the dye. Said one modern historian, "Indigo proved more really beneficial to Carolina than the mines of Mexico or Peru were to Spain. The source of this vast wealth was the result of an experiment by a mere girl."

The same year of her successful crop, Eliza married Charles Pinckney, a widower twenty years her senior who was from a prominent Charleston family. She had four children in five years and was left to manage her husband's seven plantations after he died in 1758. Many of her lands were overrun during the American Revolution, and she spent her last years living with her children, who would make their own mark. Her son, Charles, was General Washington's aide in 1777 and later was the Federalist party candidate for president in 1804 and 1808. Thomas became governor of South Carolina in 1787 and later minister to Great Britain.

Eliza Pinckney died of cancer in 1793. At her funeral, President Washington, by his own request, was one of her pallbearers.

LYDIA E. PINKHAM

FAMOUS PATENT MEDICINE PEDDLER

"Hers may well have been the best-known American female face of the nineteenth century," estimated one historian. That's amazing, because Lydia E. Pinkham was not a glamorous actress or a figure of royalty, nor had she committed some sensational crime. Instead, Pinkham peddled patent medicine, claiming to cure everything from menstrual cramps to tumors. And at a time when male doctors didn't know very much and could cure far less, women believed her in droves.

Pinkham only became famous in the last eight years of her life. She had been the tenth of twelve children of a successful Quaker farmer near Lynn, Massachusetts, north of Boston. Well-educated, she helped found the Freeman's Institute, an early abolition group that gave her a lifelong friendship with Frederick Douglass. She also taught school until 1843 when at the age of twenty-four she married Isaac Pinkham, a widower who had many plans but little success in getting rich. As her husband tried one business venture after another, Pinkham raised three sons and a daughter. Finally, her husband lost it all in the Panic of 1873, leaving the family destitute.

Meanwhile, over the years Pinkham had taken an interest—not uncommon in those days—in home remedies. She kept an extensive scrapbook on what herbs cured which ailments, and she shared her remedies with the local women of Lynn. Besides being a midwife and a nurse, she helped women with problems they were too embarrassed to bring up with their male doctors, most of whom didn't regard "female complaints" very seriously.

One remedy, in particular, became popular among Pinkham's neighbors. It was a concoction of unicorn root, pleurisy root, and fenugreek seed which was supposed to relieve menstrual pain, menopausal symptoms, and other female problems. Pinkham herself had gotten the formula out of a book, which called it "the old squaw remedy."

About the time the family was bankrupt, some women from another town knocked on the door wanting to buy some of Pinkham's concoction. It was Pinkham's sons who saw that this might be the answer to the family's problems. So Pinkham made up a large batch in her cellar kitchen, only this time she added 20 percent alcohol as a "solvent and preservative."

The first bottles of "Lydia E. Pinkham's Vegetable Compound" were sold in 1875. At the time, druggists' shelves were jammed with patent medicines claiming to cure everything. And Pinkham's was no different. Said one of her advertisements, "If a woman finds that her energies are flagging, that she gets easily tired, dark shadows appear under her eyes, she has backaches, headaches, bearing down sensations, nervousness, irregularities or the 'blues,' she should start at once to build up her system by a tonic with specific powers, such as *Lydia E. Pinkham's Vegetable Compound.*" Eventually, the product was claimed to cure male kidney disorders and female sterility—"A Baby in Every Bottle," touted one advertisement.

Years later, scientists were unable to come up with any measurable medical benefit from Pinkham's product, though they agreed that the alcohol content, which made her "vegetable compound" more potent than wine or sherry, probably helped some. Ironically, the Pinkhams were all temperance advocates, and some of the product's advertisements featured testimonials from leaders of the Women's Christian Temperance Union.

Pinkham's product was helped greatly by her sons, who aggressively distributed handbills throughout the Northeast. They began buying newspaper advertisements and used the profits from increased sales to buy more ads. By the end of the century, Pinkham's concoction was the most heavily advertised product in the United States.

Pinkham's breakthrough came in 1879, when her sons convinced her to put her picture on the bottle. Sixty years old, Pinkham had the face of a kindly old woman. With her gray hair tied in a bun and a lace shawl wrapped conservatively around her neck, Pinkham's picture was as powerful as the testimonials that accompanied it. "The doctor gave me up, then I wrote Lydia Pinkham," said one. "Trust Lydia Pinkham, not the doctor who doesn't understand your problems," said another. The company never patented the formula for Pinkham's vegetable compound, but it did trademark her picture.

Each bottle of Lydia E. Pinkham's Vegetable Compound came with a four-page "Guide for Women" which included health tips such as "Ventilate!" and "Keep clean inside and out." Pinkham also began a Department of Advice, where she personally and frankly responded to the medical questions of thousands of women. Critics later would say that Pinkham's mail-order medical advice probably caused many women to delay seeking necessary medical treatment. But on the other hand, simply by addressing female complaints, Pinkham made women aware of their special medical needs long before many doctors did. Her health book sold over one million copies, and she even wrote a book about sex "for married women and those about to be."

In 1881, Pinkham sold two hundred thousand bottles of her vegetable compound. But that same year, her two younger sons, their condition aggravated by overwork, died of tuberculosis. Pinkham had tried to cure them with some of her herbal remedies, but to no avail. Pinkham herself died in May 1883, five months after she suffered a paralytic stroke.

But her patent medicine—sold by her descendants—lived much longer. Many home remedies were put out of business by the federal government's Pure Food and Drug Act of 1906. But Lydia E. Pinkham's Vegetable Compound was just that, and the company merely had to scale back some of its more optimistic advertising claims. Meanwhile, sales continued to grow until the 1920s, finally peaking in 1925 at $3.8 million. By then, the product was also an international success, sold as "La Remède Végétal de Lydia Pinkham" in France and "El Compuesto Vegetal de Lydia Pinkham" in Latin America and the Caribbean.

The company was held by Pinkham's descendants—surviving a series of family feuds—until 1968, when its sole product was sold to Cooper Laboratories. In 1973, Cooper shut down the factory in Lynn and moved it to Puerto Rico, putting two of Pinkham's great-grandsons out of work.

"MOLLY PITCHER"

REVOLUTIONARY WAR HEROINE

There never was a woman named Molly Pitcher. There was, however, a Mary Ludwig Hays McCauley, whose act of bravery in the Revolutionary War had been all but forgotten until the ladies of Carlisle, Pennsylvania, decided to memorialize her for the centennial celebration in 1876. Thanks to some monuments and modern history books, Molly Pitcher has become the best-known heroine of the American Revolution.

Mary McCauley was only fleetingly famous during her own lifetime. The daughter of a Dutch dairyman near Trenton, New Jersey, Mary was sent to Carlisle in 1769 to become a domestic servant in the home of a doctor. A few months later, not yet sixteen, Mary married John Hays, a barber.

When the revolution began, Hays enlisted as a gunner in the Pennsylvania artillery. And as was fairly common in those days, Mary followed her husband's outfit, washing and cooking for the soldiers. Apparently she was not daunted by army life. Described by one soldier as "a coarse and uncouth-looking female," Mary was also said to be a stocky woman who smoked a pipe, chewed tobacco, and "swore like a trooper."

In the summer of 1778, after the harsh winter at Valley Forge, the American army was pursuing British troops who were on their way through New Jersey toward safer quarters in New York. On June 28, they met at the Battle of Monmouth. It was a blistering hot day, perhaps over a hundred degrees, and fifty soldiers died of thirst during the battle. Not content to stay back in the camp, Mary braved the gunshots and cannon fire and carried water from a small stream to the parched American troops. The relief she brought in a pail or pitcher gave Mary her legendary nickname.

But her greater valiance was yet to come. As she was delivering some water, Mary saw her husband fall wounded by his cannon. With too few men to keep the cannon firing, an American officer ordered it pulled back from the front lines. But Mary, who had watched her husband in training, stepped into his place and began loading the cannon. She kept it firing for the rest of the battle. Though it would make a better story, Mary did not spur the Americans to win the battle, which ended in a draw. But she did win the admiration of the other soldiers, who called her "Sergeant Molly"—legend has it that General Washington himself gave her a noncommissioned title—and made up songs about her: "Oh, Molly, Molly, with eyes so blue/ Oh, Molly, Molly, here's to you!"

Mary and her wounded husband returned to Carlisle, where he died soon after the war. Their son later fought in the War of 1812. In 1792 she married John McCauley, a man whose neighbors said he "liked work so well he could lie down and sleep alongside it." Mary left him and got work as a laundress and a nursemaid. A record book in 1811 indicates that Mary, at the age of fifty-seven, was paid $16.03 to wash and scrub the courthouse. In 1822 the Pennsylvania legislature awarded her a pension of forty dollars per year "for the relief of Molly M'Kolly, for her services during the Revolutionary War."

Shortly before she died at the age of seventy-seven in 1832, Mary watched the local militia conduct a drill. "This is nothing but a flea-bite to what I have seen," she said.

MARY ELLEN PLEASANT

THE BLACK WOMAN WHO MAY HAVE FINANCED JOHN BROWN'S RAID

There were a lot of issues that led to the Civil War, but the event that historians often cite as turning the arguments into action was John Brown's raid. That certainly was the intention of the guerrilla abolitionist, who thought that his raid on the federal arsenal at Harpers Ferry, Virginia (now West Virginia), in 1859 would unleash a massive slave revolt throughout the South. Instead, Brown's siege ended unsuccessfully after thirty-six hours, with seventeen dead and Brown headed for execution. But it did spur plantation owners to mobilize against further violence, and it catalyzed their anger against Northern abolitionists, who considered Brown a martyr.

Several of those prominent abolitionists—men like Gerrit Smith and Samuel Howe—were criticized at the time for having provided financial support for Brown's anti-slavery efforts, though the men denied knowing that Brown was planning his violent raid. But besides those well-known abolitionists, a sizable share of the money for Brown's raid may have come from a former slavewoman who later became a legend in the early history of San Francisco. The evidence of Mary Ellen Pleasant's role in John Brown's raid is sketchy. But it would not have been out of character for the black activist, whom a federal judge later would call a "crafty old woman."

Although some accounts vary, Pleasant probably was born a slave in 1814 in Georgia. Somehow she made her way to Boston, perhaps, according to one version, freed by a kindly planter who sent her away to be educated. In Boston, Pleasant married a wealthy Cuban planter whose home was used as a meeting place for abolitionists. The planter died, leaving Pleasant $45,000 and instructions to use the money to aid the fight against slavery. Instead, Pleasant moved to San Francisco about 1849 and opened a boardinghouse during the booming Gold Rush. Some of her boarders included men who would later become important California businessmen and politicians, and they took advantage not only of "Mammy" Pleasant's accommodations but also her prostitutes. Said one historian, "She handled more money during pioneer days in California than any other colored person."

In 1858, Pleasant sailed east around the Cape to Chatham, Canada, the town where John Brown and his followers had gathered to plan their raid. Some of Brown's biographers don't mention Pleasant at all, and there is no firm record that they met. But they were in Chatham at the same time, and Pleasant bought some property there, presumably as a refuge for escaped slaves.

Some accounts, based largely on stories that circulated in San Francisco, say that Pleasant delivered thirty thousand dollars to Brown, which allowed him to proceed with his raid the next year. More likely, Pleasant gave him some five hundred dollars she had collected in California (abolitionists gave Brown a total of four thousand dollars) and promised him more. When Brown was captured at Harpers Ferry, he was carrying a note that read, "The ax is laid at the root of the tree. When the first blow is struck, there will be more money to help." It was reportedly signed "W.E.P.," but officials may have misread Pleasant's first initial.

Back in San Francisco, Pleasant's influence was

more visible. She was active in rescuing slaves who were illegally held in California, a free state. In 1863 she helped convince legislators to grant Negroes the right to testify in court. In 1864 she sued two San Francisco streetcar companies who had refused to let her ride and she won.

In her later years, Pleasant lived in the home of banker Thomas Bell. Officially she was his housekeeper, but their ties were much deeper. Associates said she advised him on business deals. She designed their mansion, the "House of Mystery," which was so called because it was hidden behind a row of eucalyptus trees, and local gossip had it that Pleasant was a witch who had cast a spell on the respected banker. Seen only when she emerged for daily errands, dressed always in a plain black dress, a red plaid shawl, and a straw hat, she was the subject of a front-page newspaper story in 1899 under the headline "Mammy Pleasant: Angel or Arch Fiend in the House of Mystery?"

In 1881 a huge scandal erupted when one of California's senators was sued for divorce by a woman no one even knew was his wife. She later confessed it was a hoax, and eventually Pleasant admitted it was she who had instigated the fraud to get revenge on the senator, who had once hurt her housemate Bell in a business deal. It was then that a judge said, "This case, and the forgeries and perjuries committed in its support, have their origin largely in the brain of this scheming, trafficking, crafty old woman."

When Bell died, Pleasant was not mentioned in his will, and she was forced to move out of the "House of Mystery." She died impoverished in the home of a friend in 1904 at the age of eighty-nine. In her will,

Pleasant requested that her tombstone say, "She was a friend of John Brown's."

MADAME DE POMPADOUR

THE WOMAN BEHIND LOUIS XV

When, in 1755, the Austrian ambassador to France wanted to propose the first alliance between the two countries in two hundred years, he didn't write to Louis XV or to the king's foreign minister. He wrote to Louis's mistress: "Madame, I have often wished to remember myself to you . . . I think our offers will not give you cause to regret the trouble you may take to request the King to send someone to negotiate with us."

It says much about the sorry state of France under Louis XV—historian Thomas Carlyle called his reign a "harlotocracy"—that the Austrian ambassador's overtures were successful, prompting what is known as the Diplomatic Revolution of 1756. It also testifies to the deftness of his most powerful mistress, Madame de Pompadour. "We owe everything to her," the ambassador wrote to his queen, "and it is to her that we must look for everything in the future."

You can probably get a clearer idea of politics under Louis XV—grandfather of the ill-fated Louis XVI—by studying the correspondence of his mistress rather than his own letters. Said one historian, "A history of her rule would properly be entitled France under Madame de Pompadour."

Her ascension was nothing if not hard-won. Born into the bourgeoisie, the daughter of a financier who had to flee the country in a money scandal, Jeanne Antoinette Poisson did quite well by marrying into the family of another financier, Le Normant d'Étioles, in 1741. But she was not satisfied. She used her moderate position—and her beauty and disarming charm—to become one of the most sought-after guests and hostesses in Paris. She hosted a salon of intellectuals, including Voltaire and Montesquieu, and soon her name was circulating among the king's court at Versailles.

But apparently the king did not take the bait quickly enough, because finally to catch his eye Madame d'Étioles drove her carriage directly into the path of his hunting party. She did it more than once, and made enough of an impression that the king's current mistress ordered her banned from the hunts. That mistress died soon after in 1744.

At that time, it was so common, even expected, for a king to have a mistress that it was almost like filling a Cabinet post. The woman even had an official title, *maîtresse en titre*—the recognized royal mistress. Besides her pleasing the king, there were but two qualifications. The mistress had to be chosen from the aristocracy, and she had to stay out of politics.

Madame d'Étioles satisfied neither, but soon after she gained the king's attention again at another ball in 1745, she was installed at Versailles and was presented to the court—and to Louis's queen, Marie—in a formal ceremony. (Her husband begged her to return but she never saw him again.) Wrote one minister of the twenty-four-year-old mistress, "In her grace, the lightness of her figure, the beauty of her hair, she resembled a nymph. She was a good musician with a sympathetic voice, excelling in declamation, and she varied the King's pleasures by performances in which she played the leading part. Mistress of the King and of the universe, she was surrounded at her toilette like a queen."

Granted the title Marquise de Pompadour, she worked hard at pleasing the king. That was no small task, as Louis XV was passive and unimaginative, leaving an especially large void after the powerful flourish of Louis XIV. Louis XV almost never left his circle of palaces surrounding Paris. It was largely up to Madame de Pompadour to keep him amused at an unending stream of balls, buffets, and hunts. She staged comedies and light operas for the king, who told her "You are the most charming woman in France." Even the religious Queen Marie admitted, "If there has to be a mistress, better this one than any other."

As if she were the queen, Madame de Pompadour so imposed her taste on furniture, fashion, and the arts that in many ways she defined the age. By her patronage she encouraged the ornate rococo style of furniture, vases, clocks, frames, and other decorative arts that are now the best-known French antiques. In addition, she helped plan the Place de la Concorde in Paris and Le Petit Trianon at Versailles. She also founded the royal porcelain factory at Sèvres.

More significantly, the king's mistress imposed her taste on his government. At first content to speak for the king, Madame de Pompadour eventually spoke instead of him. She got her friends appointed to high posts, and they in turn protected her position. Louis XV came to rely on his mistress so heavily that even after they stopped sleeping together—historians record the year as 1751—another *maîtresse en titre* was not named until 1757.

And even then, Madame de Pompadour retained

her influence. It had been the previous year when she had arranged France's ties with Austria. The alliance, it turned out, was disastrous, leading to the Seven Years War against England and Germany. But it was her foreign minister, the Duc de Choiseul, who negotiated the peace in 1763, costing France much of its colonial empire in America and India.

Madame de Pompadour lived just long enough to see the damage. She died of cancer in 1764 at the age of forty-three. Louis XV, beset by war debts and the clamor of a nation frustrated with its ineffectual throne, died of smallpox in 1774. It was Louis XVI who was left to cope with his grandfather's affairs.

R

IDA ROSENTHAL

SHE INVENTED THE BRA

Just in case you haven't kept up with the evolution of the brassiere, let the woman who invented it fill you in. "Now in those days [the 1920s], the cheapest dress we made was $125, and it just didn't fit right. So we made a little bra with two pockets. Not accentuated, of course. That's a development. Since then we've made them more rounded, more pointed—oh, mama dear—like any new idea, the first airplane was not a jet."

That was Ida Rosenthal: the Wright brothers of the feminine form. Before Rosenthal's innovation, the bra was a plain piece of cloth with some hooks in the back, a sort of female cummerbund that was designed to flatten what was under it. Rosenthal added her uplifting tucks, and the way was paved for Jane Russell movies, Vargas's girls, and fumbling boys frustrated by their lack of dexterity. "Nature has made women with a bosom," said Rosenthal, "so nature thought it was important. Who am I to argue with nature?"

The daughter of a Hebrew scholar in Russia, Rosenthal immigrated alone to the United States in 1904 at the age of eighteen. She set up a dressmaking shop in Hoboken, New Jersey, and soon was successful enough to bring over the rest of her family. With her immigrant husband, William, the business expanded, and later they and a partner opened a store on fashionable Fifty-seventh Street in Manhattan. It was there that Rosenthal designed the bra that helped her dresses fit better.

At first, the Rosenthals gave the bras away free to their dress buyers. But when women wanted more, they founded the Maiden Form Brassiere Company in 1923. William, who later became an amateur sculptor, was in charge of design. He created the standardized sizes that were the forerunners of the A, B, C, and D cups. Ida, only four feet eleven inches tall, managed sales, traveling around the country and eventually the world to open new markets.

The Rosenthals sold their millionth bra in their first decade. Partly that was due to the requirements of the shapelier styles of the 1930s, and Ida deserves some credit for that, too. Wrote *Time* magazine, "Ida Rosenthal probably had a greater impact on the U.S. female form than all the couturiers in Paris." In the 1940s, Maiden Form helped the war effort by producing a "pigeon vest," a cup-shaped cloth that held a courier pigeon. Rosenthal said her company also had no trouble getting rubber for elastic bra straps during the war. "We got priority because women workers who wore an uplift were less fatigued than others."

In 1949 the Rosenthals launched their classic advertising campaign featuring a bra-clad woman who said, "I dreamed I went shopping in my Maiden Form bra." Later versions had the woman fighting bulls, winning elections, racing chariots, boxing, and riding a fire truck. The campaign didn't sit well with the women's movement in the 1960s, but Ida Rosenthal remained confident. "We are a democracy and a person has a right to be dressed or undressed," she said. "But after thirty-five a woman hasn't got the figure to wear nothing."

Even into her eighties, Rosenthal continued traveling the world in search of new business. Eventually Maidenform (as they came to be known in 1960) bras were owned by one of every three women in the United States and were sold in some 110 countries worldwide, including Papua, New Guinea, where women previously were noted for going topless.

Ida Rosenthal died of pneumonia in 1973 at the age of eighty-seven. Maidenform, which remains the largest privately owned intimate apparel company, is now run by her daughter, Beatrice Coleman.

ANNE NEWPORT ROYALL

THE FIRST FEMALE AMERICAN JOURNALIST

There is a wonderful legend about Anne Newport Royall which if it's not true ought to be. The first American female journalist with a national reputation, Royall, so the story goes, once caught President John Quincy Adams swimming naked in the Potomac, and she sat on his clothes until he agreed to give her an exclusive interview. Historians have discounted the tale, saying there's just no evidence to support it. But even a century later, President Harry Truman got enough of a kick out of the story to repeat it to an interviewer from *The New Yorker*.

Certainly, catching a president without his pants would be quite in character for Royall, often called "the Grandma of the Muckrakers." She began her writing career at the age of fifty-four in 1823, when she suddenly found herself penniless after her husband—an eccentric Virginia gentleman farmer whom she had met when her mother became his servant—died, and his relatives cheated her out of his wealthy estate.

Royall began to earn a living by traveling around the young United States and writing about her experiences. In ten years she wrote ten volumes, encompassing virtually every major settlement in the country—as far west as St. Louis and north into Canada. She wrote "pen portraits" of some two thousand prominent people she met along the way, including the French military hero, the Marquis de Lafayette, whom she cornered in his hotel room after she sneaked past his guards. At a time when communication was slow, Royall's journals—which covered everything from public buildings and ceremonies to a mental asylum and a visit to the home of General Andrew Jackson—gave Americans an idea of what the rest of the nation was like. Her books remain fascinating social sketches of the period.

A lady who had been accustomed to traveling in a carriage with attending servants, Royall was often broke as she trekked around the country. She traveled alone, sometimes by stagecoach or steamer, but often on horseback or on foot. Frequently she had to beg for meals and lodging, and often promised to include mention of charitable proprietors in her next book.

But far from clouding her writing, such hardships made her more vitriolic. Covering the commencement ceremonies at Harvard, she noted the mortar board worn by the college president: "I thought it interrupted his Rev. LL.D.-ship very much by getting into his eyes." Of another of her unfortunate victims she wrote, "The young doctor of Knoxville, in a few words, was a pert little fop, and an ignoramus besides."

Royall saved her best scathing remarks for the evangelical movement. "I would not," she proclaimed, "give a fig for any God that could not spread his own gospel or any gospel, without money. I would rather be a god of wood or stone than one who robs the poor and ignorant under a cloak." In 1829, after she found a group of Presbyterians praying under her rooming house window in Washington, D.C., Royall lashed out with such violent language that the evangelists pressed charges. Despite testimony on her behalf from the Secretary of State, Royall was convicted of being a "common scold."

The following year Royall began publishing a weekly newspaper in the nation's capital called *Paul Pry*, and indeed she did pry. It was a common sight to see Royall, a tiny-framed woman, scurrying through the halls of Congress, wearing her typical tattered dress and a three-dollar plaid coat, and carrying a green umbrella and her newspaper subscription book. Sometimes the only mistake a politician had to make to draw the wrath of Royall's editorial columns was to not buy the previous week's edition of the *Pry* or her later, aptly titled newspaper, *The Huntress*.

Though her friends included Presidents Adams and Jackson, Royall had many more enemies. On one occasion, she suffered a broken leg when she was thrown down the stairs by one victim of her words. Another time she was mobbed by students at the University of Virginia who didn't like her writing.

Royall's stories often were reckless and her gossip frequently was wrong. But she uncovered enough scandals to make politicians pay attention. Besides, she said, public officials are "fair game." She continued to publish *The Huntress* until July 1854. In October, at the age of eighty-five, Royall died with thirty-one cents to her name and owing six dollars in back rent.

If he had indeed been one of her victims, John Quincy Adams seemed more amused than annoyed when he wrote of Royall in his memoirs. "Stripped of all her sex's delicacy," he wrote, "but unable to forfeit its privilege of gentle treatment from the other, she goes about like a virago errant in enchanted armor, redeeming herself from the cramps of indigence by the notoriety of her eccentricities and the forced currency they give her publications."

S

SACAGAWEA

HELPED GUIDE LEWIS AND CLARK

For nearly a century after Meriwether Lewis and George Clark made their famous journey across the West to the Pacific Ocean, no one ever mentioned Sacagawea, the Indian wife of one of Lewis and Clark's interpreters and the only woman to make the trip. But this century has more than made up for that neglect. In about 1900, suffragists embraced the Native American as an unsung heroine, and a few popular books claimed that she had actually guided Lewis and Clark throughout their trek. To this day, there are more monuments across America honoring Sacagawea than any other woman.

In fact, the truth about Sacagawea's accomplishments is somewhere in the middle. The young Indian, also called "the Bird Woman," did not show the famous explorers their way west. But neither is it unfair to say that without Sacagawea, Lewis and Clark might not have made it.

Sacagawea was born a Shoshoni Indian in central

Idaho, probably about 1789. When she was ten years old or so, she was captured by the Hidatsa tribe that lived in what is now North Dakota. By 1804, Sacagawea either had been sold or gambled away to Toussaint Charbonneau, a French Canadian trapper who lived with the tribe. Charbonneau also bought another Shoshoni and made both women his wives.

Lewis and Clark—and the forty other men in their expedition—left St. Louis in May 1804 and arrived in the Hidatsa villages by winter. After learning that the Shoshonis were the closest Indians to the Rocky Mountains, Lewis and Clark hired Charbonneau, who knew the language, and they insisted he bring Sacagawea. When they set off in April 1805, Sacagawea carried her two-month-old son on her back.

Sacagawea was not familiar with most of the territory they crossed, but she was vital to the mission. First, her very presence calmed Indian tribes by signaling that these white men were not hostile. Also, she showed the men which roots were edible and once rescued important instruments and records that had fallen overboard during a storm on the Missouri River. Most importantly, Sacagawea helped the men locate her former tribe, from whom Lewis and Clark hoped to acquire horses and aid before they attempted to cross the Continental Divide. Without the Shoshonis' aid, the travelers faced starvation in the coming winter before they crossed the mountains.

When the expedition first made contact with the Shoshonis, Sacagawea was brought in to interpret a meeting with Chief Cameahwait. The original journals of Lewis and Clark describe the meeting: "Sacagawea was sent for, and she came into the tent, sat down, and was beginning to interpret, when, in the person of Cameahwait, she recognized her brother.

She instantly jumped up, and ran and embraced him, throwing over her blanket, and weeping profusely. The chief was himself moved, though not in the same degree. After some conversation between them, she resumed her seat and attempted to interpret for us, but her new situation seemed to overpower her, and she was frequently interrupted by her tears."

Lewis and Clark got the horses and guidance they needed to reach the Clearwater and Columbia rivers, which led to the Pacific. Clark wrote to Charbonneau after the journey, "Your woman, who accompanied you on that long, dangerous, and fatiguing route to the Pacific and back, deserved a greater reward for her attention and service than we had in our power to give at the Mandans (where they parted)." Clark later took over the education of Sacagawea's son. Jean Baptiste Charbonneau befriended Prince Paul of Württemberg and spent six years in Europe. He later fought in the Mexican War and ended up working in the California gold fields.

Meanwhile, Sacagawea and Charbonneau went back to the Hidatsa villages and later moved to St. Louis in 1810. After that, the fate of the famous Indian has been long debated. It is clear that Charbonneau returned to Fort Manuel in the Dakota Territory where, on December 20, 1812, a clerk recorded that the trapper's wife, "a Snake [Shoshoni] squaw, died of a putrid fever she was good and the best woman in the fort, aged 25 years she left a fine infant girl."

But some historians believe that the woman who died was Charbonneau's other Shoshoni wife whom he had left behind when he and Sacagawea traveled with Lewis and Clark. There are some accounts that say Sacagawea stayed behind in St. Louis with two children and later spent time with the Comanche Indians in Oklahoma. An old woman claiming to be Sacagawea turned up on the Wind River Reservation in Wyoming, where she died in 1884.

Two decades later, the exaggerated legend of the Bird Woman began with a novel called *The Conquest* by an Oregon writer named Eva Emery Dye. The book was very popular and very much fiction, but it began a movement to honor the forgotten Indian wherever she had been, or at least wherever someone thought she had been. Besides her many monuments, Sacagawea also has her name on a river, a peak, and a mountain pass in Montana.

SHAKESPEARE'S "DARK LADY"

THE OBSESSION OF HIS SONNETS

Although libraries are filled with volumes about the works of Shakespeare, scholars are forever frustrated by the fact that they know so little about the real life of the world's greatest playwright. Just about the only certain information comes from a few legal records that sketch his life, including his marriage to Anne Hathaway and the births of their three children. But what inspired Shakespeare—his daily life, who his friends were, and even when he actually wrote each of his plays—largely remains a mystery.

That is why so much attention is focused on his sonnets. Some of the individual poems have become the most popular in the English language, especially

Sonnet 18, which begins, "Shall I compare thee to a summer's day?" But many scholars suspect—and hope—that the complete collection of 154 sonnets is the closest thing to an autobiography that Shakespeare left behind. Said William Wordsworth, "With this key, Shakespeare unlocked his heart."

And the key with which scholars have tried to unlock the sonnets is a woman who may have been the love of Shakespeare's life, his so-called "Dark Lady." When Shakespeare married Anne Hathaway in 1582, he was eighteen and she was eight years older and already pregnant. Because Shakespeare apparently spent much of his twenty-year theatrical career in London away from his wife, it is assumed that the playwright looked elsewhere for love.

In Sonnets 127 to 152, Shakespeare wrote of his tormented relationship with a coarse, promiscuous, married woman, who had dark hair and equally blackened morals. "My mistress' eyes are nothing like the sun," he wrote in Sonnet 130, later describing "the breath that from my mistress reeks." In an era when fair-haired women were the beauties, Shakespeare wrote, "Some say that thee behold/ Thy face hath not the power to make love groan." But he goes on, "A thousand groans but thinking on thy face/ Thy black is fairest in my judgment's place."

The sonnets indicate that Shakespeare first became smitten with his Dark Lady when she was in trouble and he helped her. He then became obsessed with her, only to watch her have an affair with the other mystery person of his sonnets—the man to whom most of the poems are addressed. Many scholars believe that the man was the young Earl of Southampton, who was Shakespeare's patron in his early years as a playwright. He writes to his Dark Lady, "Who taught thee how to make me love thee more/ The more I hear and see just cause of hate?"

Apparently, the woman had finally ended her relationship with Shakespeare, and he was distraught. One critic called the Dark Lady sonnets "some of the most tortured and introverted of the poems; it is difficult to imagine the poet wishing to show them even to the woman, let alone make them public." The sonnets were, in fact, first published in 1609, seven years before Shakespeare died and apparently without his consent.

The list of possibilities as to the true identity of Shakespeare's Dark Lady is long indeed. Some say she was the black madam of a London whorehouse. In the nineteenth century, many seemed to think she was Mary Fitton, a nobleman's daughter who served in the court of Queen Elizabeth and had a scandalous reputation for fooling around. But Fitton, though she had two children, was unmarried, and a couple of paintings show that she had red, not dark, hair.

The most plausible nominee seems to be a woman named Emilia Bassano, the dark-haired daughter of Italian court musicians. Five years younger than Shakespeare, Emilia became the mistress of a lord, who got her pregnant in 1592 and then had her marry another court musician, Alfonso Lanier. It was during that period, scholars believe, that Shakespeare probably wrote his sonnets, because a plague had closed London's theaters.

After the sonnets came out in 1609, Emilia herself published a long religious poem that, in part, chastised men for writing poems against women. "If it were not by the means of women, they would be quite extinguished out of the world," she pointed out. Emilia's husband died in 1613, and she spent much of the rest of her life engaged in lawsuits for the rights to his estate. She died in 1645 at the age of seventy-five.

Whoever she was, Shakespeare's Dark Lady shows up elsewhere in his writings. She is believed to be Rosaline in *Love's Labour's Lost*, and the entire situation seems to be the basis for *Two Gentlemen of Verona*. But the sonnets remain the heart of the matter. Said one critic, "They are the most thrilling and intimately deep poems in our language; they are often passionate, but they are like a record that leaves out most of the facts, and all the names and dates."

LADY HESTER STANHOPE

THE FEMALE LAWRENCE OF ARABIA

If they were to recast the movie *Lawrence of Arabia* with a female star, it would be the story of Lady Hester Stanhope. "I am," she said, "the oracle of the Arabs," and she was not exaggerating. In the early nineteenth century, even the desert Bedouin tribes, who savagely protected their territory, bowed down to this small-framed British import. With great foresight, her uncle, British Prime Minister William Pitt the Younger, once told her, "If you were a man, I would send you on the Continent with sixty thousand men, and give you carte blanche; and I am sure that not one of my plans would fail."

Lady Hester never knew a normal life. The daughter of an eccentric earl who spent his time unsuccessfully trying to invent things, she was raised primarily by her flighty stepmother on isolated estates. She was twenty-seven when in 1803 she was rescued by Pitt, the boy-wonder prime minister who at the time was politically out of favor. When Pitt, a bachelor who had invited Hester to keep house for him, returned to leadership in 1804, suddenly this sheltered young woman became the most sought-after hostess in London. She also helped her uncle dispense patronage, and became the prime minister's closest confidant. "I let her do as she pleases," Pitt said, "for if she were resolved to cheat the devil she could do it."

But Lady Hester Stanhope's new career was cut short in 1806 when Pitt died unexpectedly at the age of forty-seven. No longer the center of attention, Hester tried living in Wales, but in 1810 decided to go abroad. She never returned.

With an annual pension of 1,200 pounds left to her by Pitt, Lady Hester left England with one female companion. She was greeted as royalty by ambassadors as she sailed through the Mediterranean, finally stopping in Constantinople for a year. After the British embassy rejected her plan to defeat Napoléon, she sailed on to the Middle East. She survived a shipwreck on the island of Rhodes before finally arriving in Cairo.

The legendary status of Lady Hester Stanhope developed shortly after, when she visited Damascus. In Turkey, she had begun exchanging her properly corseted dresses in favor of a Turkish man's attire. The British spinster would wear bright-colored, loose-fitting pants or robes and a large silk turban. And that's what she donned as she rode into Damascus, a city where by Moslem law women always appeared veiled and never in pants. Despite predictions of violence—if not an international crisis—Hester was greeted by cheering crowds.

Lady Hester traveled throughout much of the Middle East, which was then largely ruled by the Turks through Arabic sultans and pashas. Many of the territorial rulers were violent enemies of each other, but they all entertained Hester warmly. They also agreed she was insane to attempt to cross the dangerous Syrian desert to visit the ancient ruins of Palmyra. But instead of attacking, the Bedouin tribes eagerly welcomed her into their camps, and when she arrived at Palmyra, residents gave her a crown of flowers. "I am the oracle of the Arabs," she said, "and the darling of all the troops, who seem to think that I am a deity because I can ride, and because I wear arms, and the fanatics all bow before me."

Whether the Arabs thought that Lady Hester Stanhope was a representative of the powerful British Empire—which was hardly the case—or whether they were just amazed by her gall, she wielded very real power in the Middle East for about twenty years. Rulers sought her favor and feared her wrath, after she riled one tribe to overthrow its sultan.

But since she could never be, literally, Queen of Arabia, Hester created her own dominion which she ruled with no less authority. In 1814 she settled in an abandoned convent at Dar Djoun, located on top of a hill near Mount Lebanon. With dozens of Arab servants, she transformed the dilapidated site into a palace, a forty-room complex of one-story buildings and lush gardens, all surrounded by a massive wall. Thirty cats roamed the palace, which also housed two horses in case the Messiah returned to carry them both into Jerusalem. Lady Hester also had thirty personal attendants whom she beat with a mace and forbade, she said, "to smile, or scratch themselves, or appear to notice anything."

Her fortress occasionally became a refuge for other

European travelers who found themselves caught in the middle of the region's many territorial battles. During the siege of Acre in 1832, she housed some two hundred refugees. The last didn't leave until 1836.

Lady Hester Stanhope's reputation was also spread by the many visitors she entertained and harassed. Many prominent Europeans called on her, though some were abruptly denied an audience even after they had traveled hundreds of miles across Syria. She made her guests stand while she spoke to them, which sometimes lasted late into the night. One guest fainted. Said another, "In haranguing her visitors, there is no doubt that Lady Hester found the greatest happiness of her life."

Her personal physician, who attended her almost nightly for many years, recalled, "She fancied herself an eastern princess. I have known her to lie for two hours at a time with a pipe in her mouth (from which the sparks fell and burned the counterpane into innumerable holes) when she was in a lecturing humour, and go on in one unbroken discourse, like a parson in his pulpit."

Not surprisingly, Hester Stanhope's pension did not cover the cost of her little kingdom. Under pressure from her Arab creditors, British officials in 1838 appropriated the bulk of her pension to pay off her debts. Enraged, Lady Hester appealed to no less than Queen Victoria. "My grandfather and Mr. Pitt did something, I think, to keep the Brunswick family on the throne," she wrote to the queen. "And yet the granddaughter of the old king [George III], without hearing the circumstances of my getting into debt, or whether the story is true, sends to deprive me of my pension in a foreign land, where I may remain and starve."

Her appeal failed, and in August 1838, Lady Hester Stanhope dismissed all but five of her servants, who she then requested to wall in her palace gates. She died the following June at the age of sixty-three. By the time the British consul arrived from Beirut, the servants had fled, stealing all but what Lady Hester was wearing. She was buried in the garden. Fade out.

BELLE STARR

"THE LEADER OF A BAND OF HORSE THIEVES"

Belle Starr, the most notorious female outlaw before Bonnie, of Bonnie and Clyde, insisted she had gone straight. "Far from society, I hoped to pass the remainder of my life in peace," she wrote to a newspaper in the early 1880s from her hideaway in eastern Oklahoma. "Indeed, I never corresponded with any of my old associates and was desirous my whereabouts should be unknown to them. Through rumor they learned of it."

Starr spent her life denying that she was a gangster, and in fact, legend has indicted her far more than law enforcement officials ever did. Still, in the last months of his life, when Jesse James had become one of the most hunted men in America, he sought refuge with Starr, the woman called "the Bandit Queen," "the Petticoat Terror of the Plains," and even "the Female Jesse James." Said federal Judge Isaac C. Parker, also known as "the Hanging Judge," "She has all the accomplishments of a highwayman."

Rumored to be a fallen Southern belle turned Confederate spy, Myra Belle Shirley actually was far less rebellious. Born in southwestern Missouri in 1848, she was the daughter of a tavern owner. One of her brothers was killed by federal troops in 1863 as part of William Quantrill's outlaw gang. Her other brother died in a gunfight four years later. And after the family moved to Scyene, Texas, east of Dallas, their farm became a regular hideout for remnants of Quantrill's gang, including the four Younger brothers and their cousins, Frank and Jesse James. In 1869 Belle had a daughter, Pearl, probably by Cole Younger. She had a second child, Edward, a few years later by another outlaw.

Meanwhile, Belle had become a frequent sight in the saloons and casinos of Dallas, where she played piano. Belle was a plain-looking woman who favored flashy clothes; only her holsters with two pearl-handled pistols betrayed her real occupation. There were rumors that Belle participated in several bank and stagecoach holdups, but dressed as a man, she could never be identified in order to be charged with the crimes. More likely, she made her living by trading stolen horses and fencing other goods robbed by her male colleagues.

It was with her second husband, a Cherokee Indian named Sam Starr, that Belle created her famous hideout called Younger's Bend. Settled on the Canadian River some miles from the Arkansas border, the cabin and plot of land are near a hill that is still called "Belle's Mound," where she allegedly posted her boys to watch for vulnerable travelers or federal marshals. For a time, she bragged about her safe haven. "There are three or four jolly, good fellows on the dodge now in my section," she told one newspaper, "and when they come to my home they are welcome." Still, when Jesse James took refuge there in 1881, Starr said she introduced him to her husband as "one Mr. Williams from Texas."

In 1883 Starr faced the only indictment that prosecutors were able to make stick. The first woman ever to appear in federal court on the charge of being "the leader of a band of horse thieves," Starr—whose court appearances in Fort Smith, Arkansas, were so frequent that they became a regular source of entertainment for the locals—was hardly fazed. Wrote one reporter, "A devil-may-care expression rested on her countenance during the entire trial, and at no time did she give sign of weakening before the mass of testimony that was raised against her." Nor was she overly traumatized by the nine months (three months off for good behavior) she spent in federal prison in Detroit after she was convicted.

She dodged additional indictments in 1885 and 1886. All in all, her life hadn't changed much by February 1889, when, while her fourth husband was away on a court appearance, she was shot in the back and fell dead from her horse on a muddy road near Younger's Bend, two days before her forty-first birthday. Her killer was never found, but local gossip accused her son, Edward, who may also have been her lover and who, neighbors said, was upset over the whipping Starr had given him for mistreating her horse.

The rest of Starr's family fared no better. Her husband was killed in 1890 while resisting arrest. Edward was shot in a saloon fight in 1896. Her daughter, Pearl, became a prostitute in Arkansas. Pearl placed a tombstone on her mother's grave at Younger's Bend that said:

Shed not for her the bitter tear,
Nor give the heart to vain regret;
'Tis but the casket that lies here,
The gem that filled it sparkles yet.

MARGARETE STEIFF

INVENTOR OF THE TEDDY BEAR

Since the teddy bear was named for him, President Theodore Roosevelt deserves some credit for the invention of the world's most popular stuffed animal. But Teddy, of course, never actually made one of his little stuffed namesakes. And although—as with many great inventions—determining who made the first teddy bear is a task fraught with claims and counterclaims, most of the credit probably belongs to a crippled German spinster named Margarete Steiff.

Born in 1847 in the small village of Geingen-on-the-Brenz in southwest Germany, Steiff contracted polio when she was two years old, which left her in a wheelchair for the rest of her life. She also had a weak right hand, but she studied dressmaking and in 1877 opened a shop. She developed a successful small business, making coats, dresses, and tapestries. One day she used some spare felt to sew a stuffed elephant. "The small elephant was intended for use as a pincushion," she wrote later.

But the village children had better ideas. They pleaded for Steiff to make more stuffed toys, and soon she had created an entire menagerie of donkeys, horses, pigs, and camels. By 1886, Steiff and the workers she was forced to hire had made more than five thousand stuffed animals. She ran the business while her brother, Fritz, and five nephews began selling the toys at country fairs. Recalled one of her descendants, "She was very firm, very hard. My father was always a little afraid of her."

It was her nephew, Richard, who came up with the idea of a stuffed bear in 1902. His Aunt Margarete was not enthusiastic, but she made a few bears anyway. They hardly sold at all until the grand Leipzig Fair in 1903, when an American importer ordered three thousand of the bears, which had movable arms and legs and were covered with mohair.

Perhaps the American importer was aware of the hoopla that had occurred the previous year when President Roosevelt went bear hunting in Mississippi. Teddy was fairly obsessed with bears. Said one historian, "He dissected every bear he ever shot, and would hold his fire until the very last minute. He'd simply sit and stare at the bears' activities until they either ran away or charged him. He nearly lost his life to a grizzly."

On this hunting trip, his dogs had chased a malnourished black bear until it was so exhausted that one of Roosevelt's hunting party simply knocked it on the head and tied it to a tree. When Roosevelt saw the poor thing, *The Washington Post* reported, "he would neither shoot it nor permit it to be shot." But although legend has it that the bear wound up in a zoo, in fact Teddy ordered a fellow hunter to kill it with a knife. Soon after, a cartoon in the *Post* showed the president shielding the bear from harm. The play on Roosevelt, who boasted of carrying a big stick but wouldn't shoot the bear, captured the public's imagination.

Here is where the origin of the teddy bear gets murky. According to one version, a Russian immigrant named Morris Michtom, who ran a novelty store in Brooklyn, had his wife make two stuffed bears, which he placed in his shop window with a sign that said "Teddy's bears." The two animals sold quickly, his wife made many more, and the couple eventually incorporated as the Ideal Novelty and Toy Company, which grew into a major U.S. toymaker.

But most teddy bear books—and there are a lot—say the term "teddy bear" wasn't coined until 1906. It was at the wedding breakfast of Roosevelt's daughter, Alice, where the centerpiece at each table was a Steiff bear dressed in hunting gear. A guest called them "teddy bears," and the name stuck.

Whether or not Steiff actually had made the first teddy bear, her company probably profited the most. In 1907 the Steiff company made 974,000 stuffed bears, compared to 12,000 in 1903. Teddy bears—Steiff's and those of countless competitors—became such a craze that there was a backlash. One Michigan minister warned that the stuffed animal would destroy the instincts of motherhood.

Margarete Steiff died in 1909, but her company remains a major toymaker, and teddy bears remain its biggest seller. Indeed, teddy bears continue to be the most popular stuffed animal in America. They are the subject of three magazines—*Teddy Bear Review*, *Teddy Tribune*, and *Teddy Bear and Friends*. A psychiatrist did a study in 1988 that found that teddy bears are the most "solacing object" to children, after their parents. One police department stocks teddy bears in its squad cars to calm traumatized children.

What do you suppose would have happened if Teddy had shot the bear?

LUCY STONE

THE FIRST WOMAN TO KEEP HER MAIDEN NAME

"I wish, as a husband, to *renounce* all the privileges which the law confers upon me, which are not strictly *mutual*, and I intend to do so—Help me to draw one up—When we marry, I will publicly pledge myself to never avail myself of them *under any* circumstances —Surely *such a marriage* will not degrade you, dearest."

Such were the pleadings required of Henry Blackwell to woo Lucy Stone. And even once she agreed to march down the aisle, the trip was far from traditional, especially considering that it occurred in 1855. Besides omitting the word "obey" from their vows, the happy couple paused during the ceremony to read a speech protesting the laws of marriage, which at the time granted the husband full control over his wife's body, children, and property. But Stone's most dramatic and symbolic slap in the face of the institution of marriage was that she, unlike any before her, kept her maiden name. "A wife should not more take her husband's name than he should her's," she said simply.

Although her husband was quite willing to go along with Stone's altered marriage proposal, it is nonetheless surprising that she ever said "I do." The daughter of a prominent Massachusetts farmer who showed a marked preference for her older brother even though she did better in school and could run faster, she could not imagine following the course of her mother, who struggled to raise seven surviving children. When it was pointed out to her that the Bible said men were superior, Stone studied Greek and Latin to prove that the scriptures had been translated badly. "It will take longer than my lifetime for the obstacles to be removed which are in the way of a married woman having any being of her own," she wrote to a friend.

After teaching school to pay her way through college (her father didn't believe in it for women), Stone graduated from Oberlin in 1847 when she was twenty-eight, becoming the first Massachusetts woman to earn a college degree. She was asked to write the commencement address but refused, because only a man would have been allowed to present it.

Stone went back to Massachusetts and began conducting lectures. She was paid six dollars a week by William Lloyd Garrison's American Anti-Slavery Society, but she soon found she could earn far more by speaking for women's rights and charging her own admission. Stone, who always spoke extemporaneously, is called the "morning star" of the women's rights movement, and with good reason. It was upon hearing one of her speeches that Susan B. Anthony converted to the cause. Elizabeth Cady Stanton recalled, "Her sweet voice and simple girlish manner made her first appearance on the platform irresistible." Not to everyone, as Stone often faced hostile audiences and once was hit in the head with a prayer book.

It was during one of her national speaking tours that Stone met Henry Blackwell, a Cincinnati hardware merchant whose sister, Elizabeth, became the first American woman granted a medical degree. Blackwell, seven years younger than Stone, spent two years carefully courting her, professing his sincerity in a steady stream of letters. Stone seemed most impressed when he helped rescue a fugitive slave.

After they were married at her family's home, Stone at first took her husband's name. But after a few months she began dropping it. When she signed legal documents or registered at hotels, she wrote, "Lucy Stone, wife of Henry Blackwell." She never made it much of a public issue during her speeches. But for years, women who followed her act were called "Lucy Stoners."

Generally, using her maiden name didn't cause her

much trouble until 1879, when Massachusetts officials, who had granted women the right to vote in school-board elections, would only allow Stone to register under her husband's name. "My name *is* Lucy Stone, nothing more," she replied. "I have been called by it more than sixty years, and there is no doubt whatever about it. If the use of a foot- or cart-path for twenty years gives the right of way, surely the use of a name three times twenty years should secure the right to its use." State officials weren't convinced, but Stone didn't pursue the matter in court.

By then, Stone no longer was at the forefront of the women's rights movement. Though she had tried to continue her speaking tours after her daughter was born in 1857, she gave up because she was unhappy with the nursemaids. When she joined the suffrage cause after the Civil War, a series of political and personality disputes led her to lead a conservative split away from Anthony and Stanton, both of whom history has remembered far better.

Stone did achieve the kind of marriage she wanted. She and her husband maintained separate bank accounts. Her money paid for their house in Orange, New Jersey, a situation which won her wide publicity when she refused to pay her property taxes, calling it "taxation without representation." (The state took possession of two of her tables and four chairs to pay the tax.) Stone was not hindered by her husband in pursuing her career, but neither did she see him much, as Blackwell tended his real estate ventures in the Midwest.

Near the end of her life, Stone told her daughter, "I do believe that a woman's truest place is in a home with a husband and with children," but, she added, "with large freedom, pecuniary freedom, personal freedom, and the right to vote." After she died of a stomach tumor in 1893 at the age of seventy-five, Stone accomplished one last "first." Like no one before her in New England, she was cremated.

MARY SURRATT

HANGED, PERHAPS WRONGLY, FOR LINCOLN'S ASSASSINATION

After John Wilkes Booth was tracked down and shot for assassinating President Abraham Lincoln, four others eventually were hanged for conspiring with the failed actor. Three clearly were in on the plot: that same night—April 14, 1865—Lewis Payne stabbed and seriously wounded Secretary of State William Seward, David Herold drove Payne's getaway carriage, and George Atzerodt had prepared to shoot Vice President Andrew Johnson, but he chickened out.

But hanged alongside those three men on July 7 was one woman. Mary Surratt ran the Washington, D.C., boardinghouse where the men had met and plotted their crime. As President Johnson later said, signing her death warrant, "She kept the nest where the egg was hatched." Or did she?

Surratt's boardinghouse symbolized the end of a long road of decline for this woman from Maryland. Married at fifteen to a man in his late twenties, Surratt and her husband, John, lost their first farm in a fire. John bought 1,200 acres on credit and built a tavern and store at a crossroads, which became known as Surrattsville (now Clinton). That farm, too, had financial troubles, and by 1857 it was reduced to half its former size. During the Civil War, their older son joined the Confederate army, their slaves ran away, and Union troops raided the farm. Then after her husband died in 1862, Mary Surratt had to call her younger son home from college, where he was studying to be a priest, to take on his father's job as postmaster. The next year he lost that job to a Republican.

Almost broke, Mary Surratt moved to Washington, where she opened her boardinghouse on H Street in October 1864. Her son John became a Confederate courier, carrying secret papers in and out of Richmond, Virginia. Along the way he met Booth, who at the time was devising a plan to kidnap Lincoln in exchange for the release of Confederate prisoners. John joined the plot, and Booth began frequenting Surratt's boardinghouse for strategy sessions. According to later trial testimony, Surratt had asked her son what he and his friends were up to, and John simply told her they were discussing cotton speculation.

After the Confederacy fell and Booth decided to assassinate Lincoln, many of his group backed out, including John. Still, within a few hours after Booth killed Lincoln at Ford's Theater, police officers searched Surratt's boardinghouse. Two days later, Surratt and her boarders were arrested for questioning. Surratt was never released.

On May 12, she and seven men—including Dr. Samuel Mudd, who set Booth's broken leg, and a stagehand at Ford's—went on trial before a special nine-man military commission. Federal officials, who like the nation were traumatized by the death of the president, were intent on proving that Lincoln's assassination was part of a broad Confederate plot. Booth's diary seemed to contradict that, but prosecutors did not allow the document to enter the trial. Nor were any of the defendants allowed to testify.

The primary evidence against Surratt came from two men who themselves were threatened with their own trial if they didn't cooperate with prosecutors. They testified that Surratt frequently was seen engaged in private conversations with Booth at her boardinghouse, though they didn't know what was said. Also, twice before Booth shot Lincoln—once three days before and once on the day of the assassination—Surratt traveled back to her farm at Surrattsville. The men testified she made the trips to provide supplies for Booth's escape. Her attorneys said she simply was trying to collect back rents from her farm to settle her overdue mortgage. When Surratt's son, who had fled the country, was caught and tried two years later, the testimony that had implicated his mother was discredited, and he was not convicted.

Surratt sat through the seven-week trial in the sweltering Washington summer covered by a veil that she lifted only to be identified by witnesses. By the end of the trial, prosecutors had not produced any clear evidence that Surratt was involved with the assassination plot or even that she knew about it. Nevertheless and to the surprise of no one, she and the seven men were found guilty. Surratt and the three most directly involved in the crime were sentenced to hang, though five of the nine members of the commission recommended that Surratt's sentence be commuted to life in prison. President Johnson approved her execution anyway, and after questions about her guilt were raised almost immediately after her death, Johnson claimed he had never seen the commission's recommendation for leniency. So Surratt—after two soldiers removed her bonnet—went to the gallows.

Not all historians are convinced, but it may well be that Mary Surratt simply was a woman who tried to be hospitable to the boarders she desperately needed to avoid bankruptcy. In the hysteria after Lincoln's death, according to one historian, she was made into an example of Confederate women who "had 'unsexed' themselves by cherishing and cheering fathers, brothers, husbands and sons on the tented field." Mary Surratt may, in fact, not be a woman who made a difference. If she did, it has never been clear, at least, what difference she did make.

BERTHA VON SUTTNER

SHE MAY HAVE GIVEN ALFRED NOBEL THE IDEA FOR HIS PRIZES; SHE WON ONE, TOO

Alfred Nobel's first idea for encouraging the world to lay down its arms was not the Nobel Peace Prize. "I would like," said the inventor of dynamite, "to produce a substance or machine of such frightful efficiency for wholesale devastation that wars should thereby become impossible." A century later, that weapon has yet to be invented, and Nobel's Peace Prize—which he hoped would become unnecessary far sooner—is perhaps the highest honor in the world. That he established the award in his will—along with prizes in sciences and literature—is partly due to Bertha von Suttner, a leading European peace activist in the late nineteenth century.

They met, oddly enough, when Nobel hired Suttner to be his housekeeper. Bertha Kinsky had been born a countess, the daughter of an Austrian field marshal who died before she was born. She was raised among the Austro-Hungarian aristocracy, but after her mother gambled away the family fortune, Bertha at the age of thirty was forced to find work as a governess in Vienna. It was while caring for the four daughters of Baron von Suttner in 1876 that Bertha fell in love with the baron's son, Arthur. The baron's wife, upset that her son might marry the impoverished countess, showed her a classified advertisement in a newspaper in which Nobel was seeking a secretary and a housekeeper in Paris.

Bertha got the job. But a few days later, while Nobel was away on business, she received a telegram from Arthur that said, "I cannot live without thee." She left Nobel a note of apology and returned to marry Arthur. To get away from his parents, they moved to the Caucasus region of Russia, where Arthur became a bookkeeper while Bertha taught piano lessons to the daughters of the nobility. After war broke out between Russia and Turkey, Arthur began writing articles about the fighting and sold them to Austrian publications. Bertha, too, started writing, and together their work, which included four novels, became quite popular. They returned to Vienna in 1885, and Arthur's parents welcomed them with a suite in the castle.

Over the years, although they had met each other only briefly, Suttner and Nobel had kept up an occasional correspondence. They became better acquainted when the Suttners were living in Paris in 1886, which was also the time when they began to get involved in the European peace movement. After Suttner joined the International Peace and Arbitration Association, Nobel began contributing money. But Nobel, a brooding, lonely bachelor with a delicate digestion caused by years of inhaling nitroglycerin fumes, would not join the cause himself. "Inform me, convince me, and then I will do something great for the movement," he told Suttner.

Suttner gained her own fame in 1889 with the publication of her novel, *Lay Down Your Arms.* The story of an Austrian woman who loses two husbands to the ravages of war, Suttner's book contained battle scenes so graphic and moving that they captivated Europe. The book was translated into twelve languages, and its impact was compared to that of *Uncle Tom's Cabin.* Even Leo Tolstoy wrote her, "The abolition of slavery was preceded by the famous book of a woman, Mrs. Beecher Stowe; God grant that the abolition of war may follow upon yours." With a second highly praised novel, *The Machine Age,* Suttner emerged as one of the leading spokesmen of the peace movement. She founded the Austrian Peace Society and made speaking tours, advocating—well before her time—a unified Europe and an international "peace court" to settle disputes between nations.

In 1893, Nobel, whom Suttner had kept well apprised of her activities, wrote her that he intended "to set aside a portion of my estate for a prize to be awarded once every five years (up to a total of six, for if there has been no success in reforming the status quo within the space of thirty years, then we shall inevitably revert to barbarity)." The prize, Nobel said, would go "to the individual who has advanced furthest in the direction of a peaceful Europe." Suttner replied, "Yes, do that—very seriously, I implore you."

Nobel died in 1896, and the first peace prize was awarded in 1901 to Frédéric Passy, founder of the French Peace Society, and to Jean-Henri Dunant, founder of the International Red Cross. Dunant wrote to Suttner, "This prize, gracious lady, is your work. For through your instrumentality Herr Nobel became devoted to the peace movement, and at your suggestion became its promoter."

Four years later, Suttner became the first woman to win the Nobel Peace Prize. For almost a decade she continued her strident plea for peace while much of the rest of the world prepared for war. She was well-received in the United States in 1913, and Andrew Carnegie was so impressed that he promised her a monthly pension for the rest of her life. But the Austrians, who, confident of victory, looked forward to the coming war, considered Suttner a traitor (her face now appears on the one-thousand-schilling note).

In her acceptance speech after winning the Nobel Peace Prize, Suttner had said, "This question of whether violence or law shall prevail between states is the most vital of the problems of our eventful era. On the solution of this problem depends whether our Europe will become a showpiece of ruins and failure, or whether we can avoid this danger and so enter sooner the coming era of secure peace and law in which a civilization of unimagined glory will develop."

On June 21, 1914, after declining an operation for a malignant stomach tumor, Suttner died at the age of seventy-one. One week later, Archduke Franz Ferdinand was assassinated at Sarajevo, and World War I began.

T

IDA TARBELL

HER EXPOSÉS HELPED UNRAVEL JOHN D. ROCKEFELLER'S EMPIRE

In 1880 John D. Rockefeller so monopolized the young oil industry that his companies were refining an amazing 95 percent of all oil produced in the United States. By the turn of the century, his Standard Oil Trust was quickly pumping the Rockefeller fortune toward the inconceivable amount of $1 billion. And then a decade later, in a stunning blow to the free-wheeling age of the robber barons, the Trust was shattered by the U.S. Supreme Court.

If Rockefeller had blamed anybody for breaking up his precious oil monopoly, it probably would have been Ida Tarbell, the only woman among the writers Teddy Roosevelt dubbed muckrakers. "Not a word! Not a word about that misguided woman!" the oil baron blurted when he was asked to respond to Tarbell's deeply revealing series of magazine articles on his dirty oil dealings. In nineteen installments in *McClure's* magazine from 1902 to 1904, Tarbell laid out the record of Rockefeller's strong-arm tactics and competition-cutting devices as no one ever had before. By the time her series ended, Tarbell, said *Time* magazine later, had uncorked a "gusher of public resentment that flowed all the way to the U.S. Supreme Court."

The series, which later was published as *The History of the Standard Oil Company* in two volumes, was the high point but not the only peak of Tarbell's career as a journalist. Her fame began after she quit her job at a Pennsylvania magazine at the age of thirty-four and moved to Paris in 1891 to study at the Sorbonne. She interviewed Louis Pasteur and other prominent figures and got her stories published in *McClure's*, a struggling new feature magazine. In 1894 she joined its staff in New York, where her immensely popular articles on Napoléon and Abraham Lincoln helped make *McClure's* one of the most successful magazines in the country and gave her a national reputation.

In 1900 Tarbell began looking into the Standard Oil Company. Her background did not leave her entirely unbiased. Raised amidst the oil fields of western Pennsylvania, Tarbell had grown up hearing talk of the resentment of neighbors who had been squeezed out of the oil business by Rockefeller. Not the least was her own father, who had been the first manufacturer of wooden oil tanks until Rockefeller undercut him, causing his partner to commit suicide.

In her two years of research, Tarbell pieced together the consistent pattern of Rockefeller's monopoly. A stubborn, steady woman, often wearing a conservative high-collar white dress, her hair pulled up in a bun, Tarbell dug up copies of documents that Standard Oil had even gone so far as to invade libraries to destroy. She revealed how Rockefeller had demanded special rebates from the railroads because he was such a big customer, and how when oil producers began shipping through pipelines, he muscled into that business as well. Rockefeller spied on his competitors, and once he had forced them out of business, he raised prices. Most devastating, in the public's opinion, was Tarbell's heart-breaking account of the Widow Backus, whom Rockefeller had forced to sell her late husband's refinery for far less than it was worth.

"There was no more faithful Baptist in Cleveland than he," Tarbell wrote of her subject, whom she never met. "He gave to its poor. He visited its sick. Yet he was willing to strain every nerve to obtain for himself special and unjust privileges from the railroads which were bound to ruin every man in the oil business not sharing them with him." Her series concluded, "As for the ethical side, there is no cure but in an increasing scorn of unfair play—an increasing sense that a thing won by breaking the rules of the game is not worth winning."

Some compared the impact of Tarbell's exposé on the Standard Oil Trust to that of Thomas Paine's *Common Sense* on the American Revolution and Harriet Beecher Stowe's *Uncle Tom's Cabin* on slavery. One newspaper in Cleveland, Rockefeller's hometown, said, "Miss Tarbell has done more to dethrone Rockefeller in public esteem than all the preachers in the land."

To be sure, Tarbell was not the only writer weighing in against Rockefeller, and Standard Oil was facing a growing number of anti-trust suits from its squelched competitors. But it was four months after Tarbell's series ended that Congress launched an investigation, and the following year the government prosecuted Standard Oil under the Sherman Anti-Trust Act.

Ironically, the immediate effect of the trust breakup was to enrich Rockefeller still more, since he still retained shares in the thirty-nine smaller companies formed out of the trust, and their value initially shot up in the market. But Rockefeller's grasp on the oil industry would never be as tight again.

Tarbell left *McClure's* in 1906 to join other muckrakers in a new publication called *American* Magazine. That lasted until 1915, after which she wrote several successful books, lectured frequently, and served on government boards. After her anti-business bent taken out on Rockefeller, "the Terror of the Trusts" shocked many with her warm biography of U.S. Steel founder Elbert Gary in 1925.

Tarbell also frustrated feminists with her cool stand on women's suffrage. Though she herself had taken a vow as a teenager never to marry—"I must be free and to be free I must be a spinster," she said—she later wrote, "Women had a business assigned by nature and society . . . of more importance than public life." If she believed it, Tarbell, who died of pneumonia in 1944 at the age of eighty-six, certainly didn't pay it much attention.

ANNIE TAYLOR

THE FIRST PERSON TO GO OVER NIAGARA FALLS IN A BARREL

Besides attracting legions of honeymooners and millions more who just want to gaze at one of the world's most terrifying wonders, Niagara Falls has also regularly drawn plenty of nuts. It began in 1859 with "The Great Blondin," a Frenchman whom P. T. Barnum paid to perch above the falls on a tightrope. Others followed by swimming through the dangerous whirlpool below the falls or by floating over the lower rapids in a barrel.

But although it has since become the classic Niagara Falls stunt, it wasn't until 1901 that anyone tried to go over the falls themselves in a barrel. And then, it wasn't attempted by any world-renowned circus performer or an Olympic swimmer. The first person to take the plunge was a forty-three-year-old schoolteacher from Bay City, Michigan, who, reported one observer, "looked and acted as if she were more some plain, stout, old woman on her way to Sunday morning service."

Annie Taylor was just that. Widowed and childless —she couldn't even swim—Taylor cared nothing about the challenge except for the chance to make a bundle. Buffalo was currently hosting the Pan American Exposition, and Taylor planned to take advantage of the crowds. She hired an agent to promote her, and thousands of spectators took the bait.

On October 24, Taylor showed up with her barrel and two men who were to row her to the launch point above Horseshoe Falls, the most torrential part of the deluge. The local coroner tried to convince her that her stunt would kill her. Taylor replied, "If the authorities stop my attempt I will jump to my death over the falls and you will have work for sure."

Taylor waved to the crowd wearing a long black dress with lace cuffs and a large hat. She only changed into a shorter skirt and the heavy black stockings that she wore in the barrel once she had been rowed away from the spectators, saying, "I think it would be unbecoming a woman of refinement and of my years to parade before a crowd in a short skirt." As she sailed away, she called out, "Au revoir. I'll not say good-bye because I'm coming back."

After she had changed her clothes upstream (she made the men turn their backs), Taylor climbed into her barrel. Made of oak and bound by seven iron hoops, the barrel was four and a half feet high, four feet in diameter, and weighed 160 pounds, including a 100-pound anvil that had been anchored to the bottom to keep the barrel upright. The men strapped the schoolteacher inside to keep her from banging around, then tucked in a few pillows. After they sealed the barrel, they pumped in extra air with a bicycle pump.

Then the two men towed the barrel to the middle of the river (where there were thought to be fewer rocks) and, shortly after 4 P.M., cut her loose. The crowd gasped as the barrel plunged over the falls and then reappeared ten seconds later through the mist. A riverman hooked the barrel downstream near the tourist boat docks. After they pried the barrel open, a hand appeared and waved weakly. Taylor emerged, bruised and bleeding behind one ear. "Nobody ought ever do that again," she said.

Taylor immediately made herself available for every interview. "I prayed every second I was in the barrel," she said, "except for a few moments after the fall, when I was unconscious." She told another reporter, "It's a terrible nightmare. I don't want to experience it again. I'd sooner be shot from a cannon."

Instead, she began lecturing. But though she billed herself as "Queen of the Mist," Taylor proved to be far duller than her stunt. Appearing in a matronly, corseted black dress, Taylor spoke as if she was delivering a science lecture. Her tour possibilities soon dried up and she returned to Niagara Falls, broke.

There she found that her famous barrel had rotted. So she got a new one and posed next to it to make a picture postcard that she autographed and sold to tourists on Falls Street. She also sold all of the barrel stays, and when the originals were gone, she sold new ones.

Taylor died twenty years later when she was blind and living in a poorhouse. Near death in the county hospital, she lamented, "I did what no other woman in the world had nerve enough to do, only to die a pauper." Since then, six others—all men—have followed Taylor's barrel ride. Three lived and three died. But though her feat earned her little else, Taylor's gravestone proclaims, "First to Go Over the Horseshoe Falls and Live."

THEODORA THE SENATRIX

SHE RULED THE VATICAN IN THE TENTH CENTURY

The last place you'd expect to find a woman behind the man is in the Vatican. But the papal palace has not always been the sacred center of Catholicism that it is today. In the tenth century, when the Holy Roman Empire of Charlemagne was crumbling, and Italy was ruled by territorial princes, the papacy was controlled by the noble (a term of class, not character) families of Rome. And as one historian said, "their swinish lust was second only to their cruelty and avarice."

So it was that Theodora the Senatrix and her family came to rule the Vatican. Her husband, Theophylactus, was a Roman senator, chief of the city's nobles, and also held the title of Master of the Papal Wardrobe. Thus he was well-positioned to receive favors when his ally, Sergius III, took the pope's seat in 904 by throwing his predecessor into the dungeon. Sergius, who also was blamed for murdering two previous popes, rewarded Theophylactus by granting him substantial lands and the countship of Tusculum.

Theodora, meanwhile, took her gains closer to home. There is scant surviving description of Theodora, except from the medieval historian Baronius, who referred to her as "that most powerful, most noble, and most shameless whore." It is said that while her husband enjoyed his wealth, Theodora "in no unmanly way" took control of the Vatican. She had an affair with a priest and had him appointed Archbishop of Ravenna. After Sergius died, she got him elected Pope John X so he could be close to her. John X is remembered as the first pope to take to the battlefield, but he spent most of his time handing out favors under Theodora's watch.

It is not recorded when Theodora died, but her mantle was taken up by her daughter, Marozia. Years before, she was said to have been the mistress of Sergius, who may have been the father of her son. After Theodora died, Marozia feuded with John X and had him imprisoned, where he died in 929. She then had her son elected Pope John XI in 931. He ruled a brief five years before both he and his mother were imprisoned by the disgusted Romans.

But the lineage of Theodora did not end there. In

955, Marozia's grandson became Pope John XII. He was the worst of the lot, and in 964 he was killed by the husband of one of his lovers. Not for nothing is the tenth-century papacy often called "the Pornocracy."

JULIA TUTTLE

HER FLOWERS CONVINCED HENRY MORRISON FLAGLER TO BUILD HIS RAILROAD THROUGH TO MIAMI

For a man to send flowers to a lady is practically a requirement. But when a woman sends flowers to a man, you can expect things to happen. In the case of Julia Tuttle, it got her a city.

As late as 1895, what is now the city of Miami was inhabited by just a few hundred settlers who had hacked away barely enough mangroves to build their homes. A year later the railroad arrived and Miami had its first boom, incorporating itself in three months and growing to more than five thousand residents by the turn of the century. It was the railroad that made all the difference. But it was Julia Tuttle and her legendary orange blossoms that attracted Henry Morrison Flagler's trains to this swampy outpost.

Tuttle was a forty-two-year-old widow with two adult children when she moved to Miami from Cleveland in 1891. She had visited the village, little more than an Indian trading post, three times before to see her father, a carpetbagger legislator in the 1870s. It had created a small scandal in 1875 when Tuttle first made the long trip to the primitive community without her husband. After he died, she sold his ironworks business in Cleveland and bought 640 acres on the north side of the Miami River. Setting up house in the old officers' quarters of the abandoned Fort Dallas, Tuttle wrote to a friend, "It may seem strange to you, but it is a dream of my life to see this wilderness turned into a prosperous county."

Meanwhile, tycoon Henry Flagler, one of John D. Rockefeller's initial partners in Standard Oil, had begun building his Florida East Coast railroad. Initially started to transport his ailing wife away from the cold northern winters, the railroad helped build Flagler's second huge fortune. As he strung his railroad southward along Florida's balmy coast, he built hotels on land that the state gave him for free. By December 1894 Flagler's railroad extended to Palm Beach, and the aging magnate said he was finished.

Tuttle thought otherwise. Having attended the same church in Cleveland in her youth as they, she vaguely was acquainted with Rockefeller and Flagler. When she first decided to move to Florida after her husband died, Tuttle had written to Rockefeller asking him to help her get hired as the chief housekeeper in Flagler's hotel in St. Augustine. When that didn't work out and Tuttle had settled in Miami, she began writing Flagler regularly, urging him to extend his railroad the additional sixty-six miles to her new home. Flagler politely wrote back that he was satisfied with what he had already built and that those few who may want to travel on to Miami would have to get there by boat. Still, Tuttle continued writing, to the point that Flagler became annoyed.

At the same time, she convinced representatives

from a Tampa railroad company to investigate extending their line across the Everglades. Their soggy, mosquito-plagued trek through the alligator-infested swamp made them reconsider, but they were impressed by Tuttle's enthusiasm. After Tuttle set off fireworks on their arrival, one official wrote, "She has shown a great deal of energy and enterprise in this frontier country, where it is almost a matter of creation to accomplish so much in so short a time."

Tuttle may have been left writing her letters in vain were it not for the harsh winter of 1894–95. From Christmas Eve until early February, Florida was hit by three hard freezes that destroyed 95 percent of the state's citrus crop. The temperature dropped to a tourist-chilling nineteen degrees in Palm Beach.

But in Miami, there wasn't even a frost. Tuttle immediately fired off another letter, and finally Flagler, stunned by the damage to his domain, sent an aide down to investigate. Tuttle greeted him warmly and then did something that has become the fundamental legend of Miami. The traditional story is that Tuttle sent the aide back to his boss with a sprig of fresh orange blossoms, evidence that the freeze had not hurt Miami. In fact, some historians say she may have sent orchids or an anonymous bunch of flowers.

Whatever, it worked. Within a few weeks Flagler made the trip himself. Legend has it that the tycoon stepped off the boat and greeted Tuttle by saying, "Madame, I am Henry Flagler and these must be the shores of paradise." Tuttle offered Flagler half of her land, including a hundred acres for the train depot and every other lot in a city she hoped they would build—and profit from—together. As they sat on her front porch discussing the matter, according to one witness, Tuttle said coyly, "Mr. Flagler, just how much of that railroad do you own?" Flagler, puffing on a cigar, replied, "Just as much as I own this cigar."

By the end of the day they had a deal. It was helped by the fact that the Brickell family, who owned six hundred acres south of the Miami River, also offered half their land. And large land companies between Palm Beach and Miami pledged ten thousand acres. News of the coming railroad attracted hundreds of men who set up tents in Miami and waited for the opportunities it would bring.

The first train—carrying freight—arrived on April 15, 1896. The first passengers stepped off a week later. By 1897 some were staying at Flagler's grand, 350-room Royal Palm Hotel. Tuttle, who had begun clearing her land and had laid out the city's first street, ran into cash-flow problems and had to ask Flagler to co-sign a five-thousand-dollar loan.

A year later, Tuttle was making arrangements for a private railroad car to take her to North Carolina, where she hoped the cooler climate would relieve the agonizing headaches she had been suffering. On September 14, 1898, before she could board the train on the railroad she had brought to Miami, the forty-nine-year-old widow died, probably of a brain tumor. Remembered as "the Mother of Miami," Tuttle left an estate valued at some four hundred thousand dollars, most of it from the land she had bought for two thousand dollars seven years before. Perhaps a more profitable bouquet of flowers there never was.

MADAME C. J. WALKER

CREATOR OF A NEW STANDARD OF BLACK BEAUTY

Part of the famous look of Josephine Baker—the St. Louis–born black woman who in the 1920s became the star of the Folies Bergère in Paris—was her hair. So chic was her flat, shiny hairdo that blacks in France and northern Africa quickly bought up a hair-straightening product called "Baker-Fix." In fact, the French goop was merely a knockoff of an American product made by Madame C. J. Walker.

Though they were hardly the kind of inventions to make the history books, Madame Walker's hair-straightening products were indeed revolutionary, not only in the way they created standards of beauty for black people, but also for how Madame Walker defined the role of blacks in business.

Born in 1867 in Delta, Louisiana, Sarah Breedlove was the daughter of former slaves who cultivated a small farm. She was raised by an older sister after her parents died when she was six, and at fourteen she married a man in Mississippi "to get a home," she said.

After her husband, C. J. Walker, died when she was twenty, Sarah and her daughter, A'Lelia, moved to St. Louis, where she spent eighteen years earning $1.50 a day as a washerwoman.

In those days, the words black and beautiful had not yet been joined together. No magazines featured black fashions or hairstyles, and virtually no products were designed specifically to enhance black features. Left with only white fashion standards, many black women tried to straighten their hair. Later, during the civil rights movement, hair-straightening would be denounced as an insult to black pride.

But that was long after the night in 1905 when, Sarah said, she "dreamed" her hair-straightening formula. Concocted in a washtub and stirred with kitchen utensils, the blends of soaps, oils, and herbs became the basis of "the Walker Method." The shampoo, followed by vigorous brushing and hot iron combs, stiffened the hair, which made it easier to straighten and shape.

Walker's hair treatments became popular among blacks in St. Louis and were even more successful when she started selling her products by mail. She moved to Denver in 1906 and began selling door-to-door. More than just promoting her products, Walker sold her system. Calling herself Madame C. J. Walker, she traveled throughout the South and East, visiting black clubs, churches, and homes to demonstrate her straightening technique.

As her business expanded, Walker began hiring other black women to spread the method. Her "Walker Agents" became as popular in black communities as Avon ladies later were in white neighborhoods. Dressed in white shirts and long black skirts, they took Walker's message of "cleanliness and loveliness" throughout the United States and the Caribbean. Eventually, the Madame C. J. Walker Manufacturing Company, which she moved to Indianapolis in 1910, employed some three thousand people. With her picture on every tin of Madame C. J. Walker's Hair Grower and sixteen other products, Walker was the best-known black business person in the country.

Though Walker never gave up sole ownership of her company, she knew how to motivate her agents. She sponsored sales conventions and formed Walker Clubs, where agents could exchange ideas. The clubs were required to perform community philanthropic work, and Walker awarded cash prizes to the most active clubs. Among her many other contributions, Walker sponsored six students each year at the Tuskegee Institute. She also donated five thousand dollars to the National Conference on Lynching.

Madame Walker became one of the richest women in America, and also the richest black person, male or female. She built a townhouse in Harlem where, after she died, her daughter hosted salons for black artists and white patrons and is credited with helping to spark the Harlem Renaissance. Walker also built Villa Lewaro, a thirty-room mansion in Irvington-on-Hudson, north of New York. The "colored woman's palace," with its gold-leafed organ, drew wide attention and was considered, according to *The New York Times*, "Westchester County's most famous sight."

Walker was staying at her villa in 1919 when she died at the age of fifty-one of a kidney disease brought on by hypertension. Doctors had warned her to slow down, but she didn't. She left an estate of $2 million, two-thirds of which went to charities. Madame Walker's business did not survive the Depression. But her style—both in business and in fashion—has.

IDA WELLS

LED AN ANTI-LYNCHING CAMPAIGN

"A Winchester rifle should have a place of honor in every black home." That wasn't the Black Panthers talking. The words were spoken—more than half a century before the civil rights movement began—by Ida Wells, a black Memphis schoolteacher who made Americans pay attention to the fact that hundreds of blacks were being murdered in a cold-blooded practice called lynching.

Named after Charles Lynch, a judge who skipped the trial process and executed lingering Tory fighters after the American Revolution, lynching became epidemic after the Civil War. The term often is associated with hanging, but many victims were shot, burned alive, or cut apart. Black victims outnumbered whites three to one. In the peak year of 1892, 235 blacks were lynched.

Wells was hardly the likely candidate to confront such a threat. Born in 1862, she was the daughter of slaves in Holly Springs, Mississippi. After both her parents and three of her seven brothers and sisters died in a yellow fever epidemic when she was sixteen, Wells put up her hair, claimed she was eighteen, and got a job teaching in a rural black school for twenty-five dollars a month. In 1884 she moved to Memphis and taught in the city's black schools.

By then, the post–Civil War efforts to integrate the South were fading. And when the Chesapeake & Ohio Railroad began segregating its cars on its Memphis-to-Nashville run, Wells refused to move. She sued and actually won her case in circuit court, where she was awarded five hundred dollars in damages. But the

Tennessee Supreme Court overturned the decision in 1887. Wells continued to speak up through a column she began writing for a black newspaper, the *Memphis Free Speech*. That cost her her teaching job in 1891 when she criticized the poor condition of Memphis's black schools.

The following year, Wells's newspaper column became the initial voice in what would grow into a national movement. Three of her friends had opened a store, the "People's Grocery Company," in a black neighborhood in Memphis. The store succeeded at the expense of a white grocer, who then gathered some friends and picked a fight with the black store owners. It was, not surprisingly, the three black men who were jailed. Not satisfied, the white men broke into the jail, took the three black men out to the countryside, and shot them.

Wells wrote about the lynchings in a way that had never been done before. White newspapers, when they covered such killings at all, wrote with a tone that implied that the victims were guilty anyway and that justice had simply been accelerated. Wells wrote that the Memphis storeowners were lynched because their store was doing well.

She did not advocate bringing the lynchers to trial, knowing that would never happen. Instead, she wrote, "There is nothing we can do about the lynching now. There is only one thing left that we can do; save our money and leave a town which will neither protect our lives and property, nor give us a fair trial in the courts, but takes us out and murders us in cold blood when accused by white persons."

Many blacks heeded her call. It is estimated that as many as six thousand blacks left Memphis in the two months after the lynchings. Most headed west, and two pastors took their entire congregations to Oklahoma. In Memphis, entire blocks were abandoned, the streetcar company nearly went bankrupt, and white housewives complained that they couldn't find maids.

Wells, meanwhile, began investigating other lynchings around the nation. She wrote a series of columns describing in gruesome detail exactly how the victims were killed. She uncovered many lynchings where no actual crime had been committed. And while many black men were lynched after they were accused of raping white women, Wells found that often the situation involved an affair between consenting adults, and that the man was lynched to preserve the reputation of the woman. The rape accusation, Wells wrote, was "an excuse to get rid of Negroes who were acquiring wealth and property and thus keep the race terrorized and 'keep the nigger down.' "

Frederick Douglass, after reading Wells's articles, wrote to her: "Brave woman! You have done your people and mine a service which can neither be weighed nor measured." Memphis officials had a different reaction. Wrote the *Memphis Commercial-Appeal*, "The black wretch who has written that foul lie should be tied to a stake at the corner of Main and Madison Street." While she was in Philadelphia, a mob destroyed the offices of the *Memphis Free Speech* and death threats against Wells were rampant.

Wells did not return to Memphis. She began lecturing in eastern cities and founded several anti-lynching societies. She was well-received in England, where she spoke to audiences numbering in the thousands. Of course, lynching did not end overnight. But after the peak year of 1892, when Wells began her crusade, the number dropped steadily. In 1902, for the first time in some twenty years, fewer than one hundred blacks were lynched. Eventually, only a few scattered incidents continued to occur.

Wells's activity decreased after she married a Chicago lawyer in 1895 and had four children. She did help organize the city's first black women's clubs and also founded a social center to help the wave of blacks who were leaving the South. But when she addressed national black issues, she often was at odds with other black leaders, especially Booker T. Washington, whom Wells considered too conciliatory. "The more the Afro-American yields and cringes and begs," Wells said, "the more he has to do so, the more he is insulted, outraged and lynched." Wells gave a speech at the opening of the 1909 conference in New York that led to the founding of the NAACP, but she was considered too militant to be admitted into the new organization's inner circle.

It would be wrong to suggest that Wells by herself ended lynchings and other violence against blacks. But her epitaph—written after she died of kidney disease in 1931—is correct in saying, "She told the truth in words so stirring that she forced the world to listen."

EDITH BOLLING WILSON

WHILE PRESIDENT WILSON WAS ILL, SHE WAS IN CHARGE

According to the U.S. Constitution, if the president dies or becomes incapacitated, the vice president takes over. After that the job passes to the Speaker of the House and so on through the members of the Cabinet. Nowhere in this line of succession does the Constitution say anything about the First Lady. But after President Woodrow Wilson suffered two debilitating strokes in 1919, it was his wife who acted in his place. If she did not, as some claim, completely assume the powers of the presidency, Edith Wilson certainly came closer to the job than any other woman ever has.

President Wilson and Edith truly had a storybook romance. Wilson's first wife, Ellen, had died of kidney disease in 1914 during his first term in the White House. His spirits never completely recovered until March 1916 when he met Edith Bolling Galt, the daughter of an old Virginia family and widow of a prominent Washington jeweler. The fifty-nine-year-old president was immediately smitten; he proposed in the first week of May. Edith, forty-three, at first declined, saying she wanted to wait until Wilson was out of office. But after he won a second term, they were married in December.

Edith proved to be an able companion for her husband, who was a strong and active president. She was with him during his grueling train campaign in 1919 as Wilson tried to out-maneuver Congress and win public support for the Treaty of Versailles and his prized League of Nations. In twenty-two days the president traveled eight thousand miles and delivered thirty-seven major speeches, addressing as many as thirty thousand people at a time without a microphone. On September 26, as his train rolled from Colorado to Wichita, the exhausted president suffered a minor stroke. On the advice of his doctors and at Edith's insistence, Wilson canceled the rest of his trip, and the train sped back to Washington. By the time it arrived, Wilson had recovered enough so that he could walk off the train in front of reporters and get into a nearby car.

Then on October 2, Wilson suffered a massive stroke, one that almost killed him. His left side was paralyzed, his speech was greatly slurred, his vision was blurred, and he had difficulty swallowing. For six weeks the president was completely incapacitated, but few outside of the White House knew it. His Cabinet was told that Wilson had suffered a nervous breakdown, and the press was not told the extent of his illness until the following February. Early on, Secretary of State Robert Lansing suggested that Wilson step aside, but Edith felt sure that would kill him. "I am not thinking of the country now, I am thinking of my husband," she said. The White House physician, Dr. Cary Grayson, who had introduced the president to Edith, refused to certify that Wilson was unable to hold his office.

The president, of course, had advisors to handle many of the affairs of state, but it was Edith who controlled access to Wilson himself. She barred most visitors, including ambassadors, Cabinet members and congressmen. All papers that were sent to him, including bills from Congress, first went through her. She sent many matters on to other departments and simply set some aside. The issues that Edith passed on to the president only got there after she had summarized them and presented them in the best possible light, so as not to upset him.

Edith called the period her "stewardship." As she wrote in her memoir, "I studied every paper, sent from the different Secretaries or Senators, and tried to digest and present in tabloid form the things that, despite my vigilance, had to go to the President. I, myself, never made a single decision regarding the disposition of public affairs. The only decision that was mine was what was important, and what was not, and the *very* important decision of when to present matters to my husband."

But some in Washington, angered by their lack of access to the president, were convinced Edith was running the White House. Some senators called for a handwriting expert to examine Wilson's signature and in fact, Edith admitted that she steadied her husband's hand as he signed legislation. Many documents that left the White House also had her handwriting in the margins, beginning with the words, "The President directs . . ." One Republican senator called her the "Presidentress who had fulfilled the dream of the suffragettes by changing her title from First Lady to Acting First Man."

It is hard to determine exactly which policies Edith might have influenced, but the arrangement clearly had an overall effect on the nation. During severe strikes by steel workers and coal miners, presidential statements were issued in Wilson's name. But, as with many matters, that was a far cry from the power of Wilson's former leadership.

The difference was especially apparent in his uphill battle to get the Senate to approve the Treaty of Versailles. Before his strokes, Wilson had been unwilling to compromise to get the Senate to approve the treaty. Then as the treaty neared a vote, Edith withheld the negative reports about its chances. Some historians speculate that had Wilson been more aware of the odds against his treaty, he may have compromised. Still, just before the Senate defeated the treaty, Edith said to her husband, "For my sake, won't you accept these reservations and get this awful thing settled?" The president replied, "Little girl, don't you desert me; that I cannot stand."

Wilson never completely recovered during the rest of his term. He couldn't stand, his vision was poor, and he could concentrate for barely an hour at a time. Mentally, he felt well enough that he talked of seeking a third term. But Dr. Grayson privately told Democratic leaders of Wilson's serious condition, and he was not nominated in 1920. The nation ousted Wilson's party and elected Republican Warren Harding.

Wilson and his wife continued to live in Washington, where they took long rides in a motor car. Wilson died in 1924. Edith remained an occasional member of the Washington scene until she died at the age of eighty-nine in 1961. She died on December 28, on the 105th anniversary of her husband's birth.

VICTORIA WOODHULL

SPIRITUALIST, COURTESAN, AND THE FIRST WOMAN TO RUN FOR PRESIDENT

Cornelius Vanderbilt may have been ruthless about his railroads, but outside the office, in his later years, he was a bit of a flake. Beset with the realization of his own mortality after his wife died, Vanderbilt sought solace from spiritualists, turning to faith healers for every ache, and meeting regularly with a seer from Staten Island who passed on news from his dead mother. So it was not surprising that eventually Vanderbilt would meet Victoria Woodhull and her sister, two of the most notorious mystics of the nineteenth century. Unfortunately, no seer warned the aging tycoon that his association would give Woodhull a springboard to greater fame—and infamy.

By the time Woodhull met Vanderbilt, the thirty-year-old woman had a sleazy reputation that went back well over twenty years. Born Victoria Claflin in 1838, she had been the seventh of ten children of an Ohio drifter who put his family to work in a traveling medicine show. Victoria showed a talent for trances, and her younger sister, Tennessee, was good at séances. By their teens, the two sisters were working the Midwest on their own, frequently fleeing charges of fraud, prostitution, and, once, manslaughter, after one of Tennessee's patients died. When she was fifteen, Victoria married a real doctor, Canning Woodhull, who became an alcoholic and left her with two children, a retarded son and a daughter named Zula.

In 1868 Woodhull was traveling with her second husband, Colonel James Blood, when she announced that an ancient Greek spirit had visited her in a Pittsburgh hotel room and told her to go to New York. They apparently had no trouble meeting Vanderbilt, who was always eager to expand his mystic connections. But Vanderbilt was more interested in Woodhull's sister, Tennessee, and she became the aging widower's mistress, his "little sparrow," as he called her.

When the sisters first opened their brokerage firm on Wall Street in 1870, everyone at first scoffed at "the Bewitching Brokers," who were rumored to trade on clairvoyant messages. But when Woodhull, Claflin & Co. soon moved into lavish new offices at 44 Broad Street, it became clear that the women were acting on much more solid information. It was estimated they made seven hundred thousand dollars on insider tips provided by the Commodore about his railroads. The sisters, along with assorted members of their family, moved into a sumptuous Murray Hill mansion.

Flush with her success, Woodhull announced, "While others argued the equality of woman and man, I proved it by successfully engaging in business. I therefore claim the right to speak for the unenfranchised women of the country, and believing as I do that the prejudices which still exist in the popular mind against women in public life will soon disappear, I now announce myself as candidate for the Presidency."

With Vanderbilt's silent support and her own magnetic personality, Woodhull parlayed her notoriety in several directions. In 1871 she began publishing *Woodhull and Claflin's Weekly*, a journal—largely written by her husband, Colonel Blood, and another weird activist—that promoted free love, short skirts, and legalized prostitution. The same year, Woodhull and her sister took over the leadership of the International Workingmen's Association, an organization inspired by Karl Marx, and they used their weekly journal to publish the first American version of Marx's *Communist Manifesto*.

Amazingly, none of that prevented her from arranging to be invited to present a speech before the House Judiciary Committee in Congress on the subject of women's suffrage. It was her first link with the women's movement, and she was a smash. She was asked to address a women's rights convention that was meeting at the same time in Washington, and Susan B. Anthony and Elizabeth Cady Stanton were very impressed. Woodhull's speech later at a national women's convention in New York was so powerful that the meeting became called "the Woodhull Convention."

The more conservative members of the women's movement were appalled by Anthony's and Stanton's embrace of a woman with such a checkered past, and the controversy helped lead to a split with another leader, Lucy Stone. But Stanton defended her new friend. "The nature that can pass through all phases of social degradation, vice, crime, poverty, and temptation in all its forms, and yet maintain a dignity and purity of character through all, gives unmistakable proof of its high origin, its divinity," she said.

Stanton, it soon turned out, had been much too optimistic. As Woodhull marched seriously toward her 1872 presidential campaign, her long, colorful career began to haunt her. After her first, ailing husband returned to live in the Murray Hill mansion, Woodhull was accused of living with two husbands. One of her prime attackers was a powerful New York minister, Henry Ward Beecher, brother of *Uncle Tom's Cabin* author Harriet Beecher Stowe. Woodhull lashed back with an apparently accurate accusation that Beecher was having an affair with the wife of a prominent editor, Theodore Tilton. Woodhull was arrested for making the charge and spent Election Day, on which she garnered a few thousand scattered votes, in jail.

Though she was eventually acquitted in the case—one of the most sensational of its day—the controversy caused Woodhull to be abandoned by all her supporters, including both Vanderbilt and the Communists. Bankrupt, she lost her mansion, as her speeches drew far less interest and income. In 1876 she divorced Colonel Blood for adultery, and in her speeches she stopped talking about free love and instead called marriage "a divine institution."

Woodhull did get some help from Vanderbilt one final time, though it was after he died in 1877. He had left nearly all of his $120 million fortune to his son, William, so his other children claimed their father had been incompetent, largely based on his mystic affairs. Woodhull and Tennessee would have proved quite damaging to William's case, and when the two sisters sailed first-class for England before the trial, it was assumed that William had paid the fare. By some accounts, an additional five hundred thousand dollars went along with the tickets.

Woodhull picked up her lecture career in England and quickly attracted a wealthy banker, John Biddulph Martin, though it took six years before his family would allow the marriage. She spent the rest of her life trying to rehabilitate her American reputation and charm her way into British society, both with scant success. Woodhull outlasted her husband and her sister, who died in 1923. After that, she refused to sleep in a bed because she was afraid she would die there. Instead, she slept sitting up in a chair, and it was there she died in 1927 at the age of eighty-eight.

LADY MARY WORTLEY MONTAGU

INTRODUCED THE SMALLPOX INOCULATION TO ENGLAND

Well into the eighteenth century, there were ladies who would never appear in society unless they were shrouded by heavy veils. They were the lucky ones. Smallpox hadn't killed them, but it had left their faces deeply pockmarked, with scars they tried to hide behind veils and dimly lit rooms.

Lady Mary Wortley Montagu was one of those ladies who had survived the disease. A beautiful woman, she, too, had been left with deep scars and had been "deprived of her very fine eyelashes." But Lady Mary did not shroud herself. She got angry, and her anger helped greatly reduce the threat of smallpox for future generations.

Mary was accustomed to having her own way. Born in 1689, the daughter of an earl, she had refused her father's arranged marriage and instead eloped in 1712 with Edward Wortley Montagu, a prominent official in the court of George I. At a time when it was unheard of for a lady to write articles, she published her essays and poems anonymously and was good friends with England's foremost authors, including Alexander Pope.

In 1716, the year after she suffered her bout with smallpox, her husband was appointed ambassador to Turkey. There she saw Turkish doctors performing a procedure to prevent smallpox. Simply by scratching a healthy person with a needle that was infected with smallpox, doctors could cause the patient to develop a minor case of the disease which, upon his recovery, would leave him immune. The inoculation was not entirely safe. In rare instances, it caused a more severe case and could be fatal. British doctors, in fact, had known about the treatment since 1700, but they had rejected it as too risky.

Lady Mary was enraged. Had British doctors pursued the inoculation procedure, she believed, her own case of smallpox could have been prevented. "I am patriot enough to take pains to bring this useful invention into fashion in England," she wrote to a friend.

"And I should not fail to write to some of our doctors very particularly about it, if I knew any one of them that I thought had virtue enough to destroy such a considerable branch of their revenue for the good of mankind."

Despite the possible risk of the inoculation, she wrote, "You may believe that I am well satisfied of the safety of this experiment, since I intend to try it on my dear little son." While her husband was away, she convinced a British doctor in Constantinople to inoculate her four-year-old son. Edward got a mild fever and a few pustules, but he recovered quickly with no scars.

After the family returned to England, a smallpox epidemic in 1721 spurred Lady Mary to have her three-year-old daughter inoculated as well. It was performed by the same British doctor, and Mary invited several other doctors and prominent friends to witness the treatment. Word of the success spread as far as Leicester House, where the Princess of Wales decided to have two of her daughters inoculated.

But not everyone was so impressed. Ministers denounced the treatment as defying God's will. Said one pamphlet, "Posterity will scarcely be brought to believe, that an Experiment practiced only by a few Ignorant Women, amongst an illiterate and unthinking People, should on a sudden, and upon slender Experience, so far obtain in one of the Politest Nations in the World, as to be received into the Royal Palace."

Nevertheless, smallpox inoculation did gain acceptance, and historians credit Lady Mary Wortley Montagu with saving "many thousand British lives" every year. It wouldn't be until 1796 that Edward Jenner developed his safer vaccine method, which virtually wiped out the disease.

Lady Mary, meanwhile, went on to other struggles.

Her friendship with Alexander Pope deteriorated when she did not accept his proposal of love. Pope began writing satires and poems that savaged her reputation. She tried to fight back, but that only escalated the matter into a sensational battle of words fueled by the British press. Lady Mary finally left England in 1739, partly to escape the nasty fight, but also to get away from her bad marriage and, probably, to pursue an Italian dilettante with whom she was rumored to have been having an affair in London.

The affair didn't last, but Lady Mary Wortley Montagu didn't return to England until after her husband died in 1761. She traveled the continent on her own, settling a few years at a time in Venice and other northern Italian cities where she found life more relaxed than in stiff British society. "I prefer liberty," she said, "to chains of diamonds."

Lady Mary died of breast cancer in 1762 at the age of seventy-three. After her death, letters that she had written thirty-five years earlier in Turkey were published. Her *Embassy Letters* were a huge hit, quickly selling out and reprinted several times. So detailed and knowing were her portrayals of Turkey and British diplomats that Voltaire said Lady Mary Wortley Montagu's letters were "far superior" to those of the acclaimed Madame de Sévigné of France.

Unfortunately, Lady Mary's daughter, who by then was the wife of the Prime Minister, was so embarrassed by seeing her mother's words in print that she destroyed Mary's personal journal, which she had kept throughout her life. Undoubtedly, it was a gem. But even without it, Lady Mary Wortley Montagu—besides earning acclaim for her medical accomplishment—is considered England's foremost lady of letters until that time.

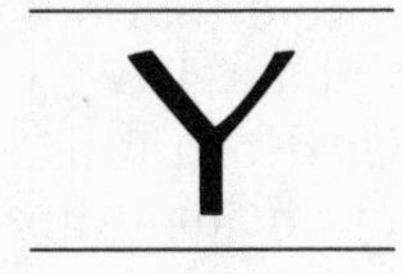

ANN ELIZA YOUNG

BRIGHAM'S LAST WIFE, AND THE ONLY ONE TO DIVORCE HIM

It has never been exactly clear how many wives Brigham Young had. By some counts, the Mormon leader got married nineteen times, but others say he tied as many as twenty-seven knots. Whatever the total, it's safe to assume that the prolific polygamist would have preferred the count had ended before his final bride.

Ann Eliza Webb was among the first generation born into the Mormon Church. Her father, Chauncy, built most of the wagons that carried the Mormons from the Midwest to Salt Lake City, and the family followed the migration in 1848. Her father also followed Young's preachings on polygamy, taking a total of five wives, a practice that Ann said almost destroyed her mother, his first wife. Polygamy, Ann said, "was the most hateful thing in the world to her, and she dreaded and abhorred it, but she was afraid to oppose it, lest she be found 'fighting against the Lord.' "

Ann had her own chance to take a stand on polygamy when she was sixteen. Young, nearly sixty, took her for a ride in his carriage one day and asked if she would ever consider marrying him. Unlike anyone else who had ever been asked that question by the powerful, revered religious leader, Ann told him no. When she was eighteen, she married James Dee, a young Mormon amateur actor. They had two sons, but Dee was abusive and—with Young's help—Ann divorced him in 1865.

For the next three and a half years, Young pursued the strikingly beautiful divorcée. Finally—after Ann said Young threatened to bankrupt her brother—they were married in April 1869. It was the last betrothal for Young, then sixty-eight. His twenty-four-year-old latest bride refused to live at Lion House—one of two large homes where most of Young's wives and some of his fifty-seven children lived—so Young promised to give Ann her own home. He bought her a tacky, tattered house with cheap furniture and a worn carpet. Like all the wives who lived away from the main residences, Ann was sent rations once a month, including a few cuts of pork, five pounds of sugar, and a bar of soap.

Eventually, Young did build Ann a nice house in 1873. But by then, his last wife had felt neglected for too long. "I was alone, tied to an old man," Ann later wrote in her memoirs. "Others were cared for, and it was more than a woman's nature could stand, to see them thus petted." To earn extra money, she took in non-Mormon boarders, including a Methodist minister, a judge, and a reporter for the *Salt Lake Tribune*. And with their encouragement, in July 1873 Ann moved into a hotel and filed for divorce, seeking two hundred thousand dollars plus twenty thousand dollars in lawyers' fees.

Being the only woman ever to walk out on Brigham Young, Ann made a big splash in the press. She granted countless interviews and began giving lectures, billing herself as "the Rebel of the Harem." The nation ate it up. In her lectures, titled "Life in Mormon Bondage" and "Polygamy as It Is," Ann gave her sympathetic audiences their first glimpse into the life of Young and his many wives. With stories of infighting among the women, and children who barely knew their father, she personalized the nation's moral horror of polygamy, a practice that was illegal, but the law was not enforced.

"Legislators," she said, "in doubt or in dread, give polygamy the benefit of their doubts or their fears, and again the question is laid over for a season. Meanwhile, anxious eyes are longing, and burdened hearts are breaking, and children are swarming forth with the blight upon their birth." In April 1874, she spoke in Washington, and her lecture was attended by many congressmen as well as President Grant and his wife. She caused an outrage by revealing that Utah's Mormon congressman had four wives, though he claimed only one. Within a few weeks, Congress passed the Poland Bill, the first national anti-polygamy legislation, which strengthened federal powers to prosecute offenders.

Her divorce case, meanwhile, proceeded slowly. Young, apparently seeing no irony, accused Ann of being an "adulteress," and offered her $15,000 to settle the case. He then claimed that his marriage to Ann was not legal, but was "a kind of mutual arrangement according to faith." In 1875, a Utah judge ruled that the marriage had been legal and awarded Ann $500 a month in alimony and $3,000 for court costs. Young refused to pay, and he was put in prison for one day.

He was released under house arrest, which ended five months later when he paid $3,600. In 1877, an appeals court ruled that the marriage was not valid, since polygamy was illegal. But Young's victory was brief, as he died four months later at the age of seventy-six.

Ann, by then nationally famous, continued her hectic lecture tour, earning as much as five hundred dollars for one appearance. In 1876 she published a best-selling book, *Wife No. 19, or The Story of a Life in Bondage.* Finally in 1882, after Congress passed even stiffer anti-polygamy legislation, her audiences began to wane, though some Mormons didn't comply until 1890.

In 1883 she married Moses Denning, a wealthy Michigan coal and lumber tycoon who had divorced his wife for her. The marriage lasted nine years. Ann later lived in Denver and El Paso as both her fortune and her health declined. Because of her ailments, she began following the teachings of a new religious leader, Christian Scientist Mary Baker Eddy. In 1908 Ann revised her book, but this time it drew little interest.

After that, Ann, then age sixty-four, was never heard from again. There is no record of her death, though stories abound. It was said that she married a businessman in the East or that she died impoverished in California. Most ironic was the story that after she died in Arizona, the Mormon Church put up the money for her burial. Her second ex-husband most assuredly would not have approved.